HOSIERY LIST.

1908.

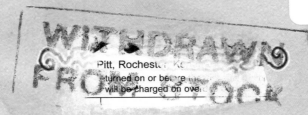

ROBERT PRINGLE & SON,

HAWICK.

(Established 1815.)

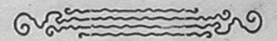

London Warehouse—67 GRESHAM STREET, E.C.

Representatives—MR B. R. CHASTON and MR G. SHAND.

Telegraphic Addresses:

"PRINGLE, HAWICK."   "RECORDATIO, LONDON."

Telephone—HAWICK, 304a.   LONDON, 12303, Central.

Pringle of Scotland *and the Hawick Knitwear Story*

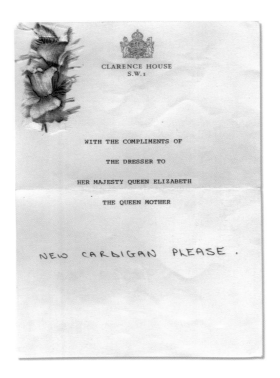

INTARSIA by Pringle
INLAID BY HAND
MADE IN SCOTLAND · 100% PURE CASHMERE

Handprinted in Scotland
by Pringle
100% PURE CASHMERE · MADE IN SCOTLAND

MADE FOR
Harrods
LONDON
BY Pringle OF SCOTLAND

STYLED BY Pringle FOR
W.S.Robertson
OF HAWICK, SCOTLAND
MADE IN SCOTLAND

Pringle
OF SCOTLAND
100% pure cashmere

Hugh Barty-King

PRINGLE OF SCOTLAND *and the Hawick Knitwear Story*

Pringle of Scotland
and the Hawick Knitwear Story

First published 2006 by JJG Publishing
Sparrow Hall, Hindringham, Fakenham,
Norfolk NR21 0DP

Copyright © 2006 Hugh Barty-King
ISBN 1–899163–83–2

Designed by View Creative
Printed in China through Colorcraft Ltd, Hong Kong

Fashion is not an inanimate object, and it is
never at rest, a distinction it shares with life
itself, of which it seems to be some special
and significant manifestation.

James Laver

The essence of taste is suitability. Divest the word
of its prim and priggish implications and see how
it expresses the mysterious demand of the eye and
the mind for symmetry, harmony and order.

Edith Wharton

The loom has received several improvements
since, till it has arrived at the Perfection of a
compleat Engine whereon Stockings of all Sorts
can be wrought with great Art and Expedition.

The London Tradesman, *1747*

KNOTTING

At noon in a sunshiny day
The brighter lady of the May
Young Chloris innocent and gay
Sat knotting in a shade.

Each slender finger play'd its part
With such activity and art
As would inflame a youthful heart,
And warm the most decay'd.

Her favourite swain by chance came by,
He saw no anger in her eye;
Yet when the bashful boy drew nigh,
She would have seemed afraid.

She let her ivory needle fall
And hurled away the twisted ball;
But straight gave Strephon such a call
As would have raised the dead.

'Dear gentle youth, is't none but thee?
With innocence I dare be free.'
By so much truth and modesty,
No nymph was e'er betrayed.

'Come lean thy head upon my lap,
While they smooth cheeks I stroke and clap,
Thou may'st securely take a nap.'
Which he poor fool obeyed.

She saw him yawn and heard him snore,
And found him fast asleep all o'er.
She sighed and could endure no more,
But starting up, she said

'Each virtue shall rewarded be;
For this thy dull fidelity,
I'll trust you with my flocks, not me;
Pursue they grazing trade.

'Go milk thy goats and shear thy sheep,
And watch all night thy flocks to keep;
Thou shalt no more be lull'd to sleep
By me, mistaken maid.'

Charles Sackville,
6th Earl of Dorset, 1638–1706

CONTENTS

THE KNITWEAR ERA

PRINGLE LEADS

ACKNOWLEDGMENTS

THE WRITING of this book in 1971 depended entirely on information received from documents and people. A list of the former will be found under 'Bibliography'. Here I would like to thank all those inside the Pringle organisation, too many to name, who at that time were ready to talk to me about the past, the present and the future with so much understanding, imagination and patience, and to take the opportunity of acknowledging the assistance of those outside the organisation who were sought out in their homes and offices, made special journeys to Rodono Mill or, by chance meeting, found themselves subject to close questioning: Mrs Francis Muir, daughter of Robert Pringle II, and her daughter and son-in law, Geraldine and Maurice Simpson, of Muchalls Castle, Stonehaven; William Mactaggart who had so recently thrown off the responsibilities of chairman and managing director held so long, and his son Bruce Mactaggat who succeeded him; Ernest Tait, ex–finance director and fund of meticulously kept statistics; Miss Saida Sime, daughter of J. Boyd Sime, last partner of Robert Pringle II, now living in Hampstead; Dick Scott, curator of the Border Museum at Hawick who produced Buckham's ledger of 1818 and the Poor Rates Roll of 1846; James Oliver, the sage of 58, High Street, ex-technical school headmaster who alone knew the meaning of 'popes'; Joe Laing, ex-managing director of James Melrose, the engineers; headmaster Basil Wilson and motor engineer William Peacock, two of the keenest members of the Hawick Archaeological Society; George Woodcock, managing director of George Woodcock & Sons, engineers; Archie Purvis, secretary of the Hawick Knitwear Manufacturers Association who produced the minute book of 1909; William Walker, recently retired organiser of what used to be the Hawick Hosiery Union which became part of the Hawick branch of the National Union of General and Municipal Workers; James Thompson, manager of the Rodono Hotel on St Mary's Loch which used to be Robert Pringle's shooting lodge; Miss McIvor and her assistants at Hawick Public Library; Robert Leslie, East Lothian County Librarian; the courteous staffs of the National Library of Scotland in Edinburgh and the town library of Haddington; Andrew Taylor, sheep farmer, of Bonchester Bridge; Alan Graham and Keith Palmer, the two enterprising young men at the Hawick branch of the British Linen Bank who remembered the vaults harboured the account books of 1809; J. T. Grieve of Torquhair, met by chance at Stow, who helped find the lost hamlet of Hoppringil; and not least, though last, the retired Pringle employees who submitted to a tape-recorded interview at Rodono Mill – Jessie Clifton; Alfred Brown; 85-year-old Bill Mitchell, the only man left who had joined in 1900 (he retired after 52 years in 1952); Miss Telfer who joined in 1916 as a girl of 14 and stayed till 1965; William Murray who joined in 1915 and retired in 1966 aged 65; 82-year-old George Middlemass who joined shortly after Bill Mitchell when there were only 145 workers at the mill, and retired in 1958; Muriel Webber; Dick Scott and Neil McCullum for reading the 1971 manuscript and giving constructive comments; Valerie Wickes; Stuart Stockdale, and Kim Winser for deciding to revive what circumstances had obliged Alan Smith to lay aside. Above all I am indebted to Stuart Beaty, the prime mover without whose initial and continuing enthusiasm there would be nothing to revive.

Hugh Bart-King, *Ticehurst, East Sussex*

ILLUSTRATION ACKNOWLEDGMENTS

Page 1, Hawick first edition ordinance survey map 1863 © *Crown copyright and Landmark Information Group ltd* (all rights reserved) 2005; Page 9, King Henry VIII and Page 13, Queen Elizabeth I, the *National Portrait Gallery, London;* Page 2, 'The Spinners', Page 5, Egyptian socks, Page 6, Knitting sheath, Page 8, Silk gloves, Page 9, Felted cap and Boot hose, Page 11, English cloth sewn hose from the *textile collection Victoria & Albert Museum*; Page 7, a course of knitting, Page 11, Spun cotton gaiters, Page 12, Machine knitted stockings, Page 14, William Lee and William Lee's knitting frame, Page 15, Silk stockings, courtesy of *Knitting Together*, www.knitting-together.org.uk; Page 165, Bond Street and Page 167: Sloane Street store courtesy of and photographed by *Keith Parry*.

PUBLISHER'S NOTE

This history of the pioneers of Scottish knitwear and the company (Pringle of Scotland) that led the way to making knitwear a fashion that has stood the test of time is illustrated with items of significance and charm which naturally tell their own rich story.

The book has two dimensions—the text which carries the reader through the often dramatic events since the invention of the knitting machine in 1591; and the illustrations. These portray the main protagonists in the story but concentrate on the dazzling shifts of fashion to which Pringle have contributed over the last hundred years.

A book with two sources of interest and two time scales.

Opposite
Twinset time:
*Dressed only in pearls she waits for
her cashmere twinset. Image, created
for the Bond street hoarding by Jonathon
Bookallil in 2002*

INTRODUCTION

It is now 2005, the 190th birthday year of Pringle of Scotland, and this makes our amazing business the oldest luxury brand in world fashion.

Pringle of Scotland holds one of the richest lives of any brand; the archives are knitted with pearls of creativity, of history making innovation, and in certain periods even raw survival.

Hugh has unveiled some of these moments and discovered some that we had not known or forgotten! His writing is that of a historian and technician; it is not a book written by a marketeer—this makes it even more enticing to read!

Since the takeover in 2000 we have worked to develop the wonderful Brand with total admiration and respect for our past and the ingenuity of the Pringle family and their board of directors, but developed with integrity and creativity for the future.

We are so grateful to the commitment and genius of these insightful people who have together made our history so rich. We intend to take this into the many decades, and even centuries, ahead of us.

Kim Winser, *Chief Executive, Pringle of Scotland Ltd*

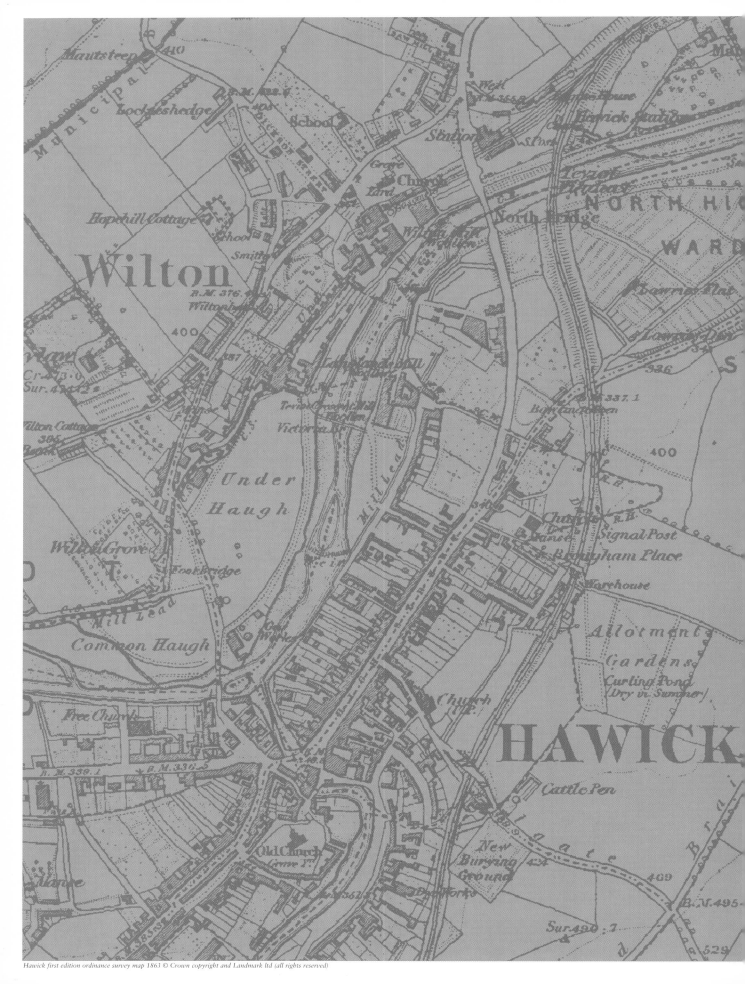

ROOTS

Upon the whole they [the manufacturers of Hawick] are a
diligent, enterprising people and deserve the notice of the public.

David Loch, *A Tour through most of the trading towns and villages of Scotland*, 1778.

Their industry is not the violent exertion of a moment, but steady
calm and persevering …Were it not for the many disadvantages
and difficulties they have to encounter, the spirit of the inhabitants
of Hawick would raise it to the first station of manufacture in the
South of Scotland.

Rev Robert Gillan in the *Statistical Account of Scotland* (entry on the Parish of Hawick) 1793.

A change of fashion has frequently been of as great consequence
as the loss of a battle, an ally, or a colony; a whole district has been
suddenly raised to the utmost pitch of prosperity and opulence by the
introduction of a particular mode of dress; whilst other extensive
occupations have been doomed to penury and unutterable distress by
a like change, perhaps effected by an insignificant thoughtless being,
who was wholly unconscious of the evils he was inflicting.

Gravenor Henson, *The History of the Framework Knitters*, 1831.

1

WOOL FOR LOOPING

Sheep on the Scottish Lowlands; hand-knitting from the Euphrates to the Dee

T HERE HAVE BEEN at least 17 different ways of spelling Hawick: Hawic, Hawich, Hauuic, Hawhic, Hauwic, Haweik, Hawyk, Hauwyk, Hawick, Hauyke, Hawyc, Hauyc, Hauwyc, Havyk, Hunewic.

It was given its name by Saxon settlers whose chief built his house in the crook of the Slitrig burn where it takes a ninety degree bend before joining the Teviot. Ha' was short for hall, and wic meant the curving reach of the river.

Hawick (Pronounced Hoik) is only some 15 miles north of the English-Scottish border, and 50 miles south of Scotland's capital, Edinburgh—in that southern part of Scotland known as the Lowlands. It is well inland, equidistant from the Irish Channel on the west and the North Sea on the east. It is in the county of Roxburghshire which was originally Saxonia, and later Marchmont. The part of it in which Hawick lies was once Tweedale-shire.

How was the activity for which Hawick is now famed attracted to so small and remote a community?

Before the development of roads and canals industries grew up alongside materials which remained raw until man devised ways of making them useful. Nature sank deposits of iron along the river Carron, and beside them rose the great foundry which turned the metal into guns and pillar boxes. Nature raised the grassy Border hills where sheep were content gently to graze and grow their woolly coats—useless to mankind until made into something useful by human hand, by manufacture.

How came the Knitwear Industry to the Scottish Border? Because here was the raw material.

This part of Britain became one of the country's richest sheep-farming areas through the devotion to the Mother Church of the man who was

Opposite
Woman Spinning:
'The Spinners' George Walker 1814
Victoria & Albert Museum

the King of Scots for almost the whole of the first half of the 12th century. His name was David, the first of that Ilk on the Scottish throne. According to his chronicler, in his endeavour to live and promote the Christian life, he 'illumined his lands with kirks and abbeys'. In the 12th and 13th centuries some 150 abbeys were founded in Scotland, and a large proportion of them in King David I's time. Many of the biggest and most prosperous were settled in the valleys and hills of the Border country.

The abbeys paid no taxes and, unlike their counterparts in England, had no obligation to maintain 'roistering troops of knights' for the king. The tenants of abbeys were exempted from war service. So when they were not praying they implemented the Rule which commended to them the dignity of labour by rearing sheep. Like the Cistercians of Fountains Abbey in Yorkshire, the Cistercians of Melrose and the Benedictines of Kelso they became experts in the breeding of these animals and kept vast flocks on the Cheviots, the Lammermuirs, in the Forest of Ettrick and in the valley of the Tweed. Kelso Abbey was granted land for grazing 700 sheep; Melrose Abbey kept 200 at Hessendean. Each of these had some 7,500 sheep during the 12th and 13th centuries. Later considerable areas of forest land were cleared to make even more pastures.

The sheep—small, scraggy and tough—were bred mainly for their wool; the mutton was sweet but scanty. It was known as Forest Wool, and was keenly sought after in Europe, particularly in Flanders and its flourishing cloth industry. In the summer the monks moved the sheep to remote 'shielings', high up in the hills, to save the grass on the lower slopes—Selkirk was 'the kirk of the shielings'. The sheep would be tended by a lone shepherd like the young Cuthbert who one afternoon, sitting on the hillside above Leader Water, was surprised to see the soul of Aidan, the founder of Old Melrose Abbey, being carried to heaven by angels, and decided there and then to leave his flock and join the monks. He probably gave them professional advice about sheep farming, and by the time he became prior a strong tradition had already been established.

The offspring of the medieval sheep which lived and died on the lands and the Border monks have been remarked upon by writers and travellers ever since. Driving through Galloway in 1725 Daniel Defoe noted the great number of sheep 'and Runts, as we call them in England'. 'The Wooll, as well as the sheep, is a very great Fund of yearly Wealth to them ... It is no uncommon Thing for a Galloway Nobleman to send 4,000 sheep and 4,000 Head of black Cattle to England in a Year ... This Part of the Country is very mountainous and some of the Hills prodigious high; but all are covered with Sheep: In a word "the Gentlemen here are the greatest Sheep-masters in Scotland".'

A hundred years later William Cobbett on a Rural Ride caught his first glimpse of Scotland as he came to the Tweed, and across the moors noted 'the valley narrow, the hills on the side rocky, cultivated here and there a little, the rest of the ground growing scrubby firs and wyns; but great numbers of the Cheviot-hill sheep feeding on them, and very pretty sheep these are. They have no horns, are white all over, legs not long, body very truss, rather larger and a great deal prettier sheep than the South-down sheep'.

In most towns on the Border there appeared a Fleece Inn; there was still one in Selkirk in the 1970s, the one in Hawick, kept by a Mr Hunter, stood at 6 High Street in the building since occupied by Stotharts. Fleece was indeed golden. It changed hands for great sums at the Border fairs. St James's Fair at Kelso dated back to the days of King David I. It lasted eight days; it continued to be held up to World War 2, but only for one day. Originally held on St James's Green, a haugh between the rivers Tweed and Teviot, on August 5, this festival of St James the Apostle, the Patron Saint of the Parish, was shifted to the old August Bank Holiday.

Bigger and more important, though less old, was Hawick Fair held on the Tower Knowe on the third Thursday of July. Here Border sheep farmers, wool brokers, dealers and buyers would settle the prices that would stay fore months to come. The last Hawick Fair was held in 1915. The principal auctions for Cheviot Wool were in Edinburgh, Leith—and Hawick.

Thus sheep and shepherd have been the backcloth to life on the Border for centuries. When the people there sing the metric version of the 23rd psalm as they often did, and not only in church, the analogy of the Lord being a shepherd and his adherents his flock was close and real. On the walls of the old farmhouses hang samplers of the Lowland Scots version. 'The Lord is my Herd, nae want sal fa' me. He louts me till lie amang green howes; He airts me stowre by the lown watirs. Na, tho' I walk thro' the deid-mirk dail, e'en thar sae I dreid nae skaithin; for Yersel are nar-by me; Yer stock an' Yer stay haud me aye fu' cheerie.

Most of the wool which the monks of Kelso and Melrose sheared from their sheep they sold to foreign buyers. There were two things they did with the wool they kept. They would press a wad of it into their wooden shoes, to ease the penance, without God or the abbot minding. The monk's weight, the heat and moisture of his hot, sweaty foot compressed and compounded the raw wool into a mat. As he walked around the cloister, into chapel and out, up the stone steps to his cell to sleep, and down to the refectory to eat, his feet were effecting a process known in Scotland as 'waulking' and by the English called 'fulling'. What the monk eventually had as a comfy lining to his clog was what both Scots and English call 'felt'.

The wool not pounded into felt was spun into yarn.

The first natural spinner was the wind which twirled the tuft which the thicket had torn from the back of the animal which had sheepishly insisted on forcing its way through. Spinning is as old as civilisation. Other materials were spun into thread before wool—the inner bark of trees for instance. For centuries thread was spun by a standing woman with a distaff in her belt and a spindle in her hand, and from the 14th century with a wheel, at first standing and, from about 1530, sitting and working it with her feet.

Sheep grew thick or thin wool, and may grades between, according to their breed and treatment. Each had its different uses. Coarse wool was used for making carpets and blankets; less coarse wool for weaving into cloth; fine wool for what concerns this story.

To most people the Woollen Industry, and the word Textiles mean spinning and weaving. Indeed, the spinning of yarn and the weaving

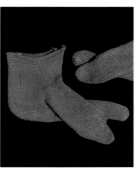

Egyptian socks:
3rd to 5th century, knitted in wool in stocking stitch using a single-needle technique and three-ply wool. Victoria & Albert Museum

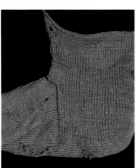

Egyptian sock:
Detail

5

of it into cloth, including the Border variety known was tweel (which through a clerical error became known as tweed), is the largest user of raw wool. But this story is concerned only incidentally with either spinning or weaving. It is concerned with what Sir David Brewster in his *Edinburgh Encyclopaedia* of 1830 called 'Chainwork'.

This he described as 'those substances, whether lineal or superficial, in which any kind of cordage or thread is linked together in the form of a chain for any purpose of useful or ornamental manufacture'. The lineal, ornamental kind, he says, is the principal application of Chainwork and is known as 'Tambouring', a succession of lineal chaining in various directions to decorate a cloth with ornamental flowers and figures. In the second type of Chainwork 'the loops of the chain are precisely the same as in tambouring; and the most simple, although tedious, way of producing this is by means of four small wires directed by the manual operations of women, or what is usually termed knitting'.

He added that the time spent on this brought it into disuse. It was rarely practised 'now' (i.e. 1830) except in northern counties and the isles of Scotland, Orkney or Shetland. It may have been slow, but it was easy. Thus John Beckmann in his *History of Inventions*:

> It may be so easily acquired, even by children, as to be
> considered almost an amusement. It does not interrupt
> discourse, distract attention or check the powers of
> imagination. It forms a ready resource, when a vacuity
> occurs in conversation; or when a circumstance occurs
> which ought to be heard or seen, but not treated with
> too much seriousness; the prudent knitter then hears and
> sees what she does not wish to seem to hear or to see.
> Knitting does no injury either to the body or to the mind.
> It occasions no prejudicial or injurious position; requires
> no straining of the eye sight; and can be performed with
> as much convenience when standing or walking, as
> when sitting. It may be interrupted without loss, and
> again resumed without trouble; and the whole apparatus
> for knitting, which is cheap, needs so little room and is
> so light, that it can be kept and gracefully carried about in
> a work-basket; the beauty of which displays the expertness
> or at any rate the taste of the fair artist. Knitting belongs
> to the few useful occupations of old persons who have not
> lost the use of their hands. Servants, soldiers, shepherds,
> and the male children of the peasants who are unfit for
> hard labour should learn to knit, for it may be a pleasant
> and profitable employment for leisure even of the male sex.

It was also portable.

> Children at the age of ten and people very far advanced in
> life may, and often do, though in a scanty measure, maintain
> themselves by their labour at this work, and the knitting can
> be carried on while travelling or watching cattle or the like;
> nor does it require much, or at least not constant light, many
> carrying on their work throughout the winter evening with

A knitting sheath:
Holds one needle and supports the knitting whilst using the other needle.
Victoria & Albert Museum

A knitting sheath:
Detail

the faintest light issuing from a few turfs—a circumstance much in favour of a country where the nights are long and the inhabitants poorly supplied with fuel or light. (Second *Statistical Account of Scotland*)

There is a well known picture painted by an artist called G. Walker, *The Wensley Dale Knitters*, which shows an old man sitting knitting, his wife standing knitting, their daughter behind them knitting and her little daughter knitting. In the background is a shepherd knitting while herding his flock. A note on a reproduction of this picture states 'in any business where the assistance of the hands is not necessary, they universally resort to knitting … a woman walked to the market three miles away to do her shopping with the weekly knitting of herself and her family safely packed in a bag on her head, knitting all the way'.

The Wensley Dale Knitters:
George Walker 1814.

The word 'knit' is said to derive from the Saxon 'crittan'. Samuel Johnson defined 'knit' as 'to make or unite by texture without a loom'. But what distinguished knitting from cloth was not so much being made without a loom as its elasticity—the fact that it could be pulled aside at the edges and it sprang back into its former shape. It could be extended without permanent enlargement or distortion. This was a unique characteristic. Moreover it would conform to the shape it was designed to cover. Instead of hanging loose like cloth, it would cling to the body. Indeed, it was often referred to as 'elastic loop hand-knitting'. Wool knitted into a web was composed of one continuous thread—like a spider's—without the separate vertical warp and horizontal weft of woven cloth. This gave it solid edges (salvages) on both sides.

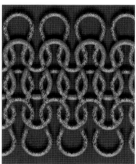
A course of knitting:
A horizontal row of loops forming a course. Photo courtesy of Knitting Together

Being one continuous thread was also the cause of its main disadvantage. If knitting was cut it would unravel itself and revert to a long and useless piece of yarn. This has given rise to the theory that the Roman soldiers' reluctance to divide Christ's seamless shirt indicates that the garment was *knitted* and not woven—'wrought' from the top throughout—for they knew that if they cut it up it would unravel.

Knitting may be as old as this, but its age is anyone's guess. This is William Murphy's:

> According to a tradition which is of almost historical validity, the art of knitting was re-discovered among the peasants of the Scottish Lowlands. The date of the discovery has never been even guessed with approximate accuracy. In the sparsely populated districts of Scotland the younger members of agricultural communities beguile the enforced idleness of winter's inclement weather by working various quaint and fanciful designs in straw, hay, plant stems and wool. Doubtless the practice led to the re-discovery of knitting, and it is very probable that the original inventor thought no more of the work than of a hundred other things he, or she, had made in the same manner. (The Textile Industries)

'Doubtless' means, as ever, there is considerable doubt. Murphy's florid note typifies the romantic theory of the origin of knitting. 'Rediscovery' implies supposed references in the Odyssey and Iliad, and to the belief that it was practised by the ancient Romans and Greeks who used the same word for both 'knitting' and 'weaving'. It is true that there seems to have been no separate word for 'knitting' in any off the dead tongues of the ancient world. At any rate, there is no identifiable allusion to it in any of the literature that has come down to us.

In asserting that knitting as known today originated in Scotland Murphy was only echoing a widely held supposition for which, however, there seems to be little evidence, let alone enough to give it anything resembling historical validity. These great text book writers, J. H. Quilter and John Chamberlain, get no further than saying, 'It is generally believed that the art was first practised in the lowlands of Scotland,' at the same time hinting that knitted fabric was found in Tutankhamen's tomb. The 11th edition of the *Encyclopaedia Britannica* asserts that the art of knitting is of a very modern origin as compared with weaving, and that no certain allusion to it occurs before the beginning of the 15th century. 'It is supposed that the art was first practised in Scotland and thence carried into England.' Similarly, F. A. Wells: 'Some authorities suggest that the art was practised there in Scotland before it was introduced to England, but whether that be true or not, the flourishing industry of the Shetland or Orkney Islands may well have developed independently. The fine wool of the island sheep favoured the production of high quality goods.'

The introduction of many 'new' activities has been lain at the door of the shipwrecked sailors of the fleeing Spanish Armada who were washed up on the shores of northern Scotland and the Shetland Islands, and knitting has been one of them. The finest wool, and the most suitable for knitting, came from the merino sheep of Spain, and the Spanish may well have learnt 'looping' from the Moors. But they would have brought it to Scotland, if at all, long before the Armada sailed.

The Victoria & Albert Museum have examples of 'ecclesiastical gloves' knitted in Spain in the 16th century. 'It has been assumed,' comments Miss S. M. Levey of the Museum's Textile department, 'in the absence of any positive evidence, that knitting was introduced into Spain (and consequently to the rest of Europe) as a result of the Arab invasion of AD 711–12.'

Perhaps the Normans and Swedes took knitting to Fair Isle? Who knows? No one knows, but everyone speculates. It would be nice (in the sense of neat), if it was 'invented' in Scotland. But William Felkin, the most important of the textile historians to have dealt with the subject of knitting, dubs it antediluvian—so simple it must have been done before the Flood. But with so many theories competing for attention, another thrown into the pool will not come amiss.
Hawick is a Saxon name, and the town was first a Saxon settlement; the English word 'knitting' comes from the Saxon 'crittan'; there is a Saxon word 'Huyk' meaning a tight-fitting dress worn by both sexes. *Ergo* knitting originated in Hawick.

The first object made of knitting—in Britain at any rate—was a woollen cap. It was of the type that had been worn by peasants in England and Scotland, only made from cloth, from the time of the Norman Conquest. From about the middle of the 15th century it came to be knitted—and in the first place in Scotland. Here it was known as the Tammy, the bonnet worn by ploughmen and later more universally: the blue bonnet which became the undress cap of the Mosstroopers.

Silk and silver gilt gloves:
16th century Spanish
Victoria & Albert Museum

There is a 16th century English 'felted cap' in the Victoria & Albert Museum in London. It was knitted with thick reddish-brown wool in plain stitch, and then heavily felted, cut and re-sewn to make two overlapping brims, and finally blocked into shape. An Act of Henry VIII of 1488 sets the price of felted *hats* at 1s 8d and that of knitted woollen caps at 2s 8d. The 'Cappers Act' of 1571 laid down that every person above the age of six years—excepting 'maids, ladies, gentlewomen, noble personages, and every Lord, knight and gentleman of twenty marks of land'—residing in any of the cities, towns, villages or hamlets of England, should wear on Sundays and holidays (except when travelling), a cap of wool, thicked and dressed in England, made within this realm, and only dressed and finished by some of the trade of cappers, upon pain to forfeit for every day of not wearing 3s 4d'.

The second piece of clothing to be knitted was what in France was called 'chaussé' or 'chaussés', and passed into English as 'hose'. The word has dominated the knitting industry ever since.

In the Victoria & Albert Museum there are a pair of knitted 'half-hose' or socks found in Egypt and believed to date from the 4th–5th century AD. They had been knitted with red, three-ply wool. Miss Levey has said the construction of these socks shows considerable technical skill—knitted from the top down.

The peoples of the world have been divided into the trousered and the non-trousered races. The Celts, who overran Britain before the Romans came, were known as the Bracati, wearers of 'braies' or breeches, the trousered people. The ancient Greeks and Romans, on the other hand, deriving from the bare-legged Egyptians, wore belted tunics, togas and mantles, and were thus the non-trousered people. In all but the Highlands of Scotland where the plaids and kilts are the direct descendants of the Roman tunic and toga, the inhabitants of Britain took more favourably to having the lower portions of their bodies covered. In medieval Britain chaussé(s) was a term used for armour for the leg, but was also used for the tight leg coverings introduced from France. In the 16th century by 'hose' was meant the entire single garment covering the man from waist to feet. The upper part around his thighs and supported on his waist was of thicker material than the lower part, and the whole garment originally was of cloth. But very soon the two parts came to be referred to separately—the upper part as trunk hose and the lower part as nether hose. Soon the two parts were physically separated and the leg covering had to be fastened to the upper part by what they called 'points'. For a time the upper part was known simply as 'hose', was later called a doublet, and then the more familiar, and lasting, 'breeches' which was a 16th century version of the old Celtic word 'braies'. In Scots they became 'breeks'.

But it is nether hose with which this story is concerned at this point. The legs were considered to be enclosed in the way they were covered by that ancient form of punishment the stocks. Each leg was stuck into a cloth stock.

Samuel Johnson explained it best. 'Stock in the old language made the plural stockken, which was used for a pair of stocks or covers for the legs. Stocken was in time taken for a singular, and pronounced stocking. The like corruption has happened to chick, chicken, chickens.' Similarly the plural of hose was 'hosen', of shoe 'shoon'. William Shakespeare felt able to use the singular word when describing a lackey

Felted cap:
Early English design of felted wool (c. 1600) Victoria & Albert Museum

Henry VIII:
Introduced the Cappers Act. Oil on copper attributed to George Gower 1588. National Portrait Gallery

9

Boot hose:
English knitted 2-ply wool (1640s) Victoria & Albert Museum

in *The Taming of the Shrew* as wearing 'a linen stock on one leg, and a boot-hose on the other'. (Boot-hose were stockings for boots, or spatterdashes—spats.) But yellow stockings, of course, were the main comic business of Malvolio's caper in *Twelfth Night*.

The making of the first trunk and nether hose was a task for a tailor, who cut the garment in its two parts out of cloth or linen with a pair of scissors, and sewed them up the back with twine. So long as the demands of fashion were limited and simple and shapeless, and the taste of the wearers undiscriminating, the tailor was kept busy, and no one thought of going to anyone else. But with the flowering of the Renaissance, young men demanded more shapely garments which would show off their dashing figures. Cloth stockings had the look of ill-fitting bandages or puttees, at their best a shapeless gaiter. To the rescue of the calves and jambs of the young Tudor nobility came the art of knitting as practised by the hand knitters.

As has been seen, the knitters had trained on woollen caps. 'It is supposed,' says the *Encyclopaedia Britannica*, 'that the art (of knitting) was first practised in Scotland and thence carried into England, and that caps were made by knitting for some period before the more difficult feat of stocking-making was attempted.'

The hand-knitted stockings clung to the figure as cloth was unable to do. What is more, the knitting came from below the needles—four of them in the form of a cylinder, as a finished stocking, without any unsightly or irritating seam. The shape of the leg would be reproduced by the knitter increasing and decreasing the number of stitches in a row as the making of the stocking progressed, effecting a more gently graduated curve than anything the tailleur could cut with his scissors.

The verb 'to knit' appears in a grammar of 1530 which belonged to one of the daughters of Henry VIII. But the word was well known in Britain before that date and appears in much earlier writings—'she that sytteth knyttinge from morning to eve can scarcely win her bread'.

Though hose was the main knitted garment, as early as 1552 an English Act of Parliament was mentioning 'knitte hose, knitte peticotes, knitte gloves and knitte slieves' which shows an enterprising variety of applications even at this time.

In 1579 Queen Elizabeth saw in Norwich a stage with women and children on it spinning yarn 'and as manie knitted worsted hose'. 'Worsted' was the name given to the type of woollen yarn, the fibres of which have been smoothed down by combing to lie in one direction (the name comes from the village of Wurthsteyde in Norfolk, now called Worstead).

Not all the first stockings, however, were knitted from woollen yarn, whether of the 'worsted' type or of the uncombed variety. As the cloth for the first hose cut by the tailor was not only woollen but also linen and silk, so also were the first hand-knitted stockings knitted with linen and silk thread as well as woollen yarn. The idea and art of knitting stockings in silk certainly seems to have come to Britain through the first samples of these lovely pieces of workmanship given as presents. Henry VIII was given a pair made in Spain and his daughter, Elizabeth, in the third year of her reign, received a pair of black silk stockings made by the serving girl of her 'silk woman' who was said 'to have quickly become so dextrous in knitting that from thenceforth Elizabeth never wore cloth hose any more'. Silk stockings were worn on ceremonial and other special occasions by royalty and the nobility, though not entirely if Prince Henry's remark to the lowly Poins in Shakespeare's *Henry IV* is anything to go by: 'What a disgrace to me to remember thy name or know thy face tomorrow; or to note how many pairs of silk hose thou hast, namely these, and those that were the peach coloured ones.' The same playwright paints a character of disreputable and humble origins as 'a base, proud, shallow, beggarly, three-suited, hundred pound, filthy, worsted-stocking knave'.

Though 'fine hose', originally copied from Spanish and Italian prototypes, was made, mainly for the nobility and by ladies and their domestic servants in the houses of England, from silk and silk mixed with wool, the craft of knitting by hand was pursued in the land of its alleged origin almost entirely with wool alone.

Hand-knitting of stockings from local, and later imported, wool, was developed on such a scale in parts of Scotland that it truly became an 'industry'. Taylor, the London 'Water Poet' visited Braemar and other northern parts of Scotland in 1618 and noted that all the lairds' hosiery was knitted by his family, their families, and servants, from the wool of their own sheep which these also had spun at home. But the great hand-knitting centre became Aberdeen.

The leading promoter of the stocking trade in Aberdeen in the 17th century was one George Pyper who directly employed 400 hand knitters and spinners. He gained the reputation of producing stockings from the delicate fibres of Highland wool of the greatest fineness in the land, costing over twenty shillings a pair.

By the 18th century the hand-knitting industry in Scotland was of a size that warranted an Act of Parliament to regulate its products—and in precise detail. An Act of George I of 1720 stipulated that *all stockings made in Scotland* should be 'wrought of three threads, and of one sort of wool and worsted, and of equal work and fineness, free from left loops, hanging hairs and burnt, cut or mended holes, and of such shapes and sizes as the patterns which shall be marked by the several deans of guild' according to specified dimensions given in detail.

The Aberdeen hand-knitting exercise was an undoubted success story. But it stands alone. It inspired nothing—no new technology, no new end products. It merely led to the making and exporting of more and more hand-knitted stockings. It never harnessed itself to the revolutionary development that came from the persistence of the country parson at Woodborough who freed knitting from dependence on the dexterity of human hands and fingers, and enabled it to become an industry different in every respect from the domestic pastime it had been before.

Spun cotton gaiters:
Women's gaiters worn over stockings.
Photo courtesy of Knitting Together

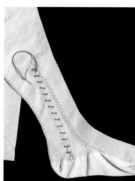

English cloth sewn hose:
17th century.
Victoria & Albert Museum

11

THE NOT SO GOLDEN HARVEST

William Lee invents the knitting machine, but reaps small reward. (1564–1610)

WOODBOROUGH is a small village close to the city of Nottingham, in just about the centre of England. When William Lee, Gentleman, was born there no one knows, but it was probably about 1564, when hand-knitting had been practised in Britain for some 100 years. There could have been someone living at the time of his birth who remembered having knitting drawn to his attention as a strange new deviation from the age-old weaving, and marvelling at it for the novelty that it was. Elizabeth Tudor was on the throne of England; Mary Stuart was Queen of Scots and on the point of marrying Henry Darnley, father of James VI.

The first known date in William Lee's life was the year in which he matriculated at Christ's College, Cambridge, which was 1579. He then went to another college, St John's, in the same university and as an undergraduate read for a Bachelor of Arts degree which he took in 1583. He stayed on as a graduate to obtain a Master of Arts degree, but this proved too much for him, and he came down from Cambridge in 1586. He went home to Nottinghamshire, took holy orders and became curate of the parish which adjoined Woodborough called Calverton. The Glebe House where he stayed was still standing when William Felkin went to make notes for his *History of the Machine-Wrought Hosiery*, published in 1867.

Considerable romance and much fanciful speculation has woven itself round the Reverend William Lee's life from this point forwards. It has been made the subject of a three volume work of fiction called

Opposite
Elizabeth I:
Refused William Lee's patent for his knitting frame in 1591. Oil on panel attributed to George Gower (1588). National Portrait Gallery

Nut Brown Maids, and the central event in it was depicted in an imaginative oil painting by A. Elmore ARA, exhibited and much admired in 1847.

William Felkin exhaustively examined all this 'evidence', and printed it fully in the nineteen page chapter of his book devoted to the subject. He concluded that the most likely version of the motivation for the parson's violent change in the direction of his life, was that of a Dr Ure who, with Felkin, made a thorough investigation of the mystery in 1833.

> It is an ancient tradition around Woodborough, his birthplace, that Lee in youth became enamoured of a mistress of the knitting craft, who had become rich by employing young women at this highly prized and lucrative industry. By studying fondly the dextrous movements of the lady's hands, he became himself an adept; and had imagined a scheme of making artificial fingers for knitting many loops at once. Whether this feminine accomplishment excited jealously, or detracted his manly attractions, is not said; but his suit was received with coldness, and then rejected with scorn. Revenge prompted him to realise the idea which love first inspired, and to give days and nights to the work. This, ere long, he brought to such perfection as that it has since remained without essential improvement the most remarkable stride in modern invention. He thus taught his mistress that the love of man of genius is not to be slighted with impunity.

So much for the romance. Such a circumstance may indeed have been the spark that fired his determination. But though conceived in a spirit of 'I'll show her!' by a hurt, resentful young man with no theoretical or practical knowledge of mechanics, the devising of a way of forming mechanically the web of loops constructed with such facility by the hand-manipulated needles was a laborious up-hill process. Obsession with overcoming the detail as each problem presented itself, and a vision of the finished accomplishment and the benefits it would bring, must soon have replaced the resentment. And one hopes that the lady in question eventually got carried away by the enthusiasm of her suitor-turned-inventor, and came to his aid with her considerable experience.

He would have needed it. It took him three years.

To perfect the practice of hand-knitting was a great thing, declared John Beckmann in his *History of Inventions*, 'but not so astounding as the invention of the stocking-loom, which was not, like most great discoveries, the result of mere accident, but of talent and genius'.

Beckmann calls Lee's machine a stocking-loom. A loom was a machine for weaving cloth or carpets involving a war and a weft. Lee's machine did not make stockings, it made knitting. As seen, the main product of hand-knitting at this time was a stocking, the leg of which was made complete as a cylinder on four needles, the heel

14

William Lee:
1563/4–1614 inventor of the knitting frame. Photo courtesy of Knitting Together

William Lee's knitting frame:
Lee's first frame greatly increased the speed of the knitting process and produced around 600 loops per minute compared to a hand-knitter's 100. Photo courtesy of Knitting Together

Opposite:
Machine knitted stockings
Thick white cotton stockings demonstrate the probable quality of Lee's original stocking frame of 1589. Photo courtesy of Knitting Together

Robert Pringle:
Who founded Pringle at the age of 20 (b.1795)

and foot of which, however, had to be made flat with two needles. The mistress of the knitting craft with whom William Lee fell in love and the young women she employed would all have been making stockings. William's aim was to make stockings mechanically, but he very soon realised that it was going to be impossible to knit the cylinder-shaped leg mechanically, reproducing the four-needle operation of the hand knitters. He therefore concentrated on a way of producing a flat web composed of a straight line of loops, each line being made simultaneously, instead of built up loop by loop one at a time, as was the only way open to the hand knitter. He conceived the idea of a hand operated machine from which would emerge row after row (or 'course') of 'knitting made from a single continuous thread, the edges of which were solid and integral. The knitting that emerged from the machine could then be doubled round to form the cylinder of the stocking leg, and the two edges seamed together with needle and cotton by hand. But with the knitting that emerged from the mouth of the machine, anything could have been made—and, as its subsequent history shows, was.

Betty Heiton:
Wife of Robert Pringle

He set to work in the Glebe House at Calverton, and the first months were devoted to the design and fabrication of a suitable type of needle or wire, as it was then called, with which a loop could be formed mechanically. What about having a wire with a springy hook on one end near a hole in the wire into which a piece of wool thrown over the hook could be sunk by something coming down from above—a sinker?—forming a loop below the hole? That was the start point. The hole gave way to a groove, and after discarding many shapes for his hooked needle, he settled for one of them, made a dozen needles of this design and hammered them into a piece of wood. Moving the row of needles on their wooden backing with his right hand and carrying a thread of wool across them with his left, he managed to produce first one simultaneous course of loops, followed by another and then another. Within a short while he had enough knitting to form a garter. The invention was under way.

Giving the iron needles the shape to perform in the way he wanted, putting holes through them, gouging out grooves—such operations alone constituted formidable tasks with the tools available to him. In the big city five miles along the road was a tradition of metal craftsmanship, and the smiths of Nottingham would have helped him and supplied him with material. The Lee clan at Woodborough and Calverton, cousins, brothers and many camp followers, contributed unskilled labour, unstinted enthusiasm and, as their experience accumulated with the months, helpful suggestions. Their master's singleness of purpose bound them as if by a spell, and inspired them with a sense of mission which was almost mystical. Indeed, the failed clergyman brought into being a dedicated order, each member of which wore on a silver chain a replica of the heart of the invention, the spring needle with the turned back barb. It was, after all, the Renaissance and not the Industrial Revolution.

The Pringle Bible:
Washed up in the Hawick flood of 1767

Having settled the form of his needles, set them in rows on a board and devised a wooden bar to come down on their springs to make a loop in the yarn, the moment came to assemble what he had achieved so far on to some kind of fixture or framework. This he made with hard wood from the forest of Sherwood. The working parts were fixed on a frame—and from this the machine got the name by which it has been known down the years, and its modern counterpart is still known today. Beckmann and Felkin misleadingly talk about the stocking-loom and stocking-weaving; but history has dubbed it the stocking frame, its product framework, and its operators framework knitters.

Having achieved the mechanical knitting of a row, Lee then proceeded to work out how to make his frame make a stocking. Here, as Gravenor Henson describes, new obstacles presented themselves.

> He wrought with great facility the top, the narrowing, and the small of the leg, but the formation of the heel and foot embarrassed the ingenious mechanic who had surmounted such seeming insuperable difficulties; it is stated that, misled by the method of fashioning stockings by the knitting needles, when he arrived at the length where the heels were to be formed, he worked the heels alone and brought the instep by the hand under the hook of the needle previous to pressing; and that he was months before he discovered the method of working them together. After having to unrove a great number of abortive attempts, perseverance at length crowned all his efforts, and the clergyman attained the height of his wishes and became the first framework-knitter. (History of the Framework Knitters, 1831)

Lee's first frame had eight needles to the inch—some 100 needles altogether producing a web about a foot in width. By removing loops by hand on the outer sides of the web to the next needles inward, he was able to narrow the width of the web, and by a reverse process to widen it. The product of the mechanical knitting frame was 'fully fashioned' from the start, as of course was the hand-knitting which it claimed to reproduce. But whereas a skilful hand knitter might form a hundred loops in a minute, Lee on his frame was able to form five hundred.

The date of Lee's invention of the mechanical knitting frame is always given as 1589, the year he completed building the first machine. It was 40 years after the destruction of the Border abbeys by the English troops of Henry VIII, 10 years after Sir Francis Drake's voyage round the world, a year after the defeat of the King of Spain's invasion fleet, the overrated Armada. Sir Philip Sidney, who had written of 'a young shepherdess knitting and singing; her voice comforted her hands to work and her hands kept time to her voice's music', had died in battle the year the young curate of Calverton had embarked on his self-appointed task of providing a less poetic alternative. There were few who ever sang as they sat at the Four Pillars of Misery, as his brainchild came to be known.

But 1589 was not the year in which the machine became publicly available. For the inventor then became operator, and for a year at least he and the members of his community at Calverton and Woodborough experimented with the making of coarse woollen stockings on the one frame they had built.

16

Walter Pringle I:
*With wife Mary Sutton,
who married in 1834*

Order document:
*18 cartloads of stones ordered
for Pringle expansion
(1820)*

Silk stockings:
*Men's and women's silk stockings
made on an early stocking frame
(c. 1700) and exhibited later
in the great exhibition of 1851.
Photo courtesy of Knitting Together*

Although the frame consisted of some 2,060 parts—needles, sinkers, jacks, clurcock, locker and bar, presser, treadles and the rest—its operation had no complicated or difficult movements. A sequence of 11 constituted the knitting of a single course, involving both the hands and the feet of the operator who sat at the frame as at a console. 'The constancy of muscular motion is favourable to the health of the stocking-maker' wrote William Felkin, who was one himself. 'The failure of the sight as evidenced by the early use of spectacles is however very common'. He considered a youth of ten or 12 years old could soon learn to work it. But that was after William Lee had figured it all out.

In 16th century England such manufacture as existed was regulated by the country's absolute ruler and his advisers. Wages were fixed by law, and no one could work at any trade unless educated to it by a term of apprenticeship. Handicrafts were confined to corporate towns which had been given a charter by the monarch. Trade was conducted by trade companies registered by the Lord Chancellor. In such a highly organised society there was no getting round the rules. With so revolutionary and unlikely a claim as that of the lapsed cleric of Calverton, the game would have to be played strictly as written, and that meant going straight to the top—the capital and the ruler who lived there, Queen Elizabeth.

It was one day in 1591, or thereabouts, that William Lee and hand-picked members of his entourage removed themselves and their precious frame to London. With them would certainly have been James Lee, William's brother, who had been his principal help-mate in the whole five-year operation. They found lodgings and a workshop in Bunhill Fields, near Aldersgate, where news of the arrival of the strange piece of apparatus soon spread, and the alleged nature of it was either disbelieved or hailed as witchcraft or a miracle.

One of the commanders of the army which had been held in waiting at Tilbury to resist the landing of Spanish invasion troops was a relative of the queen, called Lord Hunsdon. It was to this well-placed member of the court that Gentleman Lee had managed to obtain an introduction. Through Hunsdon he planned to draw the attention of the monarch to his invention and all he claimed for it, and secure from her the licence without which his frame could have no future.

The first hurdle was surmounted when he demonstrated the machine to his chosen entrepreneur and his son, Sir William Carey, at Aldersgate. His Lordship was impressed enough to recommend to her majesty that she must not fail to see it too. So, in a few days Gloriana in person, accompanied by her attendants—all strictly incognito—were ushered into the small workroom in this not too savoury part of her capital. William and James were presented to her and she saw for herself the wonder-working machine in action over which her cousin had so volubly enthused. She thanked Master Lee and his assistants, swept from the room and returned to Whitehall—a disappointed woman. Contrary to her expectation, Mr Lee's stockings were made of *coarse wool*.

'My Lord,' she wrote to Lord Hunsdon in answer to his formal intercession on Lee's behalf, 'I have too much love for my poor people who obtain their breed by the employment of knitting to give my money to forward an invention that will tend to their ruin by depriving them of employment, and thus make them beggars. Had Mr Lees made

Gentlemen's 'Short Johns':
Silk body with cotton placket
(c. 1850s)

Back detail

Whiskey House Mill:
Built in 1788, the first home to new business, Waldie Pringle & Co.
1815–19

a machine that would have made silk stockings, I should, I think, have been somewhat justified in granting him a patent for that monopoly which would have affected only a small number of my subjects, but to enjoy the exclusive privilege of making stockings for the whole of my subjects is too important to be granted to any individual.'

It was all a dreadful anti-climax. It was as final as it was unexpected. William had succeeded in going to the summit—no mean achievement—and the summit had turned him down. Mortification. But, in bringing the dread news, Lord Hunsdon reaffirmed his own faith in the invention—and not only in words. He bound his son, Sir William Carey, as an apprentice to Lee, to learn the art of framework knitting, thus making him a guarantee for the security of the machine as well as hoping no doubt to obtain for himself a share in the profits.

If the queen had expected a machine to knit silk stockings, Lee saw his only way of obtaining the essential licence was to adapt his frame to do just this. It meant a frame with 20, as opposed to eight, needles to the inch, requiring a reduction in the thickness of the needle wire, the substitution of iron for wood jacks, thinner sinkers so that five took the space of the two of the first machine, and a general overall reduction in scale. There was nothing wrong with the principle of the machine, but to make it work a fine thread like silk as against the coarse worsted wool, which it had been designed for, was very much more difficult than a mere change of scale might appear—and more costly and time consuming.

They severed their connection with Calverton. William, and his brother James and the chosen band who had come to London for the demonstration, remained at Bunhill Fields. Here for another six years they wrestled with the problems of adapting the frame to meet her majesty's requirements, supported by the encouragement, both verbal and financial, of his patron Lord Hunsdon and the manual assistance of their royal-blooded apprentice, Sir William Carey.

Lee's silk stocking frame was completed in 1598, and in that year he was able to present his sovereign with the mechanically knitted silk stockings she had expected to see issuing from his machine at the time of her first visit. She accepted them with considerable praise for their elasticity and beauty of texture—but with no offer of the hoped-for patent, or even a grant for development. William stopped attending court and concentrated on making as many more frames as his resources would allow. By the time Queen Elizabeth died in 1603, William, James and the rest of them had put together nine stocking frames.

Although he had become King of Scots as an infant on the abdication of his mother Mary, Queen of Scots, in 1567, James VI began his reign of his own account at the age of 12 in 1578. When the virgin queen of England left no heir, James found himself next in line of succession for her throne as well, and at once proceeded to London to be crowned. Before he left Edinburgh, he borrowed a pair of silk stockings from the Earl of Mar—'Ye would not have your king appear like a scrub before strangers?'—on hearing which William felt justified in believing that his chance of once again finding favour at court had revived. But James Stuart showed no more inclination to grant the mechanical stocking maker a patent that Elizabeth Tudor had done, and William Lee's life work seemed destined to evaporate in a mist of indifference.

18

Ladies 'All in one':
*All Wool undergarment
(1900s)*

Placket and tailored bust detail

The Cross Wynd Mill:
*Occupied by Waldie Pringle & Co
1819–68 (photo from 1960s)*

But one day he had another visitor at Bunhill Fields, a Frenchman who came with a letter from the Duke of Sully, Marquis de Rosny, first minister and favourite of the French King, Henry IV, who was in England as a special envoy of his master to negotiate an alliance. Lee demonstrated the frame to his French visitor, and later had an interview with Sully who invited him to bring his invention to France. In place of the cold shoulder shown by Sir Robert Cecil, he promised a warm welcome for his revolutionary process. Royal patronage awaited him and his device—in France.

As a one-time ordained priest of the protestant Anglican Church, Lee feared the kind of reception he might receive from the Catholics of France whose intolerance had resulted in such inhumane treatment of the Huguenots. With thoughts of religious persecution awaiting him if ever he set foot on French soil, he refused to go. But some years later he thought better of his decision, and with both Lord Hunsdon and his son Carey dead, he took ship with his brother James, eight of his workmen, and nine stocking frames, to Normandy. One of his leading men, a miller called Aston, chose to remain in England, and returned to his native villager of Thoroton, close by Calverton.

William's party settled in Rouen, where they set up their machines and awaited a summons to court. Sully was as good as his word, and within weeks presented William to Henry IV, who gave him an encouraging reception and endorsed all that Sully had held out. Sully told him that with the seal of royal approval he would now arrange for the consolidation and expansion of Lee's manufactory in Rouen.

William was congratulating himself that the tide was at last beginning to flow in his direction, when news reached him at his lodgings in Paris that Henry had been assassinated in his carriage when it stopped in the street on its way out of Paris to his army headquarters.

Gravenor Henson's graphic prose describes the end of this sorry tale:

So dreadful a misfortune acted as a thunder bolt upon the unfortunate ingenious man, and when, on waiting upon Sully, he found that that great minister had resigned the whole of his appointments into the hands of Mary de Medici, the Queen Regent, and that he was preparing in disgust to retire to his estate, leaving the government in the hands of Italians, his fortitude forsook him, and he gave way to the melancholy which had attacked him in London; he thought himself the most unfortunate of men; alone, unprotected, in a foreign country, after twenty-two years struggles; he sickened at the thought, and sent for his brother James from Rouen, but before he arrived the inventor of the stocking frame died of a broken heart, in the midst of strangers. This happened in the year 1610. (The History of the Framework Knitters, 1831).

He would have been aged about 46–50 at the utmost.

James Lee only stayed long enough in Paris to give his brother a funeral. He then returned to Rouen, had a council of war with the others, and decided that he and six of them would return at once to England. In the expectation that the new government would give them the aid

Wooden form:
Pattern for ladies 'All-in-ones'
(1900s)

1907

Registration for the protection of this New Design has been applied for.

The sales tool:
An illustrated catalogue
(1907)

19

1907

Sex appeal in 1907:
A more glamorous illustration
for a similar product produced
in the same year

promised to William, two of the frameworkers remained in Rouen with one of the machines which James agreed to sell to them. James took the rest to London and set up in Old Street Square. But on hearing that Aston, the member of the original team who had stayed in England, had devised a number of vital improvements, he decided to sell the old frames and use the money to build new ones on the lines developed by Aston. For this purpose James joined Aston at Thoroton, and reoccupied the old premises at Calverton and Woodborough.

Aston's improvements were wide-ranging, his introduction of the lead sinker being perhaps the most important. They made the original frames antiquated by comparison. The improved machines were found to be particularly suitable for working the 'worsted' type of woollen yarn which was spun in the nearby Sherwood Forest from the wool of the local sheep which had the longest and finest 'staple' in England. Stockings (hose) and socks (half hose) knitted from this yarn were strong enough to compete in wear with the hand-knitted hose now mainly made from extra twisted materials.

More important, the James Lee/Aston frames could be made—and sold—for less than half the cost of the original models. As each new frame left the Thoroton workshop it was copied and duplicated. Alongside the framework knitters grew up a race of 'framesmiths' able to erect and repair ('recruit') the machines. During the lifetime of James Lee and Aston the number of frames in Britain must have been well over a hundred. It had now become not so much a matter of developing an invention as creating an industry. Colonies of stocking-makers grew up, notably in Godalming, Surrey.

But the greatest number of frames were in London. Their owners soon felt large and powerful enough to form themselves into a trading company or association to maintain standards and prices, and regulate the entry of apprentices. They sought to penalise the knitters of what they considered 'fraudulent' goods, that is, not as fully fashioned as they should be.

There was widespread opting out of the rules, and large numbers of framework knitters and framesmiths took their knowledge, and often their machines, to realms outside England—to the Republic of Venice and the Netherlands—and to the country that lay to the north of the river Tweed which, although ruled since 1603 by the same House of Stuart as England, was still a separate kingdom governed by its own Parliament and nobility, and its own laws. Moreover, Scotland had to raise its own revenue which meant extracting as much excise duty from England as from any other trading nation.

20

Hoisery catalogue:
(1905)

Ribbed knee caps:
Night dresses, Cycle drawers and Tam O'Shanters are some of the Pringle products available to purchase (1905)

Opposite
Princess:
The Princess corset vest, this design was recreated as part of the 190th anniversary celebration in 2005 (1907)

1913

1913

3

BY PACKHORSE TO HADDINGTON

17th century Scotland's first manufacturers include framework knitting. (1603–1688)

T HE ACCESSION of James to the throne of England, and both kingdoms thus devolving on one sovereign, was an event fruitful of blessings to each nation. National prejudices, and a mutual resentment owing to a series of wars betwixt the two kingdoms carried on for centuries, still however subsisted and disappointed James's favourite scheme of an entire and indissoluble union. But it required almost an hundred years, though England and Scotland were governed all the time by a succession of the same princes, to wear off the jealousies and prepossessions of the formerly hostile nations, and to work such a change in their tempers and views as to admit of an incorporating and an effectual union.

George Ridpath, minister of Stitchill, whose words these are (from his *Border History of England and Scotland* of 1776) was not alone in decrying the circumstances that kept the two nations apart and hindered the northern one from developing as healthily as its thriving neighbour. Poverty dogged the Scotland of the 16th and 17th centuries; and mainly because of the almost total pre-occupation of the sections of the community who could bring wealth and prosperity with either wrangling over ecclesiastical niceties or undertaking the time-consuming activity of putting haughty neighbours in their place by kidnapping or killing, and pillaging their barns. The energies and finances of the government were largely dissipated, when not coping with raiding English troops, in useless attempts to bring these feuding nobles to heel. It was a way of life which sapped the intellectual

Opposite
Fashion plate:
A range of ladies styles and designs from a 1913 catalogue

powers of men who inherited a tradition which continued to give priority to such matters at the expense of delaying the more mundane, but no less exciting adventure, of laying the foundations of long-term social and economic prosperity.

John Keymor was one of those who ruminated on the unpleasant reality of the economic gulf that lay between England and Scotland and in 1620 set down his conclusions in a 'Memorial' which he addressed to James VI. He pointed out the serious evil of exporting raw materials and importing manufactures, quite apart from the stupidity of allowing the Dutch to fish without hindrance off the Scottish coastline. He estimated the foundation of a trade to foreign countries and the exporting of fish and manufactures would make Scotland richer by £3 million, and implored his ruler to do something about it.

In spite of the promises made in a tearful farewell oration in St Giles Cathedral, after removing himself to London in Lord Mar's borrowed stockings, James I of England made only one visit to his northern kingdom in his entire reign. But he was sincere in wanting to turn his new position to the good account of Scotland. Scotland was still feudal. The wheels of society still turned on privilege and the system demanded the sovereign granting rights as 'favours' in return for services or bribes. Thus undertakings requiring business skill came into the hands of prominent courtiers to whom grants of monopoly were given on personal grounds. A Mr Udwart had entertained King James particularly lavishly during the monarch's only visit in 1617, and two years later was granted the privilege of opening a soap manufactory in Leith. Similarly a nobleman, Sir John Hay, was given a patent in 1610 for manufacturing glass at Weems. Both failed. Nonetheless, during his long reign, as one historian put it, 'Scotland made a greater advance from barbarism to civilisation than in any whole century of its previous history'. James died in 1625, and his son Charles was crowned King of Scots in 1633. The declared policy of Scotland was now to rival the Dutch in their fishing and the English in their woollen trade. John Keymor's Memorial had been taken to heart.

When in 1642 Charles Stuart, King of England and Scotland, raised his standard at Nottingham, James Lee and Aston can only recently have died at nearby Thoroton and Calverton. During the Civil War that followed, on the strength of the Scottish Act of Parliament of 1641, three factories were established in Scotland in 1645 for the manufacture of fine woollen cloth.

Under the Protectorate which followed the surrender of the Royalists and the execution of the king, Oliver Cromwell abolished not only the monarch but also the separate Scottish parliament. When the whole of Scotland fell to General Monk's army in 1652, Cromwell proposed a Commonwealth of England and Scotland in which the people of the single nation would all enjoy the privileges of English subjects. In England it was to Oliver Cromwell that the framework knitters of London looked for state recognition of the association which, as has been seen, they had formed shortly before the Great Rebellion broke out—in 1656 he had granted a charter to the sewing needle makers. So on July 13, 1657 the Society of the Art or Mistery of Framework Knitters of the Cities of London and Westminster and Kingdom of England and Dominion of Wales presented him with a petition for a similar charter, which opened as follows:

24

The new mill 'Rodono':
*The nickname given to the new mill after Roberts hunting lodge at St. Marys Loch.
(picture 1930s)*

Rodono "quality second to none":
*Pringle make its first spun silk underwear at Rodono
(1892)*

Ladies knickerbockers:
*Finely knitted knickerbockers with elaborate Scottish motif knitted into the design
(1890s)*

"Rodono" underwear:
Pringles first brand
(1922)

The humble representation of the promoters and inventors of the art and mystery or trade of framework-knitting, or making of silk stockings or other work in a frame or engine ... Their trade is properly stiled frame-work-knitting because it is direct and absolute knitwork in the stitches thereof, nothing different therein from the common way of knitting that by the judgement of all beholders, it far excels in the ingenuity, curiosity and suptilty of the invention and contexture, all other frames or instruments of manufacture in use in any known part of the world.

And for the skill requisite to the use and manage thereof it well deserves (without usurpation as some others impertinently have) the titles of mystery and art, by reason of the great difficulty of learning and length of time necessary to attain a dextrous habit of right true and exquisite workmanship therein, which preserved it hitherto (from the hands of foreigners) peculiar to the English nation, from whence it has extraction, growth and breeding, unto that perfection it hath now arrived at. Not only able to serve your Highnesses dominions with the commodities it mercantably works, but also neighbouring countries round about, where it has gained so good repute that the vent thereof is now more foreign than domestic; and has drawn covetous eyes upon it, to undermine it here and to transport it beyond the seas.

The Rodono guarantee:
Unshrinkable
(1912)

The Lord Protector granted them their charter. When the monarch was restored, all Cromwell's acts were set aside, but the association petitioned for, and were granted, a new charter from Charles II in 1663.

The Restoration of the monarchy also restored the separate Scottish parliament, which got down to ironing out the customs which had hindered industrial progress. It enabled joint stock companies to be formed and incorporated. The making of cloth, linen and *stockings* was indicated as suitable fields for such companies. Model rules for their organisation were outlined. A 'Committee of Trade' was set up. New inventions were to be exempt from local taxes. Some 50 Scottish companies were set up between 1661 and 1707.

Charles II governed Scotland from London by means of a Royal Commissioner who at this time was his brother James, Duke of York, the future King James the Seventh of Scotland and Second of England. In the year of 1681 the Duke of York made a tour of Scotland in this capacity, and in the course of it paid a visit to James Stanfield's New Mills wool factory at Haddington. He was much impressed. The management he had to admit was English and so were the principal craftsmen, but this he felt was the prototype of the kind of commercial activity he would like to see all over Scotland.

The Duke of York let it be known that the undertakers of the New Mills project had royal approval, which immediately attracted capital. On September 13, 1681 an Act for Encouraging Trade and Manufactures ratified Privy Council ordinances prohibiting the import of linen, cambric and all stuffs made of linen or cotton wool except arras carpets. People with capital and technical knowledge were

Gentlemen's combinations:
From a 1909 catalogue

25

encouraged to settle in Scotland and found new industries. They were to receive naturalisation on condition they set up manufactures of cloth, linen, *stockings* or soap, and teaching the trade to Scotsmen. Raw materials could be imported free of custom duty and public dues for ever. The capital of such companies was not to be subject to public or local taxes. The products so manufactured would be free of export duty.

Encouraged by this demonstration of real intent from the authorities, in the second year of his New Mills operation, Sir James Stanfield decided to expand his woollen enterprise to include the new aspect of woollen manufacture which he had heard about, and probably had seen on his visits to his native England—framework knitting.

A document called 'The Book for the Managers of The Manufactory's Weekly Sederents' from June 1681 to March 1691 has survived. These managers directed the company from a 'head office' in Edinburgh. An entry for May 24, 1682 notes that they 'made an agreement with Sir James Stanfield for foure silk stoken frames for which they are to pay 2000 markes'. On June 2 the managers wrote to John Home of London to send down the two stocking frames by land; on June 12 they were approving contracts made with three framework knitters, Francis Perry, Edward Pike and John Godson 'to maintaine and keep the frames in perfect care' for 5s 6d a week.

During August the frames themselves came up from London to Haddington 'by land' instead of taking the usual sea route to Leith and thence by road, which indicates that the iron components had been broken up, put into panniers which were fixed on the saddles of packhorses which then proceeded on the long journey north and smuggled across the Cheviots to Haddington. Resort to these clandestine methods was necessitated by the bye-laws of the London Framework Knitters Association which forbad the export of frames from London—bye-laws which had the authority of the law of the land. The first recorded stocking frames in Scotland therefore entered the country as contraband. The wooden frames were made locally—a note in the managers book refers to the ordering of timberwork.

The framework knitting was carried on alongside the very much larger scale cloth weaving operation which in the heyday of the mill employed 700 people. Both stockings and cloth were taken from New Mills to a warehouse in Edinburgh and costed—to bring a profit of 3s 4d in the pound sterling. The goods were parcelled up and each proprietor of the New Mills company had the right to purchase the amount allotted in accordance with his holding, at cost price. He would then retail them at a selling price which gave him his profit. If a member did not draw his lot within 14 days it was sold by public 'roup' (auction). In this way the products of New Mills at Haddington were given wide distribution throughout Scotland.

The success of the New Mills Manufactory bolstered by its royal patronage and protected by laws forbidding import of foreign, including English cloth, exceeded all expectations. Through his connections with the army the one-time colonel in Cromwell's army, James Stanfield, now knighted, who headed the enterprise, obtained a Government contract for the supply of cloth for military uniforms, 'to distinguish sojers from other skulking and vagrant persons'. In 1683 he secured an order for uniforms for General Dalzell's Regiment of Dragoons.

26

Girl spinners:
Young girls spin yarn for knitwear production (1900s)

Greensmith Downes:
Tradesmen's materials catalogue and suppliers to Pringle (1912)

Ladies sports look:
Long line sports cardigan. Knitwear revolutionised sportswear, its ready stretch gave an ease of movement not experienced before (1913)

It was getting too much for a single unit to handle and he planned to launch a second venture to share the army contract with New Mills. Big profits were made; the capital was increased. Sir James Stanfield was riding high.

But by 1685 the canter was beginning to slow down—and there were occasional stumbles. There was an increasing difficulty in getting the right kind of skilled worker in Scotland. The Edict of Nantes, by which the French government gave protection to protestants, was revoked in 1685, and though the Huguenots weavers who feared persecution and sought refuge in England and Scotland were not in a position to bargain, most trained workers from abroad demanded exorbitantly high wages. And there was the ever-present problem of getting those workers they did have to do a full day's work and obey the managers' rules. Recalcitrant weavers and knitters who refused to toe the line were locked in a 'prison' in the factory, or made to stand in the market place for two hours at a time with a piece of paper stuck on their head proclaiming their misdemeanour in large letters for all to read.

But Sir James Stanfield's final fall was due to his son Philip, an extravagant and profligate youth who squandered his father's money as soon as he made it. He was a militant anti-cleric and once threw a bible at John Welch, the vicar of Haddington, and mocked him while he was preaching in the parish church. The Reverend Mr Welch—doubtless an ancestor of the Jane Welsh of Haddington who married Thomas Carlyle—stopped his sermon to remark that he did not know who had thrown the book but predicted that there would be more people at the death of the person who had done so than there were in the church that morning.

One summer morning in 1687 the body of Sir James Stanfield was found floating in the river Tyne which flows through Haddington. It was first thought to be a case of suicide by drowning, but suspicions were aroused by a hurried funeral and the fact that Lady Stanfield was discovered to have prepared grave clothes beforehand. The Privy Council had Sir James's body exhumed and examined by two surgeons. Their inspection of it in Morham Church led to their report that death was due to strangulation. Philip was suspected of murdering his father, and together with two servants and a women he was immediately arrested.

At his trial before the Privy Council he was 'tortured with the thumbikins' with little effect, but he was then confronted with the body of his father and made to touch it to see whether, in accordance with the custom of the day, he would reveal himself as the true murderer should the wounds start to bleed. That they did appear to do so when Philip touched his father's throat, had great weight with the jury. It was the last time this gruesome procedure was carried out at a Scottish murder trial.

Philip and his co-conspirators were convicted, and he was publicly hanged at the Cross of Edinburgh, receiving, as many were quick to point out, the same kind of death he had given his wretched and ill-deserving parent. Awaiting death in his prison cell he was reminded of Parson Welch's prognostication, and in a moment of remorse and regret for a worthless life, admitted that God was about to accomplish what he had been warned of, and more people would indeed throng to his scaffold than had come that day to hear the sermon in Haddington Church. The crime, and the previous insensible treatment of the worthy

Busy women:
Seamstresses working on underwear at Rodono (1900s)

Empress knitted silk jacket:
In 1907 Pringle developed the knitted motoring coat for 'adventurous ladies' (1915)

27

Scotch knit waistcoat:
(1913)

and respected father, gave rise to widespread feeling of revulsion throughout Scotland—of little help, however, to the enterprise which the murdered man had created, left now without its expert and energetic head at a time when the first cracks had begun to show.

Already, in June 1686, the managers were deliberating 'a sure way to prevent the want of work to the stocken workers that we may not for idle days', and in the year following Standfield's death the company began getting rid of their stocking frames.

The first Scottish mechanical knitting enterprise ground to a halt in 1689—exactly a hundred years after William Lee's frame first saw the light of day.

Henly style vest:
*Finely knited silk vest
(1920s)*

Underwear set:
*Plain shirt and trouser set
(1922)*

28

Opposite
Knitting Machine:
*Photographed at Rodono
(1900s)*

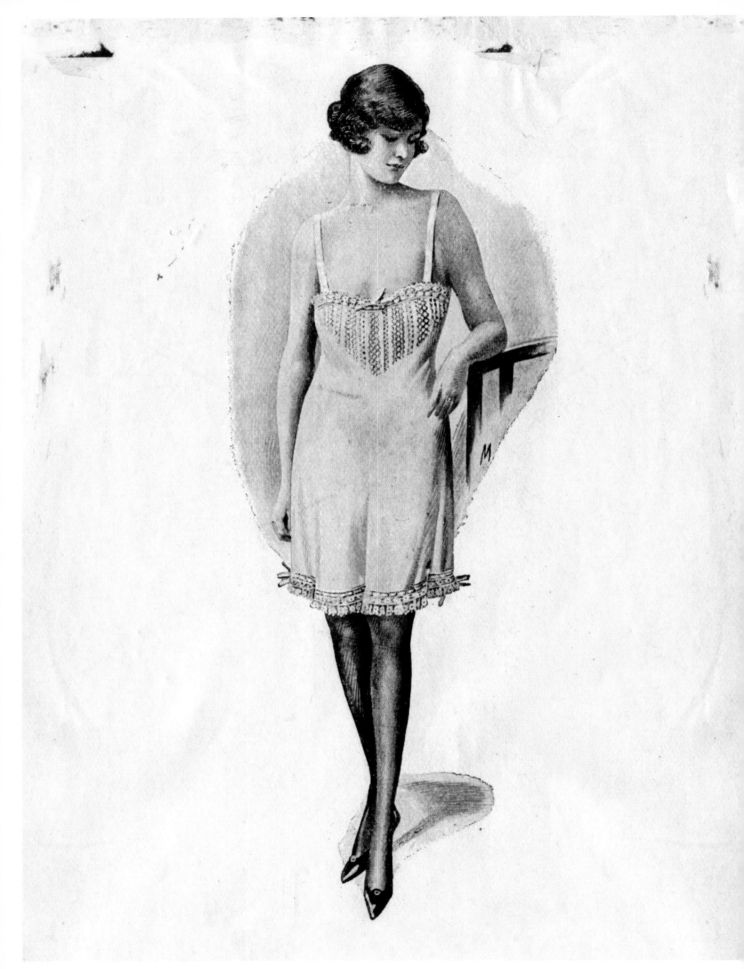

4

SCOTLAND LEANS ON LINEN

But 18th-century Hawick builds a reputation for quality—in woollen yarn. (1688–1770)

T HE YEAR of the collapse of the second New Mills manufactory— it was revived and lived on to 1712 but that is not part of this story—was the year in which the English and Scottish thrones 'became vacant' on the departure of King James II and VII and the infant Prince of Wales across the channel to France. The Dutch Prince of Orange and his English wife, both Protestants, were invited to fill the vacancy—James would not admit he had abdicated—and the engineers of the Glorious Revolution congratulated themselves on the bloodless installation of William and Mary, daughter of James I, as the new joint sovereigns. The price was war with France whose ruler, Louis XIV, insisted on recognising the pretensions of his English royal refugees, and encouraged the cause of 'Jacobitism', the triumph of which would have delayed the progress of further commercial development and put Scotland back into the age of derring-do from which it was happily emerging.

'Improvement' was the in-word of the new times. In his pamphlet *An Accompt Current between Scotland and England balanced* published in Edinburgh in 1705, John Spruel pointed out 'the same great Improvement can be attested by many worthy Gentlemen in the North,, and especially at Aberdeen, how great Increase of Profit arises upon the Industry of both rich and poor Women by one Stone of Wool, first in spinning, then in knitting it into fine Stockins, some Pairs whereof have given 10, 15 to 20 and 30s sterl Per pair, even for Women's Stockins,

Lace knit lingerie:
*Opera princess dress
(1922)*

and so are finer than Silk Stockins'. He was referring, of course, to hand-knitted stockings.

But, he went on, 'if the improvement of the Woollen Manufacture in Scotland is not improved, if the improvement is any longer slighted and neglected we shall repent it. For these have enriched England … and it might be of Advantage to Manufactories that Noblemen and Gentlemen were pleased sometimes to change their Wear from Cloth to Camblets as in England and Ireland; there are People who wait to see what is most in Fashion first in the Spring. And this would be better also for Tradesmen, and then to wear Cloth in the Winter'.

In the year of John Spruel's pamphlet, a Scottish law was passed making it illegal to bury bodies in any material but wool. But by then negotiations had already started (1702) for a treaty of union between England and Scotland, and William III had been succeeded by Queen Anne.

Union between the two kingdoms of England and Scotland came about on May 1, 1707. The crosses of St George and St Andrew were to be conjoined into a Union Jack in such manner as her majesty should deem fit.

It was an event of utmost importance in setting the stage for the birth and growth of the business with which this story is concerned.

The Act which created a United Kingdom with a single parliament, was followed by others for freedom and intercourse of trade around the newly formed Great Britain, and navigation to and from any port or place within it. Export to France was still prohibited, but it opened to Scots industrialists a wide market for any fabric wanted by the American colonies. Linen manufacture—'lawn' and 'cambric'—was begun on a big scale in Glasgow in 1725 for this purpose. Scottish linen could now be sold in England and gave impetus to the growing of 'lint' as flax was called and the manufacture of linen products generally.

The Act of the last session of the Scottish Parliament of January 16, 1707 ratifying the Treaty of Union contained a clause stating that 'Two Thousand Pounds per Annum for the space of Seven Years shall be applied towards encouraging and promoting the Manufacture of Coarse Wool within those shires which produce the Wool'—Selkirk, Berwick, Roxburghshire and the rest. The money paid to Scotland by the Bank of England was intended as indemnity for past failures such as the Darien Scheme, and to act in part as 'equivalent' to Scotland's share of the English National Debt which she now had the privilege of sharing.

The roots of a Scottish industry based on William Lee's stocking frame which Sir James Stanfield had planted at Haddington soon showed signs of growth. The efforts of the managers to get rid of the frames by renting them met with as little immediate success as the abortive rouping, but in spite of this there seems to have been quite a number of frames being worked in Scotland at the close of the 17th century, particularly in Edinburgh. Some of these would have been New Mills frames, others copies made by smiths.

James Dunlop and a number of fellow merchants of Edinburgh petitioned the Scots Parliament in 1700 for permission to erect 'a manufacty for working stockings upon frames with the same

32

Gerald Pringle:
An apprentice in the knitted coat dept. Killed in action aged 24 at Pashendale in the spring 1918 during WW1

1927

GENTLEMAN'S CARDIGAN

Cardigan:
A classic menswear design still made today (1927)

privileges as were granted other manufactories'. It is likely they were granted their petition, but there is no record of this or their having in fact established their factory.

An advertisement in the Edinburgh Courant of 1706 announced that Andrew Cockburn 'having by his care and industry improven his stocken manufactory better than any other in the Kingdom, sells all sorts of silk, silk and worsted and finist worsted stockens in his shop in the Locken Booths, at the Poll and Stokens above the Old-Kirck-Style in Edinburgh'. These might have been hand knitted stockings, but in another advertisement in the same newspaper of the same year William Williamson and Mungo Smith described themselves as 'joint owners and proprietors of the stocken-frames sometime belonging to Alexander Clerk and wrought upon by John Clerk Elder, servant' and offer all sorts of worsted stockings 'to be sold at more easie rates than anywhere else'. Stockings were in demand from men to wear above the knees with the breeches which were the fashion of the day.

But those manufacturers who looked to the Union for immediate improvement were disappointed. In spite of the £2,000 encouragement fund, the first effects were adverse. Superior English woollen goods—fine broadcloth at seven shillings a yard—flooded across the border for the first time in unrestricted quantities for which the Scots plaidings, blankets and hodden gray (coarse undyed cloth made from wool in its natural colour) were no match, spun as they were from the short, thin tar-clotted fleeces of the Border sheep. Moreover the Scottish manufacturers faced heavier taxes, a longer list of duties. Many Scotsmen migrated to England as gardeners and tailors.

But it was a matter of *reculer pour mieux sauter*.

The statesmen on both sides of the border needed a breathing space in which to get used to the new-won harmony and, so far as the industrial development of Scotland was concerned, discover how best to make up for lost time.

They took 20 years.

Once rid of the distracting episode of the pretended Prince of Wales's bid to restore the House of Stuart by the insurrection of 1715, and with a second Hanoverian George securely on the throne of the now well-established United Kingdom, in 1727 the government took the step which was to open up the development of Scotland as none had done before. This was the creation of a Board of Trustees of 21 Commissioners, seated in Edinburgh, to protect, encourage and improve Scottish manufactures and fisheries. Its first job was to gather information from the shires and boroughs, and the compilation of this miniature Scottish Domesday Book took some time. No real Plan as such was ready till 1736, but the Board at once invited applications for grants or for help in the form of experts and technicians. In his *History of the Framework Knitters*, Gravenor Henson wrote that of the 8,000 stocking frames in existence at the death of George I in 1727 'some few are said, though upon rather doubtful authority, to have been introduced into Scotland at this period, at Glasgow and Haiwck [sic]'. The bailies (magistrates) of Hawick were stimulated by the establishment of the Board of Trustees to appoint the Town Treasurer in 1728 as the person responsible for keeping in touch with the Board and to offer to any would-be manufacturers in Hawick £2 a year towards the rent of a workhouse.

Cardigan coat:
A single-breatsted knitted coat, knitted outerwear was continuing to increase in production (1922)

Princess top dress worn over corset (1922)

33

In April the same year he applied to the Board for wool sorters and combers (for worsted wool). His request was granted and the Board sent to Hawick one William Scott whose 'indolence and avaricious temper', however, was the subject of a complaint by the bailies after only a few months. He was also exacting exorbitant prices for his combing they said, 'to the great discouragement of manufacture'. They asked that the Board replace William Scott with John Scot of Langholm, who was bred a clothier (a cloth maker) in England (in spite of his name). The Board agreed but Scott took them to court—and lost. John Scot, Woolcomber, was admitted a burgess of Hawick in 1730.

Hawick was one of ten 'stations', which at this time included Edinburgh, Stirling and Galashiels, allotted £30 to buy coppers for scouring wool. A copper was bought for Hawick but never used. In 1733 a co-partnery was formed to build and run a spinning school in Hawick and the next year the Hawick bailies received a grant of £19 8s 6d from the Board of Trustees for utensils for this school, and £20 to pay the salary of a mistress from England to teach spinning of worsted 'after the English fashion'. A plea to manufacture wool instead of exporting it, to replace idleness with a Spirit of Industry came from Patrick Lindsay, Lord Provost of Edinburgh, in a pamphlet *The Interest of Scotland Considered*, which he published anonymously in 1736. Manufacture, he wrote, was in no esteem. Men of Fortune thought it beneath them to breed children to any business of that sort. 'Since war ceased to be our chief Trade, the Possessors of Law, Physick, the Business of the Foreign Merchant and Shopkeeper are reckoned the only suitable Employments for Persons of Birth and Fortune. Many Gentlemen after an expensive Education are obliged to take themselves to another Way of Life; or if they want Spirit or Discretion to continue in an idle and fruitless attendance'.

A practice which militated against any progress in the manufacture of wool was the smearing of sheep coats with tar, so that dirt and moss clung to it. Ostensibly a customary mark to identify one owner's sheep from another's, in fact it was over-done to make the fleece heavier and costlier. Over-smearing, under the guise of a tradition inherited from their forefathers for a reason that no one now remembered, was wide-spread because it brought profit. 'It was not considered the manufactories would soon discover the trick, that the wool would fall to its true value and that the merchants would go to another market'. Moreover linen became the staple industry of 18th century Scotland. Scottish linen could compete with the English product and make a profit—and the same could not be said of Scottish woollen products. It brought a new prosperity of a kind. Spinning thread from flax (lint) on the small wheel became an occupation for ladies and their maids for home use, while the poor made it for the market. In the country towns the Master Weaver called at the houses of the gentry, the farms and peasant cottages, and bought their thread which, after 'heckling', his men wove into linen checks and sheets in the shop adjoining his house. The Duke of Argyll formed a company for trading in all branches of linen manufacture with a capital of £100,000. Woollen (worsted) yarn and linen thread were woven together to form a coarse kind of cloth called 'drugget'; and a finer cloth was made from a similar mixture of flax and wool known as 'linsey-woolsey'.

1927

Spencer Lace:
Intricate knitted camisole

1927

Flapper style lingerie:
Captioned 'Ladies dress options' (1927)

Although linen became a national industry, Roxburghshire, which produced a fifth of the total wool crop of the whole of Scotland, never became as addicted to the cult as Forfar, Perth and Lanark. A mid-18th century review showed 252 lint mills in Scotland, but none in Roxburghshire. In a series of open letters to the Board of Trustees David Lock, an Edinburgh merchant, suggested that instead of giving away public money for lint seed, the increase of sheep should be the Board's first concern. Staple commodities, he said, were goods manufactured and brought to market with little or no assistance of materials from foreign countries—and now they were buying raw lint from the Baltic! That linen was the staple of Scotland was a delusion. Facts were stubborn arguments. They had convinced him that the linen manufacture ought to be so far from being considered as beneficial that it was the very reverse. By employing so many hands which might have been much more advantageously used in the woollen trade had been one great cause of the impending ruin which threatened so many of Scotland's labouring people.

'That Wool is the staple of Great Britain from Land's-end of England to the most northern islands of Zetland will be evident to any person who will give the most attention to the matter ... In short, it will be found that Scotland in every part has Wool sufficient to employ all the labouring part of men and women from the age of seven to extreme old age for the good of the country and themselves. Indeed, God and nature seems to have ordained this country for the Woollen Manufactory and denied the Linen.'

'Let any man look at the people at Leeds, Wakefield and every place where the soil and climate help them to that invaluable great article Wool, he will seem them going to church well fed and well clad, and peace and plenty in their countenances; whereas in the Linen cities and towns nothing is to be seen but misery and want, famine and nakedness.'

All the stockings that could be made in Scotland after supplying their own needs could be sold to good account in the seven provinces of Holland. Lock was told by gentlemen from England that the wool in Scotland was as fit for making stockings, coarse and fine, as any wool he ever wrought in England or got from any other place. He had held two shares in the New Mills Manufactory at Haddington and knew of their ill success, but he did not choose to make any reflections on the management of the company, but in his opinion there never was a fair and proper trial made of the project. There were three million sheep in Scotland, and without encroaching on any corn land there could be ten million. Wool was more valuable than mutton, and indeed than all the gold and silver in Peru and Mexico. With wool there was a quick return without all that fracas of sowing lint seed, dressing the flax and all that. When would the linen maker bring it to market and turn it into cash? In 18 months? 'Whereas you may have the Wool off your sheeps backs to-day, and in eighteen days have your stockings at market'.

Framework knitting was now spreading fast in England. In 1727 when destroying machines, including frames, became punishable by death and the anti-Combination Laws were revived which had been dormant since 1550, there were 8,000 frames in existence. According to Gravenor Henson's reckoning, by 1753 there were 14,000. And in

Cigarettes and slippers:
A gentleman in his stylish combinations (1927)

35

stating this he again remarked—and it would be interesting to know on what basis—that at this time 'in Scotland the hosiery trade had made some small progress at Hawick and Jedburgh, and also at Edinburgh, Perth and Glasgow'. From London where, on the request of the workers, the Government had suppressed the Framework Knitters Association, framers, skilled knitters and framesmiths were fast moving into Nottinghamshire, Leicestershire, Derbyshire and other counties in the north and west.

Some of these frames may have come to Scotland. There is known to have been activity in Glasgow at any rate. But so far as Hawick was concerned, its merchants shared the apparent universal Scottish prejudice against mechanical knitting, and chose to concentrate, with the aid of the Board of Trustees, on varieties of Woollen Manufacture other than stocking making. However, with the Hawick spinning school in full swing under its English mistress, a trade of spun, uncombed and worsted woollen yarn gathered slow but sure momentum, and became the town's principal industry. By 1750 home-spun yarn—spun, that is, in the homes of the women of Hawick on their 'muckle wheels'—was being produced on a large enough scale to be sold through a number of distribution centres on the outskirts of the town. In a couple of years the reputation of Hawick yarn had brought orders from as far afield as Newcastle, Kendal, Stirling, Boroughbridge and many other towns in both England and Scotland.

The yarn was carried to the distribution posts on packhorses—the roads were not good enough for wheeled vehicles. Their panniers returned laden with cutlery from Sheffield, leather from Kendal, dyes and other goods, which were sold at a profit. This primitive but effective bartering-marketing operation was conducted by a character called 'Old Cash' (William Oliver) and James Dickson. There was a certain amount of hand-knitting, but no more than in any other town of its size at this time. J. J. Vernon and J. McNairn made this activity one of their Pictures from the Past of Auld Hawick:

> Little things of four or five years of age learned to knit, and as they grew older that useful art was considered more a pastime than a labour. Every few minutes of spare time was devoted to knitting. Strangers passing through Hawick were struck by seeing of an afternoon so many families plying their knitting needles; tongues and fingers both busy.
>
> No woman thought it decent to go about without her knitting. In their waistbands might have been seen a sheaf of straw or quills in which was inserted the end of the inevitable wires. It was interesting to see the more elderly of the women in their print gowns, check aprons, shoulder shawls and clean white starched mutches—in many cases wearing the 'broo band'—seated on the landing of their forestairs or in their doorways, all busy at their knitting.

If, by any chance, a merchant in Hawick had wanted to hear more about this mechanical knitting business which everyone else in Scotland was sheering away from, he would almost certainly have made a clandestine visit to Glasgow. For in 1756 seven Glasgow framework knitters had petitioned the Corporation of Glasgow for a charter for

1927

LADY'S NIGHTDRESS (MAGYAR SHAPE)

Nightwear

1927

Bathing dress:
Knitted dress and trunks

their 'Incorporation of Stocking-makers in Glasgow', and on May 6 they were granted it. Many of these master stockingmakers had Scottish names like McDougall, Graham and Liddell, and as seven years apprenticeship was served at the craft before becoming a journeyman, it shows that these men had been framework knitters for many years before 1756. It was after all 50 years after the dispersal of the stocking frames from Haddington. Indeed the petition referred to a kind of sickness benefit fund set up 14 years before (that is in 1742) for those who through illness became poor and indigent. It also mentioned that the business had been set up in Glasgow 'not many years ago' and that as very few had knowledge of it, the master hosiers were obliged to hire or send for journeymen from England, Ireland (where framework knitting was widespread) and other parts. The Corporation of Glasgow in granting them a charter of incorporation stipulated that 'the stock weavers shall be obliged to stamp every pair of stockings with the word Glasgow on it upon the head of each pair'. The body later changed its name to the Master Hosiery Society and survived till 1904.

Rodono embroidery set:
(1930s)

37

HAWICK
FOR QUALITY
UNDERWEAR

As Vertue man or woman doth adorne

So (Cleane) is Linnens vertue; and is worne

For pleasure, profit and for ornament,

Throughout the world's most spacious continent.

Much more of this word (Cleane) might here be writ

But tediousness is enemy to wit,

Cleane Linnen now my verse descends to thee,

Thou that preordinated were to be,

Our corps first cover, at our naked birth:

And our last garment when we turne to Earth,

So that all men Cleane Linnen should espie,

As a Memento of mortalitie.

John Taylor, the Water Poet. *The Praise of Cleane Linnen,* 1630

Jacquard Design II

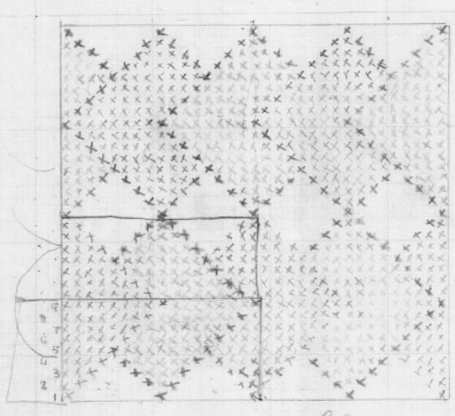

Chain

Carriers

1 Ground F.B. —
2 Black B.B
3 Red F.T.
4 Empty over chest

5

HARDIE CHANCES HIS ARM

Hawick wine merchant buys town's first stocking frame—and founds an industry. (1771–1793)

I N 1771 there was someone in Hawick with the temerity and resolution to chance his arm on at least experimenting with the mechanical stocking frame of ill-repute. He was 49-year-old John Hardie, a respected and distinguished member of the merchant community. He had the determined will of the kind to be expected from a person who chose to plough a lone furrow in a field with a possible bright future but a decidedly not too happy past.

John Hardie (his name is also spelt 'Hardy' and on his tomb in St Mary's churchyard it is 'Harday') was 'a character' and an optimist. 'Of quiet talents and decided mind' was one summing up. Stories of his eccentricities abound. But behind them all he was well equipped to withstand and return the discouraging forebodings of his business colleagues and competitors. It was not for nothing that the Hardies, as the family proudly claimed, were descended from the Hardicaustles, ancient Danish kings of England. He became a leading citizen, a bailie (magistrate) and town councillor. He inherited an independence of spirit from his father Henry Hardie, a shopkeeper, who was once fined, according to the Council records, for gross immorality in profaning the Sabbath by 'tarrying in time of Divine Service' in the house of a Mr Rennicke who kept 'a change' (a pub).

John Hardie was married to a woman called Rebecca Sawn, ran a wine and spirit shop (whisky first came to Hawick in 1755), and had a brother called 'Whether or No' (it was a great age for nicknames). But such details are of considerable irrelevancy beside the fact that some time in the year 1771 he brought to Hawick, and had installed in his shop at 37 High Street, four stocking frames which he will almost certainly have purchased in Glasgow.

41

Opposite
Jacquard diamond design:
A variation on the Argyle. The Argyle was designed in 1897 after experiments in knitting a Tartan pattern and moved from socks to outerwear in the 1920s (1930s)

He was unlikely at his age to have become a framework knitter. What he became, as a sideline to his wine and spirit business, was a hosier. It was what was known as 'custom work'.

He will have begun with one frame—second-hand probably—engaged a smith to erect it and put it in working order, and then hired a fully trained framework knitter to operate it. Within weeks, Hardie brought the other frames into use and enlisted three more knitters.

In the following year he got himself an apprentice, whose name has survived—John Potts. By the end of 12 months he was employing five men on the frames in his 'stocking shop', one of whom was probably the framesmith, and arranging for six women in their homes to do the spinning and seaming.

There is no record of John Hardie applying to the Board of Trustees for a grant for introducing a new industry to Hawick; nor for the bounty, to which he was entitled, of a shilling a stone for wool used in manufacture. He may have been too proud to apply for a grant, but so far as the bounty was concerned he would not have qualified for it, for, heretical though it may seem in the heart of the Wool Country, his first stockings were knitted with linen thread. They were of the long type worn by men over the knees to go with their breeches, the basic fashion of the day. Later his stockings were made from linen thread mixed with combed (worsted) woollen yarn. All were of the coarser variety.

It is difficult to say to what extent Hardie's frames were the 'improved' models. One of them stood at the back of William Peddie's shop in Hawick High Street until 1896, but no one ever made a detailed description of it. The frame in the Border Museum in Hawick engraved 'Gavin Lennox Glasgow no 838 WE no. 222' is thought to date from 1798.

Lee's machine, as improved by his brother James and Aston, was never again basically altered—a fact that led Bishop Gillie, wishing to introduce a topical allusion when inaugurating a church in Hawick, to compare the old stocking frame to the Roman Catholic religion which might be modified in detail but had never changed its infallible principle.

But ancillary pieces of equipment were invented which enabled the original frame to tackle operations which had hitherto been beyond it. 'A few obscure individuals,' wrote Gravenor Henson, 'sedulously engaged in devising an additional appendage to the stocking frame which has led to the most astonishing results; as no art or science in any age or country made such rapid improvements as the framework knitting during the generation which existed from 1753 to 1780.'

Appendages with names like 'Tuck Presser' and 'Side Tickler' were devised by men who emerged from obscurity to earn themselves a niche in the history of the stocking frame—Arthur Else, Robert Frost, Ferdinando Shaw, Sam Betts. An important stage was reached when William Horton introduced elasticity vertically, as well as horizontally, by knitting the stocking round from seam to seam instead of from top to bottom, and giving stripes down the leg. It was what was known as 'knotted work'. Henson sent into raptures over it. 'Nothing could exceed the beauty, durability and elasticity of these newly invented articles which from their intrinsic merit as well as novelty became fashionable, not only for stockings, but for pieces of other parts of

42

Robert Pringle II:
Partner in the business 1885
(1930s)

Jacquard chevron design:
(1930s)

male habits.' Since Horton's knotted work was not introduced until 1776, it was too late for John Hardie's first operations in Hawick.

In time for Hardie, but probably not affecting the machines erected at 37 High Street, was the so-called 'Derby Rib' of Jedediah Strutt of Belper, which produced ribbed stockings by knitting the pattern known in Scotland as 'rig and fur', alternating purl and plain. 'Purl' was a plain stitch reversed—what you see on the 'back' of knitting. It was easy for the hand knitter but impossible for a machine, until the clever Mr Strutt came out with his ribbed frame in 1758. His patents expired in 1773, but the stitch which he enabled the frames to reproduce mechanically was widely used by the industry for many years.

John Hardie's four machines were common stocking frames knitting plain hosiery in the plain 'stocking stitch' in which garments were still made for many years later. They were 'narrow' frames, that is producing a web 14 inches in width, and one web at a time. Each had a glass globe filled with water hanging from one of the cross bars through which the rays of an oil lamp would shine and be magnified to cast the maximum light on the needles and the work that emerged from them.

The work was by no means fast by any standards. Within 12 months Hardie's four frames had turned out 200 pairs of men's stockings to the order of individual customers in a variety of shapes and sizes, but no half-hose (socks). Once the operation got into full swing the Hardie establishment was producing 2,400 pairs of stockings a year.

The knitters were not paid wages, for they were not employees in the strict sense of the word. Some worked the frame in a 'stocking shop' in a team of knitters; others operated frames in their own homes. They were hirers of stocking frames who sold the finished stockings, seamed and all, to the man they hired the frame from. They also paid him for the oil they had to put into their lamps, for needles, for a boy or girl to wind the thread or yarn, for a woman (more often than not his wife) to do the seaming with cotton and a 'house-rent'. They were not obliged to work the frames at any regular hours; they came and went as they pleased. In the summer they usually worked from six in the morning to eight at night, and in the latter part of the week only; in the winter from six to nine. Every Saturday they presented to Hardie the stockings they and their seamers had completed during the week and got paid for them. There was often late-night working on Friday to make up for the days-off taken at the beginning of the week. When Hardie took the week's finished goods, he gave out a supply of yarn, the whole of which he expected to have returned to him the following Saturday in the form of stockings. Thus the system afforded Hardie and his successors no opportunity of supervision and no control over the quality and finish of these 'fashion goods'.

It was not designed to bring happy working relationships or inspire the best workmanship, but presumably it secured the maximum profit for a master hosier for whom this was the main object. On more than one occasion it was to drag the whole industry in Scotland to a sordid, wrangling halt.

Instead it was causing rioting in England at this very moment. There were now nearly 20,000 frames in Britain (45,000 in France). The earning of the framework knitters had been depreciating as each 'additional appendage' made knitting a faster operation, and the

Sportswear logo:
Appeared on stationery and catalogues (1937)

Sportswear catalogue:
(1937)

43

amount masters were prepared to pay per pair of stockings became proportionately less, on the grounds that the quantity the knitters could make each day was that amount greater.

Though the success of the English masters, with the aid of the Establishment of the day, in forcibly keeping the knitters in what they considered their place, meant low prices for the consumer of English stockings with which the Scottish variety were to find it hard to compete, none of the troubles in the south deterred the incipient industry which was making determined headway at no 37 High Street, Hawick, under the direction of Mr John Hardie. Nor did it prevent others from jumping on the wagon.

The first, within a year of his starting up, had the name of the two itinerant evangelist-stockingmakers encountered at Haddington, the brothers George and Robert Haldane. In 1772 James Haldane (son of George?) set up four narrow stocking frames in Mid Raw, Hawick. He taught his daughter to work a frame. She later married an Englishman, Bill Daykins. In 1774 the third hosier appeared in the person of John Dixon who was apprenticed to a linen draper, William Irvine, and during his time had learnt to work a stocking frame.

The following year (1775), after four pioneering years at 37 High Street, John Hardie felt confident enough to engage an Englishman, William Beck, an experienced journeyman framework knitter who had served his apprenticeship in Carlisle and been working a frame since he was 18. He also belonged to the important and growing band of 'upsetters' who, according to Brewster, 'besides setting new frames at work, have frequently more employment in repairing old ones injured by want of care or skill, than any country apothecaries who live in healthy parishes can find in curing the disorders of mankind'.

William Beck stayed with John Hardie as a journeyman for two years. In 1777, he set up as a master hosier, with narrow (14 inch) frames, in another part of the High Street opposite the Crown Hotel. When, three years later, John Hardie, suffering from unspecific 'family distress', retired, he made an agreement with John Nixon and three others to take over his stocking manufactory as a co-partnery, and to move out of the High Street shop. John Nixon took the frames to larger premises in Cross Wynd where he added several more.

In the review which David Loch made in 1778 of the extent to which framework knitting was being done in Scotland, he stated that in Hawick in Tweedale-shire situated on the river Teviot, 'Mr Hardie has four frames for stockings going and James Halden (Haldane) two'—a rare mention of names. Hawick, said Loch, was 'a village most distant from sea of any in Scotland and far from coal, yet the industry and attention of the people is such to surmount all these disadvantages'.

At Hawick the operation saw the introduction of two innovations of importance. Some time between 1780 and 1785 John Nixon decided to have stockings made to his own specification without waiting for customers to come to him with their own wool and instructions. He took the initiative of making stockings of a type for which he believed there would be a demand and then set about finding customers. For a time he probably engaged in both custom-work and non-custom-work, but finally the latter became the basis of his whole operation.

In 1785 an Englishman, John Bramble, is credited with having

'Lucerne':
Twinsets become more fashion than function! (Golf)
(1936)

'Lucille':
(1936)

Girlish glamour:
(1930s)

knitted the first stockings to be made in Hawick not of linen thread, nor thread and wool nor combed worsted wool, but from the 'woolly' uncombed wool always referred to as 'lambswool', in which the fibres stood up instead of being smoothed down. He may have been one of Nixon's men or more likely one of the independent framework knitters, of which there were probably several in Hawick.

As Robert Wilson pointed out in his *Sketch of the History of Hawick*, published in 1825, the local demand for stockings of the linen and worsted sorts was very small. 'Linen or worsted hose being not very well adapted to northern latitudes, they gradually gave way to the warm, fleecy lambs-wool stockings from the wearing of which the lower extremities are so well defined against the impressions of a cold atmosphere.'

The wool for the first all-wool stocking ('worsted' is not regarded as 'wool' in the trade) was taken from the skins of lambs slaughtered in the town for meat. A sheep fair had been started in Hawick in 1779. At the first fair 2,540 sheep had been offered, and wool was sold at 5s 6d a stone.

The Wool Country had come back into its own again.

Unlike John Hardie, John Nixon took advantage of the aid offered by the Board of Trustees, and in 1786 he sent them a petition saying he had eight frames and intended buying four more for making ribbed stockings 'a branch of business hitherto unattempted in that part of the country'. He was given a grant.

Non-custom work, use of lambswool and now ribbed frames. The pace was accelerating.

A fourth hosier jumped on the wagon in 1790 whose family was to travel on it right into the second half of the 20th century. This was William Wilson, son of the Walter Wilson known as Handless Wat who, with the aid of Old Cash as marketing man, had so successfully organised spinning in the town. William Wilson served an apprenticeship in framework knitting in Hawick, and then went to Glasgow and worked as a journeyman for 3s 6d a week. He had a frame made for himself there and brought it back to Hawick where, at the age of 26, he set up on his own as a Master Hosier.

By 1791 John Nixon was making more lambswool stockings than any other kind. In that year he made 3,505 pairs in white and various colours, and only 594 pairs from cotton, linen thread and worsted. He now employed 13 male framework knitters in Cross Wynd, 42 women spinners, nine women seamers, doublers and twiners, and a foreman—65 in all.

Parson Gillan was highly impressed. In the paragraph on the industrial, as opposed to agricultural, activities of his Hawick parish for the Statistical Account two years later, he wrote: 'Notwithstanding the disadvantages of distance from fuel and an extensive land carriage, manufactures are carried on here with considerable spirit and success. Several branches are now established but the most considerable are carpets, inkle (linen tape), cloth and stockings … Their industry is not the violent exertion of a moment, but steady, calm and persevering.'

Were it not for the many disadvantages and difficulties they had to encounter, he concluded, 'The spirit of the inhabitants of Hawick would raise it to the first station of manufacture in the south of Scotland.' Prophetic words.

Stationery:
The Pringle name comes to the fore (1930s)

45

6

JOHN PRINGLE TRIES HIS HAND

Inspires half-brother Robert to form a co-partnery at Whisky House Mill. (1794–1819)

T HE WAR with revolutionary France had been going a year when on June 26, 1794, William Beck took another apprentice. His name was John Pringle. Beck, with 17 years behind him as a Hawick Master Hosier, undertook, in the routine formula of the indenture of the day, to teach John Pringle (or 'learn' him as the phrase was) the trade of stocking-making. He bound himself to find John sufficient work as a journeyman and to behave himself as a Master and teacher, to conceal no part of the business as far as his knowledge and ability would permit. 'At any time, by giving me a month's warning and paying up the engagement, the said John Pringle is at liberty.'

John Pringle was 16 years old, as was usual for an apprentice. He was born in 1778. He was one of seven children, and the second son of Walter Pringle by his first wife Betty Heiton whom he married in 1772. There is a village of that name just to the south of Kelso. Walter Pringle I (there was to be another of that name) was the son of a Thomas Pringle by *his* first wife.

An event of 1767 long remembered and talked of was the Hawick Flood. It took place on August 5 of that year. The River Tweed and its tributaries the Teviot and Slitrig which joined at Hawick rose and roared as they had never done before. When the flood abated the frightened inhabitants crept out to survey the damage. Washed up on the bank of the river Tweed at Kelso someone found an old bible. Inside was this inscription:

> Who ought this book if ye youlld know I will you show by Letters 2 the first is T a letter bright the 2 is P in all men's sight and if you chance to read amiss look underneath and ther it is
>
> **Thomas Pringle**

Opposite
Boys at work:
Stretching knitwear into shape (1900s)

It was a rather poor acrostic—it was a great age for puzzles and secret codes. Below it was written: 'This B I B L E belongs to (indecipherable) Pringle, 1690.' On another page is handwritten 'Thomas Pringle His Bibel 1722'. On the title page of the New Testament appear two names, Thomas Pringle and Robert Pringle. The book was printed by Andrew Anderson of Edinburgh in 1678. It came into the possession of Mrs Frances Muir of Muchalls Castle, Stonehaven, Thomas Pringle's great-great-great-grand-daughter. Gravel from the bed of the 18th century Tweed was still between its pages.

It is thought that on the day his family bible was washed away, Thomas Pringle was living in a house in the part of Hawick known as Sandbed, probably in Silver Street then a main highway, as vehicles had to pass along it to cross the old bridge at Kirkstile. Though he survived the Hawick Flood of 1767 he is said finally to have succumbed to another wrathful demonstration of Nature, a snowstorm.

This is the Thomas Pringle who was the grandfather of the John Pringle indentured to William Beck in 1794. The document given to John by his new master to confirm his apprenticeship for long hung framed in the reception hall of Pringle of Scotland's head office at Hawick.

The year before the 16-year-old John Pringle started to learn how to work a stocking frame as one of William Beck's apprentices, his father married again. The first Mrs Walter Pringle (nee Heiton) had died about 1790, having produced seven children, the last of whom, Walter, was born in 1787. Walter Pringle I married as his second wife on November 22, 1793 Anny Scott; and on July 29, 1795 the second Mrs Walter Pringle gave birth to a son whom they called Robert, who was therefore a half-brother of apprentice John.

Robert Pringle I (there was to be another) was born into a Hawick that was having its first experience of machinery.

While he was learning to work a stocking frame, William Wilson saw how difficult it was to produce knitting of even texture and quality with yarn spun by hand, and promised himself that when he had the means he would buy some of those machines James Hargreaves had named after his wife Jennifer and patented in 1770. By 1797 William Wilson had accumulated enough capital to put his plan into operation, and in Rough Heugh Waulkmill he installed a number of the spinning jennies which produced yarn very much finer and faster than anything the women of Hawick could do, as well as several carding machines. Here, in Hawick's first spinning mill, he provided a separate unit for making hosiery yarn for his stocking frames.

After 200 years, mechanical spinning had at last caught up with mechanical knitting. It immediately took one step ahead when Richard Arkwright devised a spinning jenny to be driven by power, the water-frame. But a water wheel could not drive a stocking frame, for the action was not yet rotary. Its motive power remained the framework knitter's hands and feet.

Three years after Wilson set up his mill there died the man who had founded the framework knitting industry in Hawick in 1771. Bailie John Hardie died on December 22, 1800, and was buried in St Mary's churchyard. He was deeply mourned; the debt which Hawick owed him, never forgotten.

In 1801 John Pringle's seven years apprenticeship to William Beck came to an end. Though nothing is known of what John Pringle did

48

Stretching boards:
Young men stretch cashmere over wooden formes (1930s)

The pressing department

with the rest of his life, it is unlikely that after such a long training he would at once have thrown up framework knitting and engaged in some other activity. He probably continued under William Beck's banner as a journeyman—his business was flourishing—or joined either John Nixon's group or William Wilson's, both going steadily ahead. After a year, he might have joined a newcomer to the industry, Alexander Laing who, in 1802, started with two frames in Sandbed using yarn spun on spinning jennies in Kirk Wynd. He seems to have had an eye to quality, for the story goes that once he spent a day going to Glasgow by coach and showed samples of his hose to a shopkeeper called John Clapperton, who bought the lot at 2s 6d a pair. A customer came in a moment later and bought a number of pairs at once at 5s each.

John Pringle may have been diverted from his trade by yielding to the call for volunteers to meet the threats of Napoleon; to serve either 'in case of actual invasion' or 'to go against the French with gun and bayonet'. Telegraph stations were once more erected on the hills where a red flag was to be hoisted if Napoleon's troops landed in the daytime, and a barrel of tar lit if they came at night. To the consternation of the volunteer on duty beside the beacon at Hume Castle on the night of January 31, 1804, he saw what he thought was the glow of a neighbouring beacon. His orders in such an eventuality were unequivocal. Without hesitation he set fire to his barrel, and within minutes all the other beacons on the neighbouring hills were ablaze, including the one on Crumhaugh Hill at Hawick. The bells were set ringing, the drums beating. The response was immediate. Volunteers bade swift farewell to their loved ones, and thronged into the district on horse and foot from miles around; the local ladies handed out the flannel shirts and new shoes they had been storing for just this moment. Trooper James Elliot, carried away with the emotion of the hour, mounted his horse, stood on his stirrups shouting 'Here I go to Ramoth-Gilead or battle!', applied his spurs to his stead which reared and threw him to the ground. On seeing her father in his uniform with his musket in his hand, John Michie's little daughter cried, 'Shoot me yerself faither, ye'll do it cannier than the French!'

If ever there was a day for heroics this was.

It was not till next morning that they all learnt that what the man who had lit his beacon at Hume Castle had seen glowing in the dark distance across the hills, was not a burning tar barrel at a signal station, but the charwood fire at Shoreswood Colliery. The alarm had been undeniably false. If it had not been, the story of the framework knitting industry in Hawick would have taken a very different turn. As it was, the depression that followed the 'late eventful struggle' as contemporaries were always calling it, was a severe, though only temporary, setback.

Apart from any self-employed operators like John Scot (the woolcomber?) whom the Board of Trustees granted a ribbed frame in 1798, there were certainly four (Nixon, Wilson, Beck and Laing) and perhaps six, calling themselves Master Hosiers in Hawick at the turn of the century. Between them they 'employed' 22 framework knitters, each earning about 8s a week and each employing and paying a woman to do the seaming, and a youngster to wind the yarn which his master

Drying department:
Sweaters dried on wooden frames

Drying rack

49

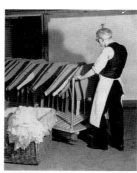

Drying rack

gave him. In 1804 William Wilson formed a co-partnery with William Watson, and it may well have been that around this time John Pringle, aged between 27 and 30, decided to have a go on his own or formed a similar co-partnery.

In the year 1807 when Robert Pringle, Walter Pringle I's son by his second wife, was a boy of 12, a co-partnery by the name of 'Waldie, Pringle, Elliot and Oliver' had an account with the Hawick branch of the British Linen Company which by now had become solely a banking organisation. The name appears in a ledger of that date.

The Pringle in that co-partnery cannot have been Robert, he would have been too young. It is almost certain to have been the journeyman framework knitter, John, who would have been eligible to form a partnership of master hosiers in any year from 1801 onwards.

John Pringle married as his first wife a Miss Oliver, and it is likely therefore that the Oliver in the co-partnery was either his father-in-law ('Old Cash'?) or his brother-in-law. It looks as if the co-partnery consisted of George Waldie, John Pringle, William Elliot (a known hosier) and James (?) Oliver.

Nothing is known of the progress, or otherwise, of Waldie, Pringle, Elliot and Oliver, hosiers, or what premises, if any, they had as a stocking shop; indeed their very existence only came to light in 1970. They may well have started life well before 1807 and continued well after 1811, and perhaps after 1815. What is known is that the period in which the four of them carried on their business was one of the most troubled in the whole history of the hosiery industry.

The war with France led to a lowering of earnings for every framework knitter in England—half of Nottingham was on poor relief in 1811. Bad harvests resulting in serious and widespread hunger added to the general misery, and with the new outbreak of Luddite rioting came the plundering of farmhouses for food.

It is of significance to this story that frames were broken, as William Felkin points out, 'not so much about wages but of cut-up work which lowered the demand for fully wrought goods and so tended to reduce prices generally'.

If circumstances led England to lower standards, there was no reason for Scotland to follow suit. On the contrary, it took the opportunity to emphasise once again the attachment it had shown, from the days of its spun yarn, to quality. As England had to withdraw, Scotland filled the breach. 'Cut-up' work was shaping or 'fashioning' stockings and other knitted goods by cutting the web with a pair of scissors, so that each row or course began and ended with a single piece of yarn severed at each end from the course above, and therefore liable to pullout.

This was opposed to the 'fully fashioned'—or un-cut fashioned—article with solid selvages which could not be unravelled, since the whole garment or stocking was made from a continuous single length of yarn, increased or decreased, as in hand-knitting, to give it shape.

The man who led the revolt against 'cut-up' goods (and low earnings) was a Leicestershire framework-knitter Samuel Slater who assumed the name of 'General Ned Ludd'. It all began when his father, who was his master, asked him to 'square up his needles' on his frame, and his answer was to take up a hammer and smash them into heaps.

50

30s catalogue 'Begonia Set':
Cashmere 'Golfer' cardigan

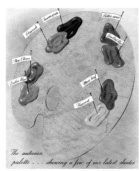

Autumn colour:
The latest shades

The pullover

The rioters were well organised in regular bands. Army and police were mobilised to deal with what a royal proclamation declared an 'insurrection'. In 1811 young William Felkin as a 17-year-old framework apprentice was told by his masters, who had 3,000 frames, to ride round to all would-be frame breakers and offer them an advance of a shilling a dozen pairs if the frames were spared. It worked.

During the war the production of 'fancy hose' went into a decline. The great variety of products made on stocking frames in England had reached a peak around 1800—silk narrowed clocks embroidered hose, warp-vandyked hose, silk tickler mitts, cotton spider net for ladies habit-shirts and the like. By 1812 most of these had been discontinued. In any event, women's fashions were loosening up; the trend was away from artificial towards more natural shapes.

The gay companians:
In partnership with Chalmers

'No woman of correct judgement' declared a writer in *The Ladies Magazine or Entertaining Companion for the Fair Sex* of the time, 'would adopt a costume that in its effect should either embarrass the motion of the limbs or give disproportion to the body. We have seen the invention of stiff and long stays, the design of which was to reduce fine shape and deformity to a level and to confound all distinction between youth and age. It will be confessed that the present fashion has recalled the privileges of the young; for no accessaries (sic) of long stays, bosom friends, cork rumps, marechale powder, or false tops, are now allowed; and no woman of real taste (unless there be a defect to conceal, would either bundle up her arms in a large puckered sleeve, or (however beautiful her neck) suffer her robe to fall off from her shoulders, so as to put her in incessant dread of its dropping off altogether, and thereby to prevent her from using her arms with ease or freedom.'

Cashmere lace:
Lace stitch cashmere with puff sleeves

51

A census of the hosiery trade taken in 1812 showed there were 28,155 stocking frames on hosiery (as opposed to lace) in England, Scotland and Ireland, of which 1,449 were in Scotland in 38 places—a big increase on David Loch's assessment in 1797. Some 2,500 out of the total number of frames were devoted to making non-stocking articles. Neither the war nor the new fashions however were yet having the same effect on Scotland as they were on the south. During the conflict, Hawick had firmly established herself in a leading position.

'The earliest manufactures in Roxburghshire,' wrote George Chalmers in his *Caledonia* published in 1810, 'arose from providing food and raiment for a rude people ... As early as the reign of King David I we have perceived the sheep washed and shorn; and we may easily suppose that their wool was by the women of every house converted into clothing. This is the natural manufacture of a country which abounds with sheep. The fabrics of wool have begun and have made some progress.

'The great seat of the woollen manufacture is Hawick, which works up more wool into carpets, blankets, narrow cloths, flannels, stockings, rugs, table covers, and saddle covers than all the rest of the county.'

The remainder of the war with France saw the quartering in the houses in the town of a hundred officers of German and Swiss nationality captured while fighting with Napoleon's army, and sent to Hawick on parole. They behaved themselves well and became a familiar part of the Hawick scene. They complained of the cold and criticised the townspeople's sober dress. However they admired seeing in practice the tenets of 'the grand constitution and the manners and the equality that we did fight for for so long'. 'I see in your streets,' remarked one of these military gentlemen, 'the priest and the shoemaker, the banker and the baker, the merchant and the hosier, all meet together, be companions and be happy.'

Good community relations nearly suffered shortly after the arrival of the 'French prisoners' as they were always being incorrectly described. One Sunday, to his amazement, churchwarden Rob Tinlin saw three men in gaudy uniforms march into William Nixon's pew for morning service. He knew there was a travelling theatrical company performing in the town, and not having been appraised of the posting of the German officers, assumed them to be actors in their play costumes attempting a profane form of advance publicity for their show. He strode down the aisle and angrily ordered them to leave the church immediately. An unfortunate start to a two-years' stay was happily averted by the appearance of the pew owner William Nixon, who had volunteered to be the parole officers' paymaster and knew the form.

William Nixon had taken over the family hosiery business with his brother Joseph on the early death of his father John Nixon at the age of 55 in 1812—a great blow for the industry. The following year, Hawick acquired an asset, however, when James Melrose started his engineering firm, to specialise in designing and fabricating machinery for the woollen industry. In 1813 Hawick got its first street lighting—oil lamps on posts—and in 1814 its last public hanging, of a man who had murdered his wife. Communications, however, were still rusty—news of the English victory at Waterloo, which ended Napoleon's attempt to dominate Europe, which had occurred one Sunday, in the summer of 1815, did not reach Hawick till the following Saturday, six days later. But it was news worth waiting for. It was the peace everyone wanted, though the rejoicing was to be short-lived.

John Pringle's first wife never lived to hear news of the defeat of the French, for she had died the year before. In 1815 John married again—a baker's daughter, Janet Kedie. It is a matter of conjecture, but it is not improbable that at this juncture in his life John Pringle, at the age of 37, decided he had had enough of the hosiery trade and withdrew from personal involvement, though helping his young half-brother, Robert, who had been attracted by his activities in the world of framework knitting and entered it himself.

Robert Pringle was indentured as an apprentice to Alexander Laing around 1808 when he was 13. When he became a fully fledged framework knitter in 1815, a new co-partnery was formed, or the old one re-formed, with encouragement and technical advice from that old hand at the game, 37-year-old half brother John Pringle, Master Hosier. It probably consisted of 20-year-old Robert, John Waldie, son of George, and Peter Wilson. In any event, it was called 'Waldie, Pringle & Wilson' and Robert Pringle took the lead.

Peter Wilson's mother had been Joan Kedie and doubtless a relation of John Pringle's second wife, Janet Kedie, so the new firm was being

52

Company stationery:
With embossed rampant lion (1940s)

Hang tag from 1948:
The ladies 'All in one' is still produced and uses the same illustration from 1907

kept in the family. Peter Wilson, 31 years old in 1815, with ten years or so as a master hosier behind him, will have been the senior partner in these first years.

An essential aspect of the new project was the acquisition of premises where framework knitting and spinning of hosiery yarn could both be carried on under one roof. In 1815 there came on the market the Whisky House Mill in Slitrig Crescent which stood beside the whisky distillery and cellars from which it derived its name. In 1787 the Duke of Buccleuch, the principal landowner of Hawick, had granted the ground to William Richardson who built a mill on it for the weaving of a rough kind of blue cloth, and 'duffle' for petticoats and carpets. Starting operations in 1788, it was Hawick's first cloth mill. It stands, a dark, stone building, enlarged but without its top (fourth) storey, and was occupied by James Melrose, the engineers.

John Waldie, Robert Pringle and Peter Wilson clubbed together to buy Whisky House Mill in 1815, and here a second Pringle framework knitting operation got under way.

To equip the mill, through which ran a 'lade' diverted from the Slitrig, they applied to the Board of Trustees for a grant towards the purchase of the machinery for preparing, carding and spinning wool and for some of Samuel Crompton's 'mule jennies' (invented 1779), all of which was going to cost them £1,622. In 1818 they received a grant of £150.

A later note by an officer of the Board on this application form stated that Messrs Waldie, Pringle, Wilson & Co carried on 'a most extensive manufacture chiefly of yarn for stocking-making, and have erected a good deal of additional machinery since the Board's grant in 1816 which they are about to extend still further. Such is the thriving state of the manufacture of wool here (Hawick), that this company, and seven others who carry on establishments on a similar scale, work night and day, and have done so for two or three years past by a double set of workmen and women'. Each company, he noted, used about 600 stones of wool a week. How many stocking frames they had is not known, but their products would have been stockings in worsted and lambswool, plain and ribbed, and maybe some of those non-stocking 'pieces'.

In 1815–16 there were seven carding mills operated by water power in Hawick, with 42 scribbling machines and 100 hand spinning jennies. Some 12,000 stones of wool were spun each year, and the yarn knitted by 510 frames into 328,000 pairs of stockings, from eight inches long to full length, in white, blue, grey and dark grey. Including seamers, spinners and winders, more than 1,000 people were employed. In 20 years Hawick had more than three times the number of frames than the Banff of 1795, and employed double the number of workers.

In 1815 another major alliance was formed in Hawick when the existing Denholm firm of Alexander Dickson and George Beattie joined forces with Alexander Laing. As Dicksons, Beattie & Laings, this group acquired land on the north side of Hawick and built Wilton Mill. Laing's contribution alone would have been 22 frames. Like the Pringle operation, it was undertaking spinning and framework knitting under one roof.

The gay companians:
Second edition of the catalogue
(1930s)

53

Hawick was now the centre of an important industry, and those employed in it had acquired a corporate sense. Though communications were bad, widespread 'tramping' provided an information grapevine to cement fraternal solidarity between north and south. Verbal descriptions at first hand were more stimulating than printed reports; and, primed by news of events in the Midlands, the framework knitters of the Border were soon straining to put their combined strength to the test. Brothers in misery unite!

Waterloo and Trafalgar were duly celebrated in Hawick High St but as 'Lurgie' Wilson, Hawick's 19th century historian, pointed out 'a twenty years' expenditure of blood and treasure like that of the late war, was infallibly to be attended with no ordinary consequences and every interest in the country has felt, or seems destined to feel, the necessary effects of that tremendous contest'. Everyone welcomed the peace, but then came the depression. The stocking trade had its share of the general calamity.

The spinning of yarn increased, however, and much of it was sent to Derbyshire and Leicestershire from where it returned to Hawick in the form of stockings very much cheaper than any made at Wilton Mill or Slitrig Crescent. Lurgie poured scorn on the inferior Leicester product, lighter in quality and comfort, not so closely knitted 'nor are they shaped or finished in such a tradesman-like manner'. The earnings of the Leicester knitters were half those of the Hawick men. The subsidising of their income from the rates—'this novel absurdity'—threatened to destroy 'the first impulses that promote men to industry as well as sap the foundations which support the national superstructure of general trade'. It was something the stocking manufacturers of Hawick had to 'bear up'.

But inevitably, with such bitter antagonism and violence across the border, the industrial peace which had blessed the infant hosiery trade in its formative years could not continue. Transportation and hanging, the extreme weapons the government were employing to deter the desperate, hungry stocking-makers of the south, held no fears for the Scots with their tradition of passionate loyalty to clan and raiding band, swearing to be true and hang together. It was as if the apparently wasted years of internal strife, when the rest of Britain was getting on with the business of industrial development, was at last paying a dividend and hardening their determination in a fight in all respects as exacting, and very much more vital, than combining to revenge the death of a chief or closing ranks to support the romantic claims of a prince across the water.

Combining of forces of either 'side' of industry—master or journeymen—was illegal, and the penalties for being caught acting as chairman, secretary or treasurer of any society of this nature were heavy. Under the so-called Combination Law of 1799 working men were not allowed to meet as a trade unless in the presence of an officer of the crown. The framework knitters of Hawick resorted to meeting in secret at night in a 'smiddy' in the part of the town known as Back Raw. So that none of them should know the identity of the all-important treasurer, and could not, therefore, have the information extracted from him by bribe or duress, at the end of each secret meeting the society's funds were placed in a bag on an anvil. On the command 'douce the glim', the man holding the lantern put his light out, and in

54

Sportswear fashion:
Promotional brochure, front cover (1940)

Sportswear fashion:
From the brochure, back cover

Sportswear fashion:
Colour card for the Gleneagles cardigan from the brochure

the darkness one of the members took the money and became treasurer until the next meeting—but no one knew who.

For a meeting held 'to swear Mr Nixon out of the trade', members of the society elected a dog as chairman—an unlikely and unworried candidate for prosecution under the Act—and proceeded to pass a resolution threatening with expulsion any member of the society who took work from Mr Nixon in the following 12 months. They formed up in procession, marched up the High Street and burnt an effigy of Nixon outside his house (a site since occupied by the Victoria Hotel).

The society first came into the open in 1817 in protest against the announcement of John Scot that he was going to pay a halfpenny less for each pair of men's stockings made—a reduction of sixpence a dozen. This was the climax to many years of tyrannical management, oriental in its crudity and severity, which had earned Scot the nickname John the Turk. The framework knitters who worked for John Scot refused to accept the new rate, and staged a 'stand oot', which became known as 'John the Turk's Halfpenny'. Nothing like this had ever happened before in Hawick. The furious John the Turk was quick to retaliate, and had the four ringleaders rounded up and taken to Jedburgh Jail, where they lay for several days without charge or trial.

In their precipitate haste to hit back at the insolent workers, the masters had lamentably failed to do their homework. The *law* did prohibit combination of masters as well as workers, and in coming together in this open conspiracy to fix a common rate, they invited prosecution which the journeymen were not slow in following up. The masters were ignominiously taken to court by those they had hoped would meekly submit to their 'rulings', but though the case was proved against them, they were all discharged.

The traditional irregular behaviour of the framework knitters can have won them little sympathy, though it was not this but a point of law which was the issue. The knitters had always given the impression that their only concern was to earn just enough money for their families' day to day needs, with no consideration for a possibly rainy morrow or improvement of their status. They had no ambition other than to maintain the status quo. They were roused when the level fell below, but never seem to have been inspired to raise it above, subsistence.

It was a matter of spending as long as possible in the alehouse—whisky was 1s 3d a bottle—before the Tam-a-Linkin called your name and appealed to your fellow-drinkers to throw you out and send you back to the stocking shop; of flying kites ('lairge dragons') or wrestling on the haugh where Glebe Mill now stands, for long enough to leave just enough time for a spell at the four posts of misery, and earn just enough cash to tide over to the middle of next week when the mad rush would start all over again.

Most of them were uninhibited poachers of salmon and game, and counted on spending regular stretches in gaol where their masters kept permanent frames so they could carry on with their knitting while they served sentence. But these Scotts and Turnbulls and Elliots, distinguished only by their nicknames of Oily, Scroggie or Bummer, had pride in being inheritors of an ancient craft and wore tall hats and white aprons at their work. Proud but poor ritualists, they stopped their frames in the middle of the day to hear one of their number read aloud the news from the single newspaper they could afford.

Gleneagles sports fashion cardigan:
The word knitwear was used for the first time in a Pringle board meeting in 1945 and registered as the new definition of knitted outerwear (illustration 1940)

Sportswear fashion:
The Fernessa cardigan (1940)

55

Sportswear fashion:
(1940)

Drawn from the same section of the community as the masters, the magistrates found it difficult to concede much to the representatives of so irresponsible a body of men who now accounted for very nearly half the employable population of the town. Admiration for their independence of spirit, liberal outlook and concern for the protection of an old craft and its standards, would have been tempered by the recognition that, underlying it all, were robust animal appetites inflamed by a heady sense of power successfully exploited. They had heard what giving in to such impulses had led to in the more 'civilised' towns of the south. Hawick at least could be spared the excesses suffered by Nottingham and Leicester.

56

Fire at Rodono:
*The fire also destroys much
of the Pringle archive
(1939)*

Charred ruins

Opposite
Austerity Style:
*The war years brings new ingenuity
to fashion conscious women
(1946)*

7

FROM STOCKINGS TO UNDERWEAR

'Robert Pringle, Hosier, Cross Wynd' rides Drouty Year and Lang Stand Oot. (1818–1831)

F OR THE young co-partnery of Waldie, Pringle & Wilson to be pitchforked into this turmoil so early in its life must have been disturbing, particularly for the young Robert Pringle at the outset of his career as a master hosier.

In 1819 the co-partnery lost its senior partner, and its first premises. Peter Wilson took over Whisky House Mill which he operated for spinning and knitting with his brother, Thomas, and also acquired the mill opposite the Tower hotel known as Tower Knowe Mill. Waldie, Pringle & Co, as it now was, acquired new premises in a mill in Cross Wynd opposite where then stood Allars Church (later a car park). The following year Robert Pringle's 21-year-old brother Andrew joined him, on completion of his apprenticeship, probably with Laings as Robert had done. Nothing is known of the Waldie, Pringle operation at Cross Wynd, how many were employed, how many frames, how many jennies. The output would have been plain and ribbed stockings as at Slitrig Crescent, and certain amount of hosiery yarn.

Smarting from their humbling experience in the courts which their discharge had hardly mitigated, and determined to meet their English competitors on their own ground of cheaper and lower quality goods, in 1822 the master hosiers of Hawick made another concerted attempt to reduce the cost of stocking-making—and this time less clumsily. Each announced individually the reduced rates they were prepared to pay. There was no question of bargaining, just take it or leave it. The reaction of the framework knitters was instantaneous—they left it. The Hawick stocking industry ground to a halt.

The stoppage lasted nine months, some say fourteen. Whichever it was, it earned itself the name of The Lang Stand Oot. Once again

Opposite
Phyllis Calvert:
British actress and starlet visits Rodono (1940s)

there was one master whose men were not on strike—William Beck. He refused to join his fellow manufacturers in the reduction of rates, and his business continued as usual.

The strikers had little money in their society's treasury, and there was a spate of fund-raising raffles, plays and concerts in the town hall—which not only produced the wherewithal but gave the bewildered families of the knitters, used to a busy day of seaming, spinning and winding, something to do. Contributions of sixpence and a shilling a week were collected by framework knitters in Edinburgh, Dumfries and Carlisle, and sent to aid their brothers at Hawick.

Nor did their stand go unobserved in the capital. A delegate representing the journeymen was invited to London to give evidence before the Royal Commission enquiring into the working of the Combination Act, the repeal of which was seriously being considered. The man chosen was a Robert Scott who, in forbidding and unfamiliar surroundings, greatly impressed his hearers. He was entertained by the great Joseph Hume, leader of the movement for reform. The evidence he gave with such clarity of thought and depth of feeling was a major factor, along with the plodding activities of Francis Place, the tailor of Charing Cross, in the decision, made in 1824, to repeal the obnoxious law. The Hawick manufacturers immediately closed ranks in a legally recognised Association.

When the manufacturers finally yielded, the proudest man in Hawick was John Pringle's old master, William Beck, who was so admired for standing aloof from his fellows on this issue, that the journeymen presented him with a silver cup. The object of this unique gesture can still be seen in the Border Museum at Hawick, a symbol of a far-seeing refusal to let slip, for short-term gain, the town's precious reputation for quality.

In the midst of all this, or perhaps at its conclusion, Robert Pringle married—December 23, 1823. His bride was Charlotte Paterson 'of benign face and disposition'. It was a confident step at a time when, the stoppage apart, business was at a low ebb.

Writing his *Sketch of the History of Hawick* in 1825, Robert 'Lurgie' Wilson reported that the stocking trade did not appear to be expanding any more. The older established houses, he said, were doing less business due to 'general stagnation and loss' throughout the whole kingdom. Trade was not in a healthy state owing to the profitless returns. This was something to which the Government should direct its attention rather than the building of new churches—a dig at the so-called 'Waterloo Churches' built in thanksgiving for victory over Napoleon. 'The late eventful struggle' was still casting its shadow.

But the general picture he painted was rosier. 'The stocking trade of Hawick is placed in the centre of an extensive district where the raw material is abundant as well as peculiarly adapted for the manufacture either of ordinary or superior hose ... Hosiers, in consequence of close proximity to the wool-growers, are not only enabled to pick and choose, but have the wool laid down at their warehouses carriage free without adulteration or risk.'

He was glad to report that the Border sheep farmers were 'now abandoning tarry propensities of their fathers'—smearing with tar to make wool heavier was out.

60

The Bulletin arrives:
Issue 4 with a message form the chairman and news of recent events (1949)

40s twinset:
From an early photographic fashion catalogue

The fashion and habits of the age, too, tend greatly to diminish the growth of tarry wool. The blunked blue or hoddin gray which the outer garments of our forefathers displayed would not be so suitable an accompaniment to the mechanical waists, flowing surtouts and divers coloured *inexpressibles* in which our modern dandies strut with such perpendicularity and show. Alas! 'old times are changed, old manners gone' There is something equally filthy and unnatural in bespattering beautiful sheep with abominable tar, nor is it easy to account for the introduction of such a practice, seeing how comfortably these 'inhabitants of the mountains' have been clotted by nature.

Times were indeed changing, and after 55 years of intense activity and growth the industry could afford to take a deep breath and prepare for the important new stage in its development which now lay in store.

There were a number of bank failures in 1826, and an early victim was the respected and now elderly William Beck whose activity spanned all but four years of the entire life of the Hawick hosiery industry to date. His business collapsed in 1826, and shortly afterwards he died. The three founders of Hawick's prosperity had now passed from the scene—John Hardie, John Nixon and William Beck. The pioneering days were over.

There is no real clue to the date when Waldie, Pringle & Co ceased to be a manufacturing partnership, but it would seem to have been around 1826, though it remained in name as the owner of property. The writer of the Hawick section of Pigot's *National Commercial Directory of the Whole of Scotland* of 1826 stated that 'J & W Waldie' introduced the manufacture of stockings and woollen cloth to Whisky House Mill, and in John Wood's 1824 map of Hawick the name 'John Waldie' is printed over the site of the mill in Slitrig Crescent. Pigot's Directory also gave as manufacturers of stockings and yarn spinners the name of 'Waldie, Elliot & Co' at Tower Knowe Mill, and 'Wilson & Elliot' in 'The Crescent' (Lynnwood Mill?).

By 1826 Robert Pringle had emerged, at the age of 31, as the head of the firm at Cross Wynd. This was an auspicious year for him, as a Pringle dynasty now seemed assured. On March 1, 1826, Charlotte bore him a son—her second child. They called him Walter after his grandfather, Walter Pringle II.

It was the year the mill lades of the town's eight watermills ran dry and the workers came to the conclusion that perhaps after all the harnessing of Mr Watt's steam engine to their spinning jennies might be more an asset than a threat—the Drouty Year. There was no rainfall from May to August. With water as their only source of power many of the spinning mills were idle. Though the knitting frames did not rely on water power, they needed to be fed with yarn, so the whole cycle collapsed.

To William Wilson the Drouty Year of 1826 brought home the unsatisfactory extent to which the industry depended on the whims of nature and he decided to import yarn from abroad in finer gauges than any to be found at Hawick Fair—the first time this was done in Hawick. The insuppressible John Scott (the Turk) took advantage of the drought to install more carding and spinning machines, towards the cost of

40s glamour:
From an early photographic fashion catalogue

40s glamour

40s dash:
The classic men's cardigan changes little over the decades

which he obtained a grant of £65 from the Board of Trustees, who also gave £200 to Dicksons and Laings to help equip their Wilton Mill.

But the Drouty Year gave the mill owners a fright. If it happened once it could happen again. Next time they would be prepared. Many of them clubbed together to build artificial lochs in the hills above their mills. Williestruther (for Slitrig) Pond and Philhope Loch (for Teviot) were two. The latter was nine miles away. In times of water scarcity the owners paid a shepherd to open the sluices of the loch, which had filled up in wet weather, at 3 am, so that the water would flow along artificial burns to reach and swell the Slitrig or Teviot in time for the mills' opening in the morning. Part of one of these miniature canals was diverted by a music loving miller to operate a water organ en route, and then return to play its less artistic role in turning the water wheel.

But the principal significance of 1826 to this story is that this year saw the introduction to Hawick of the 'broad' frame with the row of needles 16 inches to 30 inches in width, which enabled the manufacturers to make men and women's knitted *underclothing*.

The broad frame dates from the invention in 1801 of the multiple slurcock, a double-ended wedge to release jacks from their springs. This enable several stocking webs to be knitted at the same time. But more important, it meant that a much wider fabric could be knitted, opening the door to the production of machine knitted *garments*.

Robert Pringle, William Wilson and the Nixon Brothers were among the first to install 'braid' frames in Hawick. James Hogg, as has been seen, experimented with making a variety of 'pieces' on his frame which were not stockings or socks. Another Hawick framework knitter, Andrew Tait, was similarly rewarded by the Board of Trustees in 1817. They were greatly impressed by the ladies muffs and tippets fleeced with white swansdown which he had made on his frame for the Duchess of Buccleuch. They presented him with the broad 24-gauge frame for which he asked, and which, according to the record, 'he wrought till near his end'.

A third inventive knitter of the town was Matthew Lyon who, in 1823, claimed a premium for having found how to make on a stocking frame a new kind of manufacture of silk and wool for gentlemen's cloaks, two of which he presented to George IV when in Scotland, who rewarded him. The Board, however, had other views. 'Having examined the specimen produced [they] considered the manufacture to be undeserving of any encouragement.'

The trend was away from 'fancy work' to the plainer but more lucrative underwear, a term that was applied to any article of clothing which was not the final garment which the wearer put on indoors over everything else. The first underclothes made in Hawick were known as 'broad frame slack work' (20 gauge) and consisted of long-sleeved shirts, short-sleeved shirts, double-breasted shirts, men's pants, and men's knee drawers. All these garments were of wool. The women seamers of stockings now also applied themselves to the mounting and trimming of underwear.

Since the Restoration, linen was the material used for a gentleman's underclothes. Cotton was linen's social inferior. At the end of the 18th century men wore footed long drawers under their pantaloons and trousers, and short drawers under their breeches. The notion was that a close fitting garment next to the skin gave warmth. At the beginning

62

Savile Row:
The showroom
(1947)

Savile Row:
The showroom

George Sand:
A director of Pringle in Savile Row
(1947)

of the 19th century most gentlemen were wearing knitted woollen (worsted) underclothes—thick and extra-thick. For the one fabric that clung close to the body was knitting. A gentility took possession of the fashion scene which was to last for the next hundred years. Legs became known as 'limbs'; breasts as 'bosoms'; a gentleman's trousers his 'nether integuments' or his 'inexpressibles'. They found an expression, however, for his underwear—'clean linen'—even when it was made of wool.

The word pantaloon incidentally derives from a stock character of the Venetian improvised, masked comedy of the Renaissance artisans, the *Commedia dell'Arte*. This was an elderly bore, first called Il Magnifico, whose comedy line was always to be bragging about his military exploits in planting the flag bearing the lion crest of St Mark all over the world. It was a tag line that occurred over and over again in his improvised dialogue—'plant the lion', ' plant the lion', 'pianta leone'—so much so that audiences dubbed him 'Piantaleone' which became 'Pantalone' and in English 'Pantaloon'.

Gradually the Hawick framework knitters turned to underwear. This is not to say that stockings were abandoned. On the contrary, Brewster's *Edinburgh Encyclopaedia* published in 1830 reports that in Hawick 'the manufacture of lambswool stockings, in particular, from the introduction of machinery has of late years made very rapid progress, and is still on the increase'. Twelve thousand stones of wool was being spun annually on more than 100 spinning jennies and carded by 44 water-powered 'engines'. Three-fifths of this was manufactured into stockings (328,000 pairs a year) on upwards of 500 stocking frames. Carpet and blanket manufacture was in a decline. The remaining two-fifths of the yarn was sold to manufacturers in others parts of Britain. It was going to be some time before Hawick underwear got a mention in contemporary records, but it made a start. The whole output—underwear and stockings—was in an event covered by the generic term 'hosiery'.

Technical improvements were introduced—not without the familiar initial resistance of the workers—to give the new development a boost both in quantity and quality. In 1826 a safety device known as 'Tumbling Tam' was invented to stop the operator from 'coming through the work'. On the narrow frames, and on the first broad frames worked in Hawick, the operator had to carry the yarn across the needles by hand. For some time in England this had been done by the newly invented 'carrier', a device which did it automatically and twice as quickly. One day in 1827, an Englishman called Sayers 'on the tramp' from the Midlands, brought one of these new gadgets with him to Hawick and used it on the broad frame at the stocking house where he obtained employment. It was the first time this had been seen in operation in Hawick and caused a great stir. There was the usual reaction that the innovation would result in a reduction of wages. The resentment piled up, not so much on the invention itself, as on the head of the wretched Sayers who had dared to introduce so subversive a device of such obvious detriment to the interests of every honest framework knitter. Feeling ran so high that Sayers feared for his life, and each night barricaded himself into the house of the Mr Stewart in the High Street where he lodged. While at work he kept

Savile Row:
New London offices

Savile Row:
The lobby

63

Savile Row:
Hallway

a loaded pistol beside him on the bench of his frame. Finally Sayers found Hawick too hot for him and fled the town—but the ingenious 'carrier' remained.

Most employers with broad frames had carriers attached to them at once. The gadgets speeded up-production to such an extent that, in order to keep their costs per pair of stockings or garment at a rate which would bring them a reasonable profit, they had to reduce the amount they paid the stocking-makers for each article. There was the usual dispute, followed by the usual agreement. Twelve shillings a dozen was paid for long-sleeved shirts with a reduction of two shillings for short sleeves. Men's long pants (20 gauge) were paid at the rate of 13s 3d a dozen, and the short knee drawers at one shilling a dozen less. For men's ribbed stockings the knitters were paid 12s 6d a dozen.

A Hawick framesmith, William Prowett, informed the Board of Trustees that anyone who wanted to make lambswool shirts and drawers was obliged to have 'a set of frames on purpose for them'. He however had found a way of making the old frames wider and thus was able to make shirts and drawers on them equally as well on the new broad frames. He was rewarded.

No sooner had they reconciled themselves to the inevitability of accepting the broad frame and the carrier, than the hosiery and cloth workers of Hawick had to face the implications of steam power.

The replacement of hands by donkeys and then by water had been disturbing enough. A number of Arkwright's 'water-frames' had been used in Dicksons & Laings at Wilton Mill since 1810; and in 1830 they had Shaw & Roberts of Manchester install one of their power looms now widely used in the cotton industry but adapted to weave the type of cloth made of a mixture of yarns known as tweel. Their operation embraced yarn, knitted goods and cloth.

When in 1784 James Watt came up with an idea for turning a wheel neither by hand nor by donkey nor by water. His invention, though it cost more, had the promise of a degree of dependability and power hitherto undreamed of. In 1831 James Melrose built a steam engine of William Wilson & Sons in their factory at Langlands to drive his spinning and weaving machinery—Hawick's first.

Robert Pringle noted this development with mixed feelings. He knew that as water power could not help his stocking frames, neither could steam—their action was still not rotary. It is true that William Dawson of Leicester had invented an irregularly notched wheel—a cam—which, as it revolved, acted on horizontal bolts equipped with springs, the notches pushing up bars in the order of the pattern required. 'Dawson's Wheels' had shown the way but the industry had been slow to take it up. It was not until the 1840s that steam driven rotary stocking frames were used even in Nottingham, and not till much later in Scotland.

But the volume of manufacture in Hawick, confined though it was to hand frames, increased; and the Board of Trustees handed out more and more grants. Dicksons & Laings, on the strength of their power looms, received £200, so did William and Joseph Nixon. Peter Wilson got £100 for his new machinery at Tower Knowe Mill; William Watson got £95. William Wilson & Sons' high standards were complimented on being awarded a premium of £5 for a dozen 'Gents Electoral Saxony Vests'. 'These under vests were beautifully manufactured' the commissioners agreed. They gave Wilson another

Royal letter:
With thanks from Elizabeth (1947)

William MacTaggart (left):
Appointed in 1923 as a trainee manager, he becomes chairman in 1960. Recieving the Royal Warrant (1948)

By Appointment To
Her Majesty The Queen
Manufacturers of
Knitted Garments
Pringle of Scotland Ltd

£5 for 'stocking wrought underclothing'—a fine transitional phrase.

But the technical improvements and the new means of power which turned the wheels round more quickly, to say nothing of the gas lighting which had transplanted oil in Hawick in 1830, would be of no avail if these only increased volume and lowered cost, and failed to deliver what the public wanted and the promoters of fashion skilfully persuaded them to want. Gravenor Henson, whose great work *The History of the Framework Knitters* was published in 1831, had some pertinent remarks to make on this. His 'country workmen' were the knitters of Leicester and Nottingham, but the point he makes applies equally to Hawick, if not more so.

> The Londoners ... had a manifest advantage over the country workmen, as they were at the seat of fashion, and when they had meditated or produced a fancy article, they had immediate facilities of introducing it to the notice of the leading persons in the fashionable world, or to the milliners, haberdashers and tailors whose genius could direct them in the proper path for success; and who, by applying and making up the articles in an elegant fancy manner, could give them that arrangement and form which increased their beauty, which is the principal study of their business, and at which they aim to excel. One of the greatest misfortunes which has befallen the hosiery manufacture is its removal from the seat of fashion, as the workmen in the country are far removed from all knowledge of the wants, wishes and taste of the every-varying votaries of new modes of dress, who are constantly seeking for something strikingly new to introduce, to excite public attention to the wearer; as in a large crowded community nothing draws so much notice of regard as an elegant tasteful peculiarity of dress, which is much heightened by the introduction of a newly-invented fabric.
>
> A handsome person, an elegant gait or demeanour, high rank, or extensive riches or possessions, a cultivated mind, personal abilities or accomplishments, are all unavailing except to a few celebrated persons, to excite that attention or respect so natural to the self-love and self-consequence which seems inherent in the human breast; but a well-dressed figure having some peculiarity in the arrangement or fabric of the habit worn, instantly excites general attention; and though frequently met with sneers and taunts by the beholders, they are compelled to admire, and in a short time they endeavour to excite the same attention to themselves by imitating the pretended absurdity.
>
> The most successful fashions have been the most derided and sneered at on their introduction by the wearers, whose personal vanity induced them to adopt that method of making themselves conspicuous. Notwithstanding the sarcastic sneers at macaronies, bucks, beaus and dandies, the majority of the human race are incessantly imitating the whims and caprices of these 'exquisites' who are inwardly envied and admired, while they are openly treated with affected ridicule. In a state of society like that of Western Europe where the population

Designer's sketch:
Hand intarsia design
(1951)

65

Otto Weisz and guest:
Otto, designer for Pringle and father of the twinset, designs for Pringle from 1934–69
(1940s)

relies so much on the produce of their manufactures for a subsistence, these fops and belles are of the greatest utility, and however puerile their affectation may seem, they are persons of the greatest consequence in the state; a change of fashion has frequently been of as great consequence as the loss of a battle, an ally or a colony; a whole district has been suddenly raised to the utmost pitch of prosperity and opulence, by the introduction of a particular mode of dress, whilst other extensive occupations have been doomed to penury and unutterable distress by a like change, perhaps effected by an insignificant thoughtless being, who was wholly unconscious of the evils he was inflicting.

The defeat of armies, the conquest of states, a revolution or change of government or of dynasties, has frequently not had half so great an effect upon the human race as a mere change of fashion. The dreadful evil of pestilence, famine or war have not inflicted more misery than has been felt by particular districts and even states from the operations of the silent, progressive and unsuspected march of a change of mode of dress. The people of England, though the most interested of any nation on earth, have paid the least attention to this important subject, and her nobility have left this might engine entirely at the disposal of the *petit maitres* of Paris.

Bulletin:
More news reported
(1951)

66

Opposite
Intarsia designer sketches:
(1951)

⑤

⑦

⑦

VOGUE

APRIL 15

2 Summer Fashion Plans
charted and priced

Travel Clothes
for a new kind of
land cruise

50 CENT

8

HALF SCOTLAND'S FRAMES IN HAWICK

'Robert Pringle & Son, Walter's Wynd', hosiery makers to the élite of Victorian Society. (1832–1868)

ROBERT PRINGLE, master hosier, is certain to have read Gravenor Henson's wise observations and, if the progress of his firm under his guidance is any indication, he took them to his heart. But besides the steady development of his business, Robert Pringle began to take part in the affairs of his home town as a councillor, police commissioner, member of the parochial board, and above all as a member of the powerful Hawick Kirk Session. He had a lively interest in politics and was an active supporter of the Liberals, successors to the Whigs and representative of the commercial section of the community who stood for economic development, social and constitutional reform.

When the people of Hawick heard of the passing of the Reform Bill in 1832, the stocking-makers decked in scarlet and white ribbons and carrying a brand new silk flag headed a procession of shoemakers, glovers, tanners, skinners and wool sorters, through the streets. They marched to the music of three bands. They bore a proudly displayed copy of the Reform Act and a bundle of sticks firmly tied together signifying Union is Strength (which then no one connected with the Roman lictor's fasces later adopted by their political opposites, the Fascists). There was a banner with a portrait of Earl Grey, and a certain John Laurie in Highland dress held a magnificent Scotch thistle, the wool combers' teazel. It ended with an open air feast on Upper Haugh—at two bob a head!

Robert Pringle, the man of industry who looked to the future, will have smiled as he read in his newspaper of that great reactionary Sir Walter Scott predicting the passing of the Reform Bill as the prologue to the downfall of Britain. For the romantic novelist it was the signal

Opposite
American Vogue:
Cashmere makes the cover (1955)

for the weavers and framework knitters of towns like Hawick to lay low landowner and property, and the monarchy would follow.

It was indeed not long before the stocking-makers of Hawick and their friends, unhappy that the Reform Bill had not been passed in its entirety, let their radicalism get the better of them. They knew which of the 300 were the Tory voters, and as some of the latter were on their way to the poll at the next general election, a group lay in wait, seized them and threw them into the Slitrig. As a result there was an attempt by a number of MPs to disenfranchise Hawick. The action of the stocking-makers of Hawick, they said, amounted to 'tumultous assembly'. It was a near thing. The motion to deprive Hawick of its newly won franchise was only lost by 22 votes.

The year of the passing of the Reform Bill saw the death of another of the Hawick hosiery pioneers, William Wilson. His family was unconnected with the Peter Wilson who had been a member of the second Pringle co-partnery—Peter had now retired from hosiery altogether and taken to grocery. One of William Wilson's sons also struck out into a new field—James Wilson, a Hawick hatter went to seek a career in London in 1823, founded the weekly review *The Economist* in 1843 and became Financial Secretary to the Treasury and later financial adviser to the Government of India.

In 1840 the stocking-makers of Hawick, 16 years after the repealing of the Combination Laws, formed themselves into an official body which they called the Hawick Framework Knitters' Society, though their activities as a union representing the workers had continued without break. They took the opportunity to re-think their whole cause and commit to paper in the form of a Memorandum a formal statement of what they considered to be their position.

> That various grievances subsisted between employers and employed' was the first premise. The second was 'that besides the general system of oppression to be immediately adverted to, the manufacturers have acted in many instances towards individual workers with peculiar injustice and severity.

The grievances were then spelt out.

> Injuries sustained by the workmen in consequence of the rules followed by the manufacturers in regard to employment; injuries sustained in consequence of the manufacturers when they give out yarn, etc. to the workmen, refusing to give a note or ticket of the weight and value thereof; acts of oppression to particular individuals.

The rules followed by the manufacturers were those insisted on by the early framework knitters who were reluctant to see themselves as 'employees', but merely wanted to be given yarn which they could knit into stockings at any time of the day or week on a machine, the capital costs of which was low and its operation easy and hardly 'skilled'.

On one occasion they stopped work in protest against the cut rate a cloth weaver insisted on paying them for the barrel of urine they had contracted to supply him with for scouring. A barrel was put outside

70

Yarn gathering:
(1950s)

VISIT OF H.R.H. PRINCESS MARGARET
TO 'PRINGLE OF SCOTLAND' 11TH JANUARY, 1952

H.R.H Princess Margaret:
Visit to Rodono
(1952)

The Milling process:
Making the garment soft to handle
(1950s)

the stocking shop for collection at the end of each day, and the annual payment of eightpence was collected at New Year and shared by all who had contributed this by-product of their beer drinking. During the Wash Barrel Strike the containers were upset in the street.

The basic trouble was that neither side trusted the other. Both were at fault. In 70 years there had been little sign of any positive attempt to understand the others' point of view, but the formation of the Hawick Framework Knitters Society was a step in the right direction.

When in 1842 the 16-year-old Walter Pringle II put his first foot on the hosiery ladder by becoming an apprentice, Felkin reckoned there were some 2,605 stocking frames in Scotland (2,365 on woollen hose), of which 1,200 were in Hawick—just about half the total. But in the mid-1840s only 620 of them were at work. In Hawick Robert Pringle was ninth in size in a list of 12 hosiery factories. He employed 20 men and three boys (under 18). The largest employer was William Laidlaw with 220 (but he made tweeds too), the smallest J & J Kyle with 16. A total of 933 were employed on hosiery in Hawick in 1846.

In 1849, the year Walter Pringle II finished his apprenticeship, a railway link was opened with Edinburgh—important more for the coal which could be brought to the town on the goods wagons to burn in the new steam engines than the passengers in the coaches. It also brought an outbreak of cholera, and there was a big demand for the 'cholera belts' knitted on the rib frames. Ironically this was a welcome relief to the framework knitters of Hawick where yet another recession had brought considerable unemployment. More and more Hawick 'industrialists' with no real interest in hosiery were buying frames and renting them out to stocking-makers as far away as Lockerbie, Langholm and Dumfries. In the circumstances whole families migrated from the town. But in their place came Englishmen with names like Hunt, Brown, Turvill, Godfrey and Smith, and with them their national game of cricket—the first cricket match in Hawick was played on the Brewery Haugh in Slitrig Crescent in 1849. By 1856 the population of Hawick had grown to 7,800, an indication of healthy industrial progress, but once again it was to be checked by a period described by contemporaries as one of 'unprecedented suffering and distress' throughout Britain. Some put this down, so far as Hawick was concerned, to the failure of the stocking frame to adapt itself to full fashioned lambswool hosiery. Thomas Slater, secretary of the Hawick Framework Knitters Society, claimed that the recession could not be laid at the door of the stocking-makers who on no occasion had put impediments in the way of employers over machinery. On the contrary, 'amicable adjustment' had been reached over the price of work produced by each improvement to the frame as it was introduced.

The changes in recent years had been the 3-deck ribb making a saving of 1½ to 2d a dozen; the Broad Dandy making a saving of 1s a dozen on half hose over the narrow frame; the Double Carrier for working striped tops, a saving of 3d to 4d a dozen. Striped shirts wrought with the hand on a broad frame were paid for at a rate of 9d a dozen for 30 stripes, but by using a double carrier they cost 4½d a dozen. All these savings, Slater pointed out, were to the *employer*.

Slater was accused of placing an embargo on the introduction of certain machinery and even of paying men to leave Hawick who were willing to work the improved frames. This he hotly denied, but

Designer sketches:
(1951)

made the point that the signs of revived activity in England was not in the new machinery 'but in the old-fashioned machine which always rises to the ascendant in brisk times ... An obstinate old brick is the old-fashioned frame. It does not know when it is beaten and will surely die game'.

The Report of Factories for the district of Scotland of the year ending April 30, 1859 stated gloomily: 'At Hawick the hosiery trade, formerly the staple one of the town, is on the decline and, it is feared, will leave the district altogether.'

It was an uncomfortable possibility to live with, announced from so high an authority. But throughout the period a note of optimism permeated the speeches of the Hawick hosiery masters at the now annual New Year's Eve 'soirées' held sometimes in the Subscription Rooms, sometimes in the largest wareroom adorned with 'mottoes' of suitable moral uplift, evergreens and banners. It was an opportunity to cement good employee relations and inject, without spoiling the fun (which anyway came with the ball afterwards), a necessary modicum of religious indoctrination.

It was a great age for metaphor. The chairman painted a dramatic word picture of The Past as a Dream seen from the Mountain of Retrospection; a reverend reminded the guests of the need for good deeds to fill the web of life. In a speech ostensibly devoted to the new concept of a Savings Bank, a director showed how up to date he was by saying that business was now done at 'railway speed', so punctuality and carefulness in the execution of work was all the more necessary. Machinery would never deprive men of work, he said, and illustrated how mechanical improvement had in fact increased the trade of the town. A brief reference followed on the importance of education and the dangers of intemperance, and a hint that employees might give a little more co-operation.

Another invited the attention of his hearers to one of the characteristics of the time, the conversion of all kinds of refuse to useful purposes—the savings of the scourings of their manufactures formerly thrown in the river but now by a chemical process reconverted into soap, making of wrapping paper from the stalks of burnt hop plants; coal tar providing fast-colour dyes.

The year 1858 had witnessed that great triumph of science, the unification of Great Britain and America by the submarine telegraph cable—'instantaneous connection'. It heralded peace and the advancement of civilisation. Who knows but they would be speaking with India, China and Japan next, and 'in the course of time over the entire globe send sun-outstripping messages to every corner of the earth'.

It was in this year, when the hosiery business seemed to be on the verge of another great leap forward, that Robert Pringle I, the founder of the firm, died at the age of 64.

Charlotte bore Robert Pringle eleven children—four sons and seven daughters. Their first-born was a girl, whom they called Charlotte; their second was Walter born March 1, 1826.

Walter is said (in his local newspaper obituary) to have served his apprenticeship 'in the drapery trade' and afterwards to have 'had a position in a large establishment in London'. No details of this exist but it may have been a department store like Whiteleys or Harrods.

Harvey Nichols:
Advertising
(1950s)

The Common Riding issue:
A local Hawick festival is celebrated
(1950s)

Designer sketch:
(1951)

From his sojourn in the metropolis Walter Pringle II would have gained an understanding of fashion and a sense of the needs, not only of Britain as a whole but of the Empire and foreign countries, which the Hawick hosiery trade was now making ready to satisfy.

Four-fifths of the woollen yarn used by the Hawick hosiery firms was now imported from abroad, and was of the finer gauges which gave the products, and in particular the underwear, the fine quality garment for which there was an increasing demand, especially by women. Ladies underclothes now entered the stock lists, though not yet on any big scale.

Their popularity had waxed and waned over the years. In the 1770s there was more money about for spending on underclothes, and in the fashionable world it was a matter of class distinction for the ladies to wear layer upon layer of scrupulously clean underclothes. But the French Revolution brought reaction, dismissing elegance as a symbol of the now despised cult of social refinement. All superfluous underclothing was discarded, and there was a swing towards dresses that aped the classical modes of ancient Greece, reducing weight by the use of the flimsiest materials. From about 1806, ladies wore drawers of white knitted silk, knitted cotton and 'lawn' (a kind of fine linen resembling cambric), and long 'pantalettes', or 'trowsers', stretching below the calf and meant to be seen. By the 1830s women's drawers were generally accepted—but not by the 'lower orders'.

Women had usually worn more underclothing than men because their lives were less active and their outer dress was of lighter materials. They were, moreover, reluctant to add to bulk, or give an appearance of bulk, on the upper parts of their bodies. For six centuries the chief part of a woman's underclothing had covered the lower half of her body; while men preferred to keep free the use of their legs and wore heavy warm underwear on the top half.

Body cleanliness has only been of importance in the last 200 years. In Queen Elizabeth's day the outer clothes had to be protected from the skin below. In Victorian times body cleanliness became identified with Society. Frequent changes of underclothing became a necessity for the leisured classes who bristled at the idea of any part of the body coming into contact with outerclothes, so—long pants.

The 1840s saw the introduction of a new undergarment for men and women, the merino lambswool woollen vest, or under-vest, worn next to the skin—women called it a 'camisole'. But the young ladies with their mainly sedentary indoor life found wool next the skin too hot and uncomfortable. By the 1860s there was a swing towards clothes that gave ease and comfort freed from the considerations of fashion and social rank. Tight lacing took a back seat and the middle and lower classes adopted styles giving greater freedom of movement—even factory girls wore crinolines, introduced around 1857. When chemical dyes began being used in 1860, women's underclothes, all white up to then, became coloured—solferino and magenta were the first shades. More daring still, they started being embroidered. A writer in the *Englishwoman's Domestic Magazine* of 1866 protested 'the amount of embroidery put upon underclothing nowadays is sinful'. But when the crinoline cage went out of fashion, small waists came in, and corsets re-appeared. Women wore high neck vests with long or short sleeves of merino wool or flannel, and drawers trimmed with frills;

Royal visit:
Factory tour
(1952)

Twinset fever:
Anne Crawford, actress
(1950s)

73

Stars of the silver screen:
Jean Simmons and twinset
(1950s)

in winter scarlet flannel knickerbockers.

Those who wore the garments and those who made them, as novelist Disraeli so eloquently demonstrated, comprised 'two nations'. If William Blake had visited Hawick he might not have dammed its mills 'satanic', but the town of 1859 suffered from gross overcrowding, the lack of any proper water supply or sanitation. There was a high death rate in the town. The system under which the framework knitters earned their weekly payments in proud independence from the masters, was to all intents and purposes the same as that of 1819 which had caused the grand remonstrance of their handbill. They still paid a weekly rent for frame and floor space, oil and soap; they still paid their seamers and trimmers; and still the old hand frame, with its chickerty-burr throbbing rhythm, was the common means of mechanical knitting. There had been steam-driven rotary frames in Nottingham since 1848, and John Laing had installed one in 1858, but it was a freak.

In 1862 another clergyman, an American this time, with an appropriate surname, the Reverend Isaac Nixon Lamb, invented the flat knitting machine, with flat, that is horizontal, needle beds. He soon modified this, however, so that the beds were each inclined at an angle of 45 degrees. Isaac Lamb introduced this to Britain in 1866, and sold the patent rights for Europe to a Monsieur E. Dubied after it had been shown at the Paris Exhibition of 1867. Lamb himself supervised the building of large models of his machine in Leicester to knit the type of woollen waistcoat first designed to meet a request from Lord Cardigan for a warm garment for his troops in the Crimea (1854–56).

Catwalk show at Savile Row: *(1950)*

In this year 1862 was born in Buccleuch Street, Hawick, the baby whose life was to link this dark age with the middle of the 20th century, Walter Pringle's son Robert. He was joined two years later (1864) by a sister Mary (Mamie). Mary was to journey with Robert into a then unbelievable world of television, air transport and atomic energy.

In 1862 came another stage in the transport revolution, which had begun with the opening of the railway to Edinburgh in 1849, when another line was opened to Carlisle on July 1, the day after the last mail coach had made its final run. It might have given the town's captains of industry a hint that a new era had dawned, but, if it did, the advents of innovation was regarded with suspicion and unease.

It took many years before any such machine as Lamb's became acceptable to either masters or journeymen framework knitters in Hawick. In 1865 one of the former told the Parliamentary Commissioners enquiring into the employment of children in industry 'we mean to use the hand frames because we see no advantage in power, and machinery is very apt to get out of order' and encouraged young children of seven to work in the stocking shops doing winding.

The Report of the Commission stated: 'The portion of the hand frame hosiery manufacture carried on in Ireland and Scotland is very small and is confined almost entirely in Scotland in the towns of Hawick and Dumfries ... The hand frames at Hawick all work from 6am to 8pm with no special times for meals ... The children must work as long as the men ... The great number of handlooms still existing in cottages and small workshops renders it impossible to enforce school attendance.'

New stationery: *The hand drawn logo makes its entrance (1950s)*

Thomas Laidlaw of Hawick told the Commissioners: 'My opinion is handloom weaving will dwindle away. For weaving all manufacturers prefer power; but hand loom frames for hosiery will remain as there is not sufficient gain in them to make the change pay.'

'The manufacture of hosiery,' continued the Report, 'is carried on in Scotland to any important extent only in the town of Hawick where it is confined chiefly to one particular class, woollen; and also in or near Dumfries.'

A move towards something resembling joint consultation took place in 1867 with the establishment in Hawick of a Board of Arbitration and Conciliation, with nine employers and nine work people—as had been operating in Leicester and Nottingham for some time. Eight hundred hand stocking frames were now being operated in Hawick every day. Half of these were making stockings and socks (half-hose), and the other half shirts, drawers, vests and other underclothes. There were in addition 90 power and rotary frames at work, of which two-thirds produced fully fashioned goods.

Keeping down manufacturing costs had for a long time been the concern of the masters, but now it was equally as important to keep an eye on the rising charges involved in marketing the goods whose volume was growing monthly. More sensitive perhaps to this aspect of the operation than many of his competitors, Walter Pringle complained at a half yearly meeting of the Hawick Chamber of Commerce, of which he was a respected member, about the delays in the transmission of goods by rail. 'Hopeless to teach North British Railway directors that low fares must increase dividends!' he was heard to murmur in a very meant-to-be-heard aside.

Walter Pringle conducted his co-partnery under the name adopted by his father when he joined it after his apprenticeship, 'Robert Pringle & Son'. In 1867 this was one of ten leading hosiery manufacturers in Hawick.

At the end of 1867 began a series of events which led to Walker's firm securing the factory from which it has never budged. On December 11 the old part of the 60-year-old Wilton Mill built by Alexander Laing in 1804, and now belonging to Dicksons & Laings, was burnt to the ground. As a result of this Dicksons & Laings made a bid for the old firm of Nixon & M'Kie which was accepted, all the Nixon & M'Kie frames and other machinery being moved to Wilton Mill. Walter Pringle then offered to purchase Nixon & M'Kie's premises at the converted brewery in Walter's Wynd, and then 'disponed' the property to him in a document dated July 1, 1868.

Robert Pringle & Son were home.

Prima Ballerina:
*Margot Fonteyn and her
Pringle twinset
(1950s)*

Margaret Lockwood:
*Actress and sweater girl
(1950)*

75

Scottish starlet:
*Moira Shearer
(1950)*

THE
KNITWEAR
ERA

It is the accepted thing for Pringles sweaters to be far, far in the lead ... This brochure will tell you why Pringles are due for the leadership of another season. It was Pringles who really styled the Sweater—made it more than something for rugged wear. They made it the Key Piece of the ensemble, the utterly charming accent. It was Pringles who introduced Sweaters that were the softest, supplest, finest things that could be made from cashmere. It was Pringles who brought to Sweaters these rare and beautiful colourings. This as much as anything helped to fix their leadership. And here are the new Pringles with colours so exquisite they'll take your breath. Women love to wear the Style-modelled Sweater with this famous label.

Introduction to a *Pringle Sportswear* brochure of the 1930s

The essence of taste is suitability. Divest the word of its prim and priggish implications, and see how it expresses the mysterious demand of the eye and mind for symmetry, harmony and order.

Edith Wharton

9

QUALITY SURVIVES MECHANISATION

Under Robert Pringle II, technical innovations, overseas markets developed. (1868–1899)

W ALTER'S WYND is a narrow, short, straight lane that dips sharply off Hawick High Street to the bank of the river Teviot. It must have always been One Way—sometimes up, sometimes down—for two vehicles cannot pass in it. Walter was a tailor who once had his shop there, but before he gave his name to the street, it was known as Horsleyhill's Wynd after the Scotts of Horsleyhill, whose town house was at the top of the street. What remains of this house can still be seen in the 'pended' building, in the 1970s used as a shop, to which the Pringle of Scotland sign is fixed to direct motorists to the mill.

Walter's Wynd was the old North Port to the town, the only way the town could be entered from the north. It was a question of fording the river at the point where the street meets it—it is still broad and shallow here. If the water becomes unfordable, the only other way of getting into Hawick from the north was by a ten mile ride along the south bank of the river to Ancrum Bridge. When the bridge was built over the Teviot in 1741, Walter's Wynd's role as the North Port ended. It is only some 200 yards long, and on the lower half of it, on the left as you go down, there stood in 1869 the cluster of buildings surrounding a courtyard, varying from one to three storeys high which William Ainslie had built as a brewery and the Nixon brothers had converted into a hosiery factory. (Joseph Nixon was in charge; his brother William looked after the spinning at Lynnwood Mill.)

'Factory' was now the word. The stocking shop in which a framework knitter could operate his frame in the corner of the shop which he had also come to regard as 'his', was becoming obsolete. Moreover, the workers with their tradition of independence had to submit to the discipline of regular hours, to a system. Those who objected to factory regimentation in 1870 retained their self respect

Opposite
Actor John Mills:
Visits Rodono
(1960s)

by joining the decreasing ranks of men who operated frames in their homes. In 1970, 85-year-old Bill Mitchell who retired from Pringle in 1952 recalled that, when he first came to work at Walter's Wynd in 1900 as a boy of 15, there were several hand frames still being worked in Hawick.

But the factories were there to stay. Indeed, in Hawick the system had been anticipated in a way very advanced for the time, when the power frames which John Laing installed in 1858 proved they were capable of knitting six pieces at the same time. Laing gave his workers a regular weekly wage based on the time they had spent in the factory, as opposed to paying them for each piece. He was the first in Hawick to do so. None of the other hosiers followed suit. He gave his men from 14s (70p) to 20s (£1) a week, and the boys 4s (20p) to 10s (50p). This added up to the average earnings of the framework knitters in the town still on 'piece work'. Laing's men had the advantage of receiving an assured 'wage' irrespective of the fluctuations of the trade which made the earnings of the men in the stocking shops, and in their homes, so unreliable.

It is unlikely that Robert Pringle & Son joined John Laing in this bold experiment. They had few, if any, power frames. Besides, when at the time of their move from Cross Wynd to Walter's Wynd there came yet another trade depression with the Franco-Prussian War, many of their workers were laid off. There was widespread unemployment in 1876. Some couple of thousand framework knitters left Hawick.

It was also a year of personal tragedy for Walter Pringle. In 1870 his wife Mary (née Sutton) died of tuberculosis at the early age of 36. For her son, Robert, deprived of his mother when only eight, it was a terrible shock. But two years later, at the age of 44, his father married again. Walter Pringle's second wife was 30-year-old Mary Douglas, daughter of a Hawick physician, Dr John Douglas. Walter Pringle lived with his new wife and the children of his first marriage, Robert and Mary and John, at Langlands.

The next year Robert Pringle & Son, along with all the other hosiery manufacturers of Hawick, celebrated the trade's centenary—coupled with that of its principal denigrator, Sir Walter Scott. Soirée speakers vied with one another in their comparisons of the enlightened 1871 with the crudities of 1771. Hours of work, they said, had been shortened, wages increased, homes improved. The general state of society had advanced. The town's attempts to establish the manufacture of carpets, hats, blankets, gloves, leather thongs, whips and linen tape had come to nothing. All these trades had disappeared. But the hosiery trade, now a hundred years old, had not only survived but was vigorous, and—with a dig at the south—'the production of a good article is the best means than can be adopted to increase it'.

As a centenary recognition of the impracticability of hiring out power frames, frame rent—one of the hated 'reductions'—was dropped in 1871. But as a conciliatory gesture it did not go far enough. Worse, it directed attention to the continuance of the other main grievance of which they were also 'celebrating' the centenary, the seaming charge.

William Trotter, secretary of the Hawick Framework Knitters Society, sent a circular letter to all the masters formally demanding the abolition of all charges. The reply of Robert Pringle & Son was short and to the point:

Five pages from the new catalogue:
Illustrated for a Scarborough boutique (1950)

In reply to yours requesting us to free the workmen from the charges of seaming, oil & C, we have only to state we cannot accede to your request. The rise obtained last year we consider as much as the trade can sustain.

Other replies were almost identical.

On October 24, 700 framework knitters thronged the Corn Exchange to hear William Trotter read out the replies he had received from the masters; and on November 16 the masters called a public meeting at which Walter Pringle made a speech justifying the point he had made in his letter. Hawick, he said, was the great seat of the hosiery trade in Scotland and it would be a serious misfortune if it were to lose its prestige through a strike. 'The hosiery trade is historically associated with our town …'

But the framework knitters of 1872 were in no mood to be invited to take part in anything as remote as preserving and extending the hosiery trade. They were not concerned with what might or might not happen in 1922 or 1972. Their responsibilities were related to the Hawick of 1872, to their families now. If the masters were so incapable of seeing their point of view, even to discussing some kind of compromise, there was nothing for it but another Stand Oot.

The employers agreed that if there had to be a strike, it was better having it in October than June when large orders had to be taken at fixed prices. Both sides remained intransigent over Christmas and into the new year. But on January 15, 1873 William Trotter and his committee met Walter Pringle and the other master hosiers in the Tower Hotel for the last time. Then old arguments were gone over once again, and the masters had to admit that in view of the firm attitude taken by the workers and their representatives, there was no alternative but to yield. Their spokesman William Elliot came to the door of the hotel and announced to the crowd that a settlement had been reached, and they had conceded to most of Trotter's demands. 'We hope it will be for the good of the trade, although we fear the contrary,' he added.

It was not only to Trotter's society that the Hawick hosiery manufacturers conceded, but to the march of time. The whole operation needed re-thinking—in the light of the faster and more expensive machinery creating a bigger gap between master and employee, in the light of the master's need to obtain a sure return on the bigger investment he had at stake, in the light of the human problems of those whose hands and feet no longer supplied the motive power, whose pride as craftsmen thereby suffered and needed compensating. The dispute, the strike and its conclusion enabled everyone involved to look afresh at a state of affairs which was fast threatening to stifle innovation and progress. For most, even though perhaps grudgingly, a future based on a new interdependence of master and man held out promise. But for some time it was not worth participating in. One firm at least, John Wilson & Sons, decided to call it a day. They sold their entire stock to a new firm, formed only in 1868, called Innes, Henderson.

During the strike the second Mrs Walter Pringle bore two children, her daughters Jane and Catherine; and on October 24, 1873, when it was all over, a son John Douglas.

The pace of the technological revolution accelerated—indeed many

Bulletin:
(December 1955)

manufacturers were reluctant to install new machinery for fear of it quickly becoming obsolete. The power rotary frames were succeeded by the so-called 'Patent' frames of William Cotton of Loughborough introduced in the south in 1864 but not in Scotland till the 1880s. In the hand frames the needles had operated horizontally and the sinkers vertically; in Cotton's frame the needles were vertical. Steam engines, many built by James Melrose, were installed in Hawick to augment water power; and then the day came when the water wheel turned a generator which made electricity which drove an electric motor which turned the shaft.

It was in this age of technological advance that the young Robert Pringle II spent his boyhood.

He was only seven when his father's firm moved from Cross Wynd but looking back 70 years later he was able to remember being carried round the ware-room—not to be confused with the warehouse—by the foreman, Sarah Scott. He had his first lessons in Hawick at Moodie's School in the same street as his home and then attended Nest Academy, Jedburgh. Later he went to the Edinburgh Institution (Melville College).

In 1878, when he was 16, he was formally indentured as an apprentice to Robert Pringle & Son. 'Coming fresh from school in July without any holiday,' he wrote, in 1942, 'I found it very hard to be at the mill at six o'clock every morning, and I fear I sometimes had a little snooze in the yarnstore, where I was learning the hand frame under the late Willie Sinclair.'

Elsewhere he says Willie Sinclair encouraged him to take it in easy stages and not wear himself out—'I think you have peddled enough, lie down amongst the yarn!' For he had had to rise with all the rest of Hawick's working population when the town bell rang at 5.20 am and told them it was time to get up if they were to be at work by six.

Apprenticeship was now four years. Robert Pringle was paid 5s (25p) a week during his first year; 7s (35p) in his second; 9s (45p) in the third; and 12s (60p) in the fourth. The mill had few power frames, he remembered, 'but had about 200 stocking-makers, as they were called, but they made underwear as well as stockings on their hand frames'. (Bill Mitchell reckoned there were only 160 people employed altogether in 1900 when he joined.)

The stockings were of lambswool and of a cheap type in various colours selling at 8s 9d (44p) a dozen. 'Fancy' stockings were sold to wholesalers at 8¾d (4p) a pair.

'The "count" day, Saturday, was always a very busy day, and Alex Scott and I were often kept as late as three o'clock before all the men had "counted", the only thing we had for lunch being a pie from Helen Riddle's. In these days the firm had only one clerk, namely Alex Scott, and he was a most efficient and trusted employee. The office was up a very narrow steep winding stair which led to the public office and my father's private office.'

When his son came of age in 1883 Walter Pringle suggested to him that it might broaden his outlook if he took a trip to America and Canada. 'But it had to be a business trip to gain some experience, and also to allow me to see the country and have a little pleasure before settling down to business at home. I accordingly collected a hamper of samples and sailed from Liverpool in the Inman steamer *City of Richmond* in February of that year.'

Marketing opportunties:
*A stand at the Ryder cup
(1955)*

Bulletin:
(February 1957)

Two days out from Liverpool they ran into a storm and the liner's propeller broke. The propeller was mended but after three days it broke again. Outside New York they ran on to a sandbank. Five tugs failed to move the liner. One wire rope after another snapped under the strain. Robert Pringle finally reached New York harbour on board a tug, sheltering among the bags of mail. The voyage had taken 17 days.

> We only had two customers in New York as we were then doing wholesale trade only, namely Arnold Constable & Co, and Mr Hazelton. The latter we had dealt with for many years, and he gave me a good order, but alas he failed soon afterwards and we had a bad debt of £500.

He went on to Canada where he had adventures with ice boats on Lake Ontario, was nearly precipitated over the frozen Niagara Falls by a frisky horse, and indulged in some hard tobogganing and snow-shoeing in Montreal. Here he also received 'a splendid order' from Samuel Carsley & Co. He was back in Hawick in June in time for Common Riding.

The main activities of the latter take place on horseback but the young Robert Pringle's great love was cycling. He was captain of the Teviotdale Cycling Club. Highlight of the year's programme was the championship race on penny-farthings from Mosspaul, some 20 miles south of Hawick, to the Oak Tree (?).

> After I returned from my trip (continued Robert Pringle in his 1942 recollections), the firm resolved to change their trade from wholesale to retail, and it was my job to get new customers which I found was a very uphill fight. Up till then our trade had been chiefly with the Glasgow and London wholesale houses, and in Glasgow we had all the leading houses such as Stuart & McDonald.
>
> Mann, Byars was one of our largest accounts, and Mr Dunn was the gentleman in charge of the underwear department. He was very difficult and, I am afraid, not always pleasant. From his desk he could see me standing quite near waiting until he came out, but he would sometimes greet me with 'Well young man, and what do you want?' When I said I had called to see if he had any orders for me, very often he would say 'I want nothing today.' However, when he was in a more approachable mood, he would say that he would see what he could do for me, but he was never very friendly, and I always dreaded calling on him. I could never be sure of his mood. He was the most difficult customer with whom I had to deal.
>
> Our trade in those far-back years was chiefly lambswool shirts [vests] and pants, ladies' wool, combinations and vests; and we also did a big trade in ladies' wool hose, principally in black and grey. The average price of these hose was about 7s 9d (39p) a dozen, so it took a good many dozens to make up any volume of business.

Child Care:
*Post war optimism
(1950s)*

Bulletin:
(June 1957)

83

H.R.H Queen Elizabeth:
*Princess Anne in a Pringle cashmere
with embroidered corgi
(1959)*

Walter Pringle admitted his 25-year-old son Robert as a partner in
Robert Pringle & Son in 1885, seven years after he had completed his
apprenticeship. Trade was not too good elsewhere, but in Hawick
there was full employment day and night, with one firm competing
with another at fever heat.

On July 5, 1887 Robert Pringle married. His bride was 21-year-old
Edith Villiers Price, second daughter of Joseph Price. Edith was born in
Hamilton, Ontario, but at the time she met Robert was living in the
family home in Upper Tooting, London.

Robert was now well into his stride, and relieving his father of
much of the running of the mill, in particular in regard to development.
In November, 1892, he had a visit from the Mr Ford who was head
of a firm called Ford, Ayrton & Co. 'I have come to you,' Ford told
Robert Pringle, 'as, in my opinion, you are the best firm to handle my
silk, and I am prepared to confine it to you in Hawick, providing you
can see your way to take it up and run it.' He produced a 10lb bundle
of silk and attempted to sell Robert the idea that Pringle should start
making ladies silk combinations and vests.

'It was a great step,' Robert recollected, 'to jump from lambswool'
and botany yarns to spun silk. I made up my mind I would try it, so
I bought the 10lb bundle and made samples. It took some little time
to get the goods perfect, but after many trials I was satisfied that they
were right and would sell. I took samples to London and the result
was most gratifying. We continued with silk underwear from 1892
onwards and became known as "The Silk House for Hawick",
as we were considered to make the best silk even when other firms
entered the trade, which they did soon after.'

The material which presented the main competition in the realm
of underwear at this time was flannel. 'Flannel for underwear,' stated
a fashion note in the *Hawick Advertiser* of January 11, 1895 'is most
serviceable for everyone, very young infants excepted. It has the peculiar
merit of keeping the vessels of the skin constantly open … Those who
lead an exposed life should, above others, adopt flannel underwear
as far as they are able, for when working under wide differences of
temperature, they are constantly attacked with diseases resulting from
a sudden chill on violent perspiration. Many folks object to wearing
flannel next the skin as it irritates—but this is a healthy action of the
skin.' But, in spite of the flannel lobby in the local press, Pringle's knitted wool and silk goods became increasingly popular.

There was a trend too towards colour. 'There are tastes however
that only delicate colour effects can satisfy' stated the same note,
'and flesh tints, heliotrope, lavender and light blue and other delicate
shades have been provided to satisfy their wants … Lightweight woollens
will be worn more than ever before.' Underwear was moving into the
20th century.

Walter Pringle knew little of these new developments, for during
the last two years of his life he was unable to attend to the running of
his now substantial business. The cancer in his body was slowly eating
away his strength, and he died on April 3, 1895 at the age of 69. He
was survived by his second wife Mary (née Douglas) who was 52; by
her children, Douglas, Jane and Catherine, and by two of the children
of his first marriage, Robert and Mary.

Walter Pringle II had never been physically strong, but in spite

The Cashmere Bar:
Detail

Harvey Nichols:
*The Cashmere bar, the place
to be seen and buy cashmere
(1953)*

84

of this he managed to make Robert Pringle & Son one of the most prosperous firms in Hawick. In the 36 years since taking over from his father Robert Pringle I, he proved its staying power and demonstrated its potential in the important export field in which its future lay. As one of his obituarists wrote 'he made Hawick hosiery a specially quoted article in the markets of the world'. Like his father, he made a point of maintaining the most friendly and cordial relations with his work people. All of them held him in veneration and respect. He interested himself in municipal affairs and for some time sat as a town councillor and magistrate. In politics he was an ardent Liberal and took a prominent part in promoting the cause of Liberalism throughout the Border.

In his lifetime Walter had always made up the balance sheet himself, but on his death Robert Pringle, now senior partner at 33, decided to call in a firm of chartered accountants, J. Aikman Smith & Well of Edinburgh. His half-brother 24-year-old Douglas, already showing himself a man of exceptional business talents, joined him as a partner in 1897, mainly to handle the factory side of the business, leaving Robert free to travel and build up sales.

A large part of Robert Pringle's time as the century came to a close was spent in London where fashion trends were created and propagated.

'I realised that to get a grip of the retail customers,' he recalled in his 1942 memoir, 'new ideas must be introduced, and from time to time we made some very good, special improvements which gradually led us into a very nice trade. Fortunately Mr J. P. Jones, our representative at 21 Noble Street, was well known in the London trade, and I had to spend a long time with him every year going round the various firms and trying to make openings. We cultivated the ladies' trade more than the men's, and consequently most of our improvements were in the ladies section.'

In 1895 ladies' combinations were knitted full-fashioned to follow the general outline of the female form. But the shaping of the bust was normally done by cutting the fabric and sewing it in an additional piece of material. The inside seams created by this operation had always been a source of irritation and discomfort to the wearer, but no one found a remedy until Pringle's framesmith, Ben Wood, given the problem, came up with a technically unbeatable method of fashioning ladies' combinations the whole way up without cutting and inserting, He had invented the long-awaited Seamless Gore.

> As soon as he had perfected it, I took a sample to London and it turned out to be a great hit. I found however that I & R Morley had struck the same idea, so neither of us could patent the invention, but it certainly revolutionised the ladies' underwear trade.

The old century went out with a boom for the Hawick Hosiery Trade—and with the meaning of 'hosiery' now shifted almost entirely away from stockings to underwear. In January, 1899 James Henderson, head of J. Henderson & Co, held a reception to celebrate the wedding of his daughter in South Africa. He took the opportunity to review the state of trade in Hawick on the threshold of the 20th century.

In ten years, he said, there had been great changes. The hand

Telegram news:
*Cashmere evening coat delights
(1957)*

Hardy Amis:
*Mr Amis collaborated with Pringle
to create exclusive cashmere pieces
(1959)*

85

Cavanagh cashmere coat:
*Cashmere evening coat delights
(1957)*

frame had had to give place to the power frame, and the introduction of steam power had caused the manufacture of hosiery to pass largely into the hands of women.

> With the help of steam power Hawick has held its own in the hosiery trade with its competitors. I believe the number of hands employed now is in excess of that number of any former period when hand frames were the only machines in use. Certainly the production is very much greater.
>
> It is to be regretted that the stocking and sock trade is now so small in the town; but the time may come when it may be revived, and a share of that branch may come our way. Meantime we are glad that underwear is in great demand. Long may Hawick be famed for excellence of quality!

There was a time when there had been well over 1,000 hand frame knitters in the town, but by 1899 there were under 250. The last hand frame apprentice was Henry Anderson who began his training in 1892 and then indentured himself for a further four years on the steam frames of Robert Pringle & Son. The steam frames had killed the hand industry, but there was still a certain cachet in a garment being 'hand-made'. But the terminology had now shifted. The word 'frame' was reserved for the machine which made the main knitted fabric in plain 'stocking stitch' which formed the body and sleeves of garments; the name 'knitting machine' was applied to the hand-operated machines by which a standing operator made the 'fancy' knitted fabric in various widths for components like cuffs and collars. 'Hand-frame' denoted the improved broad 'stocking frame' as invented by William Lee, operated by the hands and feet of a sitting framework knitter. Its products were 'hand-made'.

The Hawick Framework Knitters Society had consisted of the latter, and by the end of the century membership had dwindled to 50. It was wound up and its remaining funds of £215 divided. At the meeting held to execute this final piece of business in January, 1899, William Easton, the stockingmaker employed by Lyle & Scott who acted as treasurer, failed to appear. They waited some time, and a member volunteered the information that he had been seen in the street earlier that day. When the winding up formalities had been completed without him, the committee went to the Chief Constable and told him that not only Mr Easton was missing but £125 of their funds. The magistrates issued a warrant for his arrest and he was picked up in Jedburgh and charged with embezzlement. He was convicted and sent to Jedburgh Jail for 12 months.

86

Men's fashion show:
(1950s)

Bulletin:
(September 1959)

Opposite
Gentlemen's fit session:
(1950s)

10

FROM UNDERWEAR TO OUTERWEAR

Success of Norfolk Jackets brings Knitted Coat Department; war widens home market. (1900–1920)

THE RANGE of Pringle underwear being made in the small mill at the foot of Walter's Wynd by some 150 workers at the end of the 19th century was surprisingly extensive.

The 47-page Winter Hosiery List of September 1, 1899 followed by the 40-page Summer Hosiery List of the same year indicated a wide variety of styles, materials, qualities and sizes. Ladies and gentlemen in 1899 had two sets of underwear—heavy for winter, light for summer.

The goods offered were indexed under 'Men's Wear' and 'Ladies' Wear'. The main headings under 'Men's Wear' were: Shirts, Boy's Dresses, Trousers, Night Shirts, Combinations, Body Belts, Knee Caps, Golf and Cycle Hose, Dresses (Moran's Patent Flap). To modern ears these may not sound like items of underwear at all, but 'shirts' meant vests, 'dresses' combinations, 'trousers' long pants. The Americans called combinations 'union suits'.

There were many types of men's 'shirts' alone: Shetland; Lambswool; C. B. Shirts; Natural Cashmere and Fancy; Ribbed Cashmere; Elastic and Stout Merino; Spun Silk; Silk and Wool; M.C. and Wool. Boy's shirts were available in lambswool, Merino and Llama.

Shetland was the heavier type of wool from the Shetland Islands. Cashmere was the soft goat's wool from Tibet which had superseded alpaca as the fashionable material in the 1850s. Merino was fine wool from Australian sheep which had been crossed with Spanish-bred merino sheep from South Africa in 1795. Llama was the soft wool of the South American camel of that name which, with the Alpaca and Vicuna, once lived in the Andes but also came to be bred in Australia.

'Silk and Wool' was another of Robert Pringle's 'improvements'. 'Another great hit,' he wrote, 'was the 29 P. plaited spun silk in ladies' vests and combinations, and this we had patented and ran for a good many years. Up till then there were many cut-up plaited goods on the market, but our invention was to make fashioned goods and still

89

Opposite
Elvis in Hawick:
(1960s)

continue the plaiting. It took a lot of working out, but eventually Ben Wood again managed to perfect an appliance which narrowed and widened and made spun silk on the top and wool below. We had one customer, James Spence & Co of St Paul's Churchyard, whose buyer Mr J. A. Jones took a tremendous fancy to the 29 P. ladies' combinations. He advertised them as 'Luxurio' and for many years whenever I went to London he gave me an order for one hundred dozen.'

Shirts and most other underwear were made in six sizes shown in the List as Sml, Slr, Men's, Popes, O.S. and Ex. O.S. These were: small, slender, men's, a size midway between men's (36 inch) and outsize (40 inch) known as Popular (38 inch) which got contracted to Pops and became for some unknown reason 'Popes'; outsize and extra outsize.

Shetland shirts (vests) were available in 14 qualities. For instance 202 Popes—the cheapest and coarsest quality in this size—cost 28s 6d (£1.42½) a dozen; whereas the highest quality 280 Popes cost 55s 6d (£2.77½). Double-breasted Shetland shirts were 3s extra (15p) with short sleeves 2s (10p) less. The prices of course were wholesale charges made to retailers.

Shetland trousers (pants) had spliced seats, and if, instead of stretching to the ankles, they only came to the knee—Knee Drawers—the cost was 3s (15p) less. Lambswool shirts could be had not only double-breasted but double-backed—at 9s (45p) extra. You could specify silk spliced elbows. You could have your lambswool trousers fitted with silk spliced knees. But not if you were Extra Outsize.

Fancy Shirts (Long Arms Single Breasted) and Fancy Trousers came in six types;: Beaconsfield; Salmon; Natural Shades; Australian Llama, Natural; Australian Llama, Self-Grey; Fancy Tweeds. The first were the cheapest and the last the most expensive.

Ladies' Wear was listed under: Vests, Dresses [combinations], Drawers, Cycle Dresses, Cycle Drawers, Night Dresses, Bodices, Body Belts and Knee Caps. Vests came in four types: Lambswool, Perfection, Scotch Ribbed, Ribbed; and dresses in the same plus spun silk and smocked.

Llama drawers could have a Shaped Band for 2s (10p) extra and made in Pure Fast Black for 5s (25p) extra. Spun Silk Night Dresses were the most expensive items on the Ladies' Winter Underclothing list. Boys and Girls underwear were listed separately—including Kilt Dresses in seven sizes and four qualities.

'We have pleasure in intimating,' read an announcement given a page to itself, 'that we have secured the sole right to manufacture "The Moran Patent Flap Combination" in Fashioned Goods which we make in most of our regular numbers.' Printed in red on the same page was the information: 'All Goods Stamped with our trade mark "Rodono Finish" we guarantee Unshrinkable.'

The development of the unshrinkable process was a major break-through, and it was featured in all the marketing. 'We would beg to draw special attention to the fact that our ALL WOOL AND SILK & WOOL GOODS are now being treated by Our Special Process, and all Garments stamped with our Trade Mark, the "Rodono" Finish we Guarantee Unshrinkable, and any Garment shrunk in washing will be replaced.'

It was just becoming the fashion for each manufacturer to distinguish

Newspaper advertising:
Pringle at Simpsons department store Piccadilly
(1965)

Rodono model:
(1960s)

Stuart Beatty:
Otto Weisz's successor
(1960s)

his product by his own trade mark or brand name. 'Beaconsfield' and 'Perfection' were examples in the 1899 Pringle catalogue. 'Rodono' was the name of the shooting lodge on St Mary's Loch in the Yarrow valley which Robert Pringle leased from the Earl of Wemyss. He applied it as a name which was not only distinctive but local, first to the unshrinkable finish, then to certain garments, and finally to the mill in Walter's Wynd. The name derives from the old Scots word for a Rowan tree or Rodon tree, of which there are many in the Meggat Vale, once known as the Barony of Rodona. Earthworks still mark the site of the Rodono Chapel which stood just south of Chapelhope Farm by the Loch of the Lowes two miles from the house, which was built in 1856 for one David Turnbull. It became the Rodono Hotel. The 'o' ending which may sound more Italian than Scots is, however, common on the Border—Kelso, Minto.

In the Summer List the men's shirts and trousers were in lighter materials like gauze (from Gaza), elastic and stout merino.

Ladies' Dresses (Sleeveless), of Indian Gauze, for Evening Wear, were trimmed with lace. There were Ladies' Cycle Dresses and Cycle Drawers in Gauze Llama; Children's Sleeping Suits with Smocked Sleeves.

Buyers were invited to send their orders by telegraph, and special code numbers were given for each item to save lengthy descriptions on the telegram. If you wanted Ribbed Arms, you added R.A., if Short Sleeves, S.S., and so on.

The combining of vest or chemise with drawers into a combination garment had first been introduced at the end of the 1870s, but at the turn of the century Greensmith Downes, the Edinburgh mail order drapers, were still able to write in their catalogue that 'the theme of the moment' was the coming popularity of the combination garment for men.

'It is, in our opinion,' wrote the Riding Correspondent of *The Field*, 'a great improvement on those ordinarily worn. For golfing, fishing, riding or participation in any sport where bodily freedom is essential, it is exceptionally comfortable, as there is nothing to ruck up, nothing to work down, one thickness, and complete covering from neck to ankle.' Another combinations' fan ' T.P.O' wrote: 'There is a prejudice among men against the Combination Garment but those who have tried them are full of praise of what I may term their negative advantages. In fact, the wearing of Combinations results in the avoidance of discomfort ... If you once try the single garment, I do not think you will go back to the two.'

The busy days which ushered in the 20th century were short lived. 'The close of 1899,' stated an editorial in the Hawick *Advertiser*, 'found good trade, high prices and a bright outlook, but ere January of 1900 had run its course prices, trade and outlook alike were on the wane.'

Robert Pringle countered the apparent wane in prices, trade and outlook with an innovation. In 1901 he conceived the idea of trimming the tops of ladies' vests with lace, and he bought a lace-making machine. A new heading appeared in the 1902 List, 'Fancy Lace Top Vests' in nine qualities. Next year there were also Fancy Lace Top Dresses [Combinations], and a special and more expensive version of each known as 'Princess Patterns'. Later there were Fancy Lace Top Spencers and Bodices.

Hand linking:
The process of attatching sleeves to sweaters (1960s)

Modern milling:
(1960s)

91

Pringle Annual:
The Bulletin is streamlined (1964)

I think the next big hit after the seamless gore,' wrote Robert Pringle, 'was lace tops for ladies' combinations, vests and spencers. We had a small experimental frame by Ben Wood, and it was really his idea that perfected the machine. It was a shell pattern, and I found when going round the London shops that this was a great inducement to the buyers to put down orders for ladies' goods ... After the shell pattern, 'Princess' tops came in and I may say we were the first to show them in London.

It was true, as he claimed, that 'the lace top goods which we made were the first in the market' but Robert Pringle was in fact introducing to a wider public a hand-made fashion which had been in vogue for some 30 years or more. In 1876 a fashion writer was protesting 'underclothing has reached a luxury unknown in any age. The most modest lady has now her chemise and drawers trimmed with flounces of real lace alternating with tucks, frills and insertion. A fashionable chemise looks like a baby's christening robe. Ladies' underwear had come a long way from the shift.

It was this similarity which underwear was beginning to have to outerwear which stimulated hosiery manufacturers like Pringle to adapt the techniques they had learnt in developing lace top vests and combinations to the manufacture of the outerwear that eventually became their sole product.

The move towards outerwear was in no small way due to the prompting of the new partner whom Robert Pringle invited to join him at this time, James Boyd Sime. Aged 40 in 1906, Boyd Sime came from a family of Galashiels tweed manufacturers. At the time he joined the co-partnery he was a director of the tweed firm of Sime, Williamson which he had founded in Hawick with his brother William and Fred Williamson. He became interested in hosiery when he devoted part of his Hawick factory to the manufacture of knitted goods which he successfully marketed through a mail order company which he established called Athenic Mills. A man of considerable resource and energy, he had other business interests in Hawick, besides being a pianist and organist of professional standards and a mainstay of the local amateur operatic society.

Bridging underwear and outerwear were the Bathing Suits and Dresses which appeared in both Men's and Ladies' Lists of 1902. On the last page were two 'lines', as they say, which may have been made at Walter's Wynd or may have been bought in from outside suppliers; Travelling Rugs and Fleecy Tam o'Shanters. It would be nice to think that the Pringle power frames at Hawick were being applied to the mechanical production of tammies which, as seen, are believed to have been the first article of clothing ever knitted (by hand) in Britain—and that in Scotland. But 'bought in London Goods' were a big feature of Pringle's trade at this time and these probably came under this heading.

'Real Shetland Goods Kept in great Variety—Shawls, Spencers & C' declared a line on the last page of the 1903 List, in which a page was devoted to Ladies' Ribbed and Plain Bodices, at the foot of which was a note that Spencers were available in the same qualities at the same prices.

92

Arnold Palmer:
Golfing legend had a close association with Pringle (1965)

Arnold Palmer:
(1965)

Bouby golf trophy:
Featuring the rampant lion (1950s)

The shape of the spencers was due to the eccentric Lord Spencer burning his coat tails while standing in front of the fire. He had them neatly trimmed by his tailor and walked out into the street to create a new fashion—and secure a firm place for his name in the history of British clothing. By 1905 spencers had earned an entry in the index of Pringle's List, though still linked with bodices. 'Spencers and Bodices, Fancy Lace Top and Ribbed & Plain.' A full-page plate showed a young lady with her hair up in the fashion of the time, fingering a hand mirror and wearing her knitted woollen spencer buttoned to the neck. It had a leaf decoration at the top and a ribbed 'skirt' clinging firmly to her slim waist.

It was the first item of Pringle 'outerwear'.

Throughout the centuries the two layers of garments had continually been changing places, the outer receding into the unseen background—Pantaloon's trousers becoming underpants for instance—and the lower layer becoming the upper layer. The warm bodice or spencer worn by ladies under their dresses coming to the surface to be seen and admired—largely because manufacturers like Robert Pringle & Son made them so attractively—was an example of the latter. The object was now no longer to conceal but to display the human form, and for this there could be no more suitable a medium than elastic, springy knitting—as the young men of Queen Elizabeth's day had found out 300 years before.

Formal wear was still starchy and restricted by etiquette and 'class'. But now ladies and gentlemen began to have two wardrobes, one for the formal occasion for which the rules had been laid down long ago and were still strictly adhered to, and another for when they indulged in country activities which demanded more relaxed clothing. Ladies had a walking costume with 'sensible' underclothing which gave them as much freedom of movement as possible; 'combs' took the place of voluminous petticoats. Men like Robert Pringle who got carried away by the penny farthing cycling craze—the 'cads on castors'—needed rational and 'sanitary' clothing suited to this energetic sport—short pants in absorbent 'stockingette' for instance (how successfully the original product of the frame managed to keep in the act!). For lady cyclists the only possible form of nether hose was that immortalised by American Amelia Jenks after her marriage to Mr Bloomer.

The emancipated young ladies who played tennis with such abandon also wanted garments which enabled them, to run and swing their arms without too much fatigue—or perspiration. Rinkomania—the addiction to indoor roller skating—which swept Britain at this time demanded flexibility from the waist down.

The popularity of sport broke down class barriers and opened up the market for the kind of garments which Pringle and the other Hawick 'hosiery' manufacturers now began to produce. When the fielders were out on The Vine cricket ground at Sevenoaks no one could tell the Duke of Dorset from his tailor, they were all dressed the same. Furthermore, the informal, comfortable, lighter weight, more colourful clothes—under and outer—which men and women and children wore for golf, walking, cycling and skating gave a taste for more comfortable clothes for everyday life.

A 'sports' garment which was an even stronger link between under

Pringle Annual:
A dynamic new rampant lion is introduced
(1964)

Bill and Arnold:
Bill Rogers and Arnold Palmer

93

Ryder Cup sports shirt:
75/-
(1967)

and over wear than either the bathing dress or the spencer—particularly in view of its name and the wide currency it has today—was the Sweater. As seen, Robert Pringle & Son's Summer Hosiery List of 1899 featured Men's Sweaters and Boys' Sweaters.

The sweater got its name from originally being something in which (as the Oxford Dictionary of Dr James A. H. Murray, a native of Denholm, puts it) 'a horse or a man in training is exercised to produce profuse sweating; a woollen vest or jersey worn in rowing or other athletic exercise originally in order to reduce one's weight, now commonly put on also before or after exercise to prevent taking cold'. The word and the garment first came into use around 1882. Like a bathing dress, it was both outerwear and underwear combined, for it was first worn next the skin, though of course later over a thinner 'sweat *shirt*' of a lighter material like cotton.

Pringle's Men's Sweaters of 1899 were available in the usual small, slender, men's, popes and O.S. sizes in six qualities.

In 1902 Men's Sweaters were only supplied in men's size, but in seven qualities. By 1909 they had become 'Gent's Sweaters', and there were not only Boys' Sweaters but, for the first time, Girls' Sweaters—for children of the female sex, not young ladies.

The main breakthrough in Pringle's ladies' outerwear came in 1907 when there appeared in the Hosiery List of that year two new headings in the index: Knitted Blouses and Norfolk Jackets, and 'Centenary' and Special Norfolk Jackets (Seamless), with full page plates illustrating these fine garments with their mutton chop sleeves and smart design worn by well-proportioned Edwardian open-air girls with the latest in feather decorated straw hats perched on their elaborate hair-dos.

'At this time the knitting machine portion was not large,' wrote Robert Pringle in his memoir, 'but we turned out ladies' Norfolk Coats. A very different style to those worn today [1942] but they were a novelty in the trade and took very well. We also had these coats in a cable stitch, having invented an idea whereby the cable stitch could be manipulated quite easily. This style of coat was very successful and it was called the "Minto".'

Knitted coats and jackets of this kind were of course being knitted at home by hand. At first the machines merely copied the hand-knitted garment and indeed made a point of resembling them. But soon mechanically knitted outerwear assumed a respected character of its own. Underwear never suffered in this way—no one attempted the fine gauge knitting of a pair of combs in public. Moreover mechanically knitted underwear was always coming out in new forms. The Pringle List of 1907, for instance, introduced 'the pleasing novelty' of Vertical Stripes for Gents' Underwear. 'These goods are strikingly effective, and are not *cut up*, being fully fashioned in every particular, thus ensuring ease and comfort to the wearer'.

They were another of Robert Pringle's 'hits'.

'We also had a special hit in vertical stripe men's shirts and trousers [vests and pants]. These turned out to be a great success in the men's trade, and we did a large trade in these novelty goods for many years.'

94

Skirt packaging:
(1960s)

Extract from the Bulletin:
Golf fashion shows at the tournament
(1960s)

Cashmere explained:
Promotional brochure
(1960s)

As the new century got into its stride, the spate of activity with which it began lost its momentum, and it was brought home to the leaders of the Hawick hosiery trade that that kind of prosperity was far from self-generating. If the ups and downs of the ever-recurring trade cycles were to be faced with equanimity, some degree of co-operation among the competing firms was essential. As the scale of the operation magnified and turnovers rose, the economics of success became more precarious and the margin of profit finer. The key to the latter was the most expensive item on the balance sheet, labour. In 1908 the hosiery workers reorganised themselves into a new 'trade union', as the name now was.

In May 1909, Grierson, secretary of the Hawick Hosiery Union, sent the managing-director or senior partner of every hosiery firm in Hawick a letter seeking their agreement to the union altering one of its rules. Informally the masters all came to an agreement on how they should reply, but this was the kind of thing many of those who received the letter considered should be formally discussed and minuted by a body representative of all the employers. Consequently a meeting of 14 hosiery firms was called in the Burgh court room at Hawick to consider the matter.

Robert Pringle, his half brother Douglas (who, on June 6, 1907 had married a girl called Marie Martin), and his other partner James Boyd Sime, attended the meeting as representatives of Robert Pringle & Son. These were joined by two Laings, two Scotts, two Innes, a Henderson, a Wilson and a Bonsor. At a second attended by Robert Pringle, Douglas Pringle (in the chair), and Boyd Sime, it was agreed to form a Hawick Hosiery Manufacturers Association.

In 1910 Robert Pringle's son Gerald, now 17, entered the firm as a trainee-apprentice—the fourth generation of Pringles preparing to take over a family business with a reputation in Hawick which had never been higher and a mounting prestige in Britain and overseas for quality underwear—and now outerwear.

A Knitted Coat Department was formed in 1910 in recognition of the growing importance of this side of the business. 'We have pleasure in drawing the attention of our customers to the fact that we have now a very large and comprehensive range of the latest styles in high-class Knitted Coats. During the past year we have made this department a special study and have been obliged to greatly enlarge our factory to cope with this growing demand for these useful and handsome garments. In our range will be found all styles from Norfolk Jackets to full length Steamer Coats, beautifully finished and made in weights suitable for all requirements, and in a choice selection of colourings embracing over fifty of the best and newest shades.'

There were now seven qualities of Norfolk Jacket. The technique of designing, knitting, milling and finishing these garments evolved, as seen, from the women's 'dresses' or combinations which now passed the peak of their popularity and were on their way out. A final attempt to keep combs in favour with customers was the launching of the 'Interchangeable Part' Combination in 1907 'with the object of enabling wearers to renew those parts which are subjected to the greatest wear. Special parts are provided that can easily be inserted in place of parts badly worn, thus greatly prolonging the life of the garment'. But their days were numbered.

Golfing tournament:
Pringle models at a tournament fashion show
(1960s)

95

There was a boom on all other fronts however. An anonymous writer in the *Hawick Express* of December 27, 1912, who called himself 'Scotsman', thought it worth remarking that employment in hosiery in Hawick now rivalled tweed. There had been falling off for repeats for the spring trade during the mild weather at the end of the year, but the season on the whole was good. Winter trade had opened up early and there was great demand in the autumn. Several manufacturers could have done more but they would not have been able to give delivery in time notwithstanding every factory running overtime with night shifts.

> Some years ago the hosiery trade was mainly carried along on hand frames worked by men and male youths, but there are few of those frames now in existence, and this industry has been completely revolutionised by the introduction of power frames and machines of great variety; and female labour now predominates. Apart from the usual underwear garments in lambswool, llama, silk and India gauze; a great feature of the trade now is the manufacture of high-class garments in ladies jackets, also woollen vests and scarves—some manufacturers refused orders for the latter as the demand was so great. Some firms purpose putting down additional machinery but they find a difficulty in getting more suitable workers, many having gone abroad and elsewhere.

But to those who read the newspapers, and in particular to Gerald Pringle who was now halfway through his apprenticeship, it was obvious that it would not be long before events unconnected with trade cycles and labour problems would be curtailing the demand for the extensive range of Pringle underwear, bathing suits, night clothes, stockings and outerwear which now issued from Walter's Wynd.

In the section headed 'British Or Foreign?, A Plea For A More Thoughtful Patriotism' in the sixth edition of *The Book of Scotch-Made Underwear* published by the Edinburgh mail order house of Greensmith Downes in 1912, the writer deplored the way the British public were giving preference to foreign goods in cases where the value was infinitely inferior to those of home production.

On August 4, 1914 the possible enemy became an actual one. Gerald Pringle had completed his four-year apprenticeship and immediately joined up. To the surprise of his brother and Fred Williamson, and no doubt of Robert Pringle too, James Boyd Sime, who was 50, enlisted as a private. Many Pringle employees joined the Border regiments. In 1970 William Murray who retired in 1966 at 65, recalled getting his first employment with Pringle in 1915 as a hosiery warehouseman, having two years as a soldier in the army of occupation in Germany, and returning in 1920. Another who joined during the war was Jemima Telfer who came to the mill as a girl of 14 in 1916 and retired in 1965. One of her vividest recollections was the strict discipline maintained in the flats by foreman Jimmy Hill.

With the nation at war, public demand for Pringle's products did indeed fall off, but within a short time all the Hawick mills were receiving large orders from the War Office for woollen jerseys, stockings

Patriotic packaging:
Cashmere and knitwear is transported in plastic bags to protect from dust (1960s)

Dusseldorf:
Cashmere store (1960s)

Dusseldorf:
Store interior

and underwear for soldiers, sailors and airmen, to say nothing of members of the women's services who, when they returned to civilian life, remembered the comfort of the garments to which the war had introduced them, and had acquired a taste for their cosy informality which they were never to lose.

World War I brought a rise in the cost of raw materials everywhere, and yarn was no exception. Certain of the Hawick hosiery manufacturers wanted to make it the reason for raising prices, and a committee of the Association proposed a minimum advance of two shillings a dozen on all merino goods. When their resolution came up for approval at a full meeting of the Association in November 1914, Robert Pringle & Son, as represented by Robert and Douglas Pringle, was one of five firms who objected strongly. The slight rise in the cost of merino warranted no such action, they said. It could not be justified to customers. In any event 'the arbitrary fixing of prices by the Association savoured of a ring, and was against the best interests of the trade, and contrary to the objects of the Association as well as out of its scope'.

Robert Pringle supported Thomas Henderson in his contention that members of the Association should be left to settle their own prices, and seconded his motion for rescinding the resolution. Douglas Pringle also spoke against it.

But two member firms had already acted on the committee's resolution and raised their prices. The representative of one of them protested that, if it was not part of the Association to deal with increases in prices, what good was it to any of them? Others spoke in similar vein, and a vote was taken. Eight firms, including Pringle, with 1,868 votes were for rescinding the resolution; 1,560 votes for keeping it. Thomas Henderson's motion was declared carried. The committee in question saw in this a vote of no confidence and resigned *en bloc*. After only five years, the new employers' association was in danger of splitting down the middle. But the would-be price raisers bowed to the majority feeling and agreed to re-form.

There was a depleted staff to celebrate the firm's centenary, but there was a special 1815–1915 edition of the annual Hosiery List which devoted a whole page to the latest Ladies' Directoire Knickers and several to what were now called Ladies' Sports Coats (Woollen). The latter came in 17 styles. There were also five styles of Ladies' Sports Coats in artificial silk and four styles of Ladies' Sports Coats in spun silk. A note added that caps and scarves could be made to match all coats. The fullness of the range reflected the general mood of 1915 that the war would only last a few months. Technically the ability of the machines in all departments to produce quality goods in quantity reached a new peak. In 1915 a framework knitter at Walter's Wynd produced as many garments in a day as his counterpart at Whisky House Mill of a hundred years before made in a fortnight.

Production of ladies' outerwear such as Norfolk jackets and sports coats meant a reorientation of the marketing exercise, and much of it fell on the shoulders of the London end of the operation. London Office and Warehouse first established in the 1880s at 21, Noble Street, Falcon Square, E.C., had moved to 67, Gresham Street, E.C. in 1902. J. P. Jones, the first Pringle London representative, died in 1906. B. R. Chaston who came from George Brettle & Co as London representative, knew most of Pringle's customers and

Arnold Palmer:
Pringle embraces new wools—'Orlon' from Dupont was perfect for Pringle sportswear (1966)

97

introduced considerable new business.

These first warehouses were both in the business part of the capital known as The City. But by the centenary year of 1915 the firm had acquired a somewhat smarter address in keeping with its merchandise, particularly the more fashion-conscious outerwear, off Regent Street, at 35, Great Marlborough Street, W.I. in the West End of London, nearer to the big department stores and couturiers who were Pringle's customers.

On October 12, 1917 2nd Lieutenant Gerald Pringle of the 6th King's Own Scottish Borderers was killed in action at Passchendaele in Flanders during some of the bitterest fighting of the war in which 300,000 lost their lives. He was 24. When peace came with the defeat of Germany in 1918, Robert Pringle found himself with neither a son nor a brother to whom he could hand over the business. Douglas Pringle, now 46, had decided to retire. His health had been failing him and he went to live in the south of England where it was warmer. His wife Marie had borne him two children, a daughter Elizabeth in 1908 and soon after a son, John. His mother (née Douglas), Walter Pringle's second wife, died in 1915. So Robert Pringle invited an old friend from among his customers to join him and James Boyd Sime, now returned from his army service, as a third partner. This was Herbert Benyon Johnstone who in 1919 was buyer for the large and old-established London department store of John Barker & Co of Kensington.

In 1920 there were 16 members of the Hawick Hosiery Manufacturers Association. According to the return they submitted for fixing subscriptions, Robert Pringle & Son had 7,143 inches of needles. Innês Henderson with their two factories were the largest with 16,538 inches; Lyle & Scott had 9,574. Next biggest after Pringle (the second oldest) was Walter Wilson (the oldest) with 4,684.

Together Robert Pringle, James Boyd Sime and Herbert Johnstone, with B. R. Chaston and his team in London, directed their attentions to applying this considerable array of needlepower, and the even greater fund of technical expertise and fashion sense accumulated over a hundred years of trading, to meeting the demands of the very much changed society thrown up by the greatest upheaval the modern world had yet experienced.

Bermudan boutique:
The hight of fashion. Pringle open a boutique in Bermuda and advertise 'Scottish cashmere is not the cheapest, but it is the best'
(1969)

98

Opposite
Newspaper advertising:
These striking illustrative and typographical adverts appeared in national and local newspapers across UK
(1960s)

Men who know wear *Pringle*

available
at all
eading
tores

11

ATTENTION TURNS TO CASHMERE

William Mactaggart and Arthur Oddy take charge. (1921–1940)

T HE GREAT WAR brought abrupt ends not only to young lives with promising potentials but to fashions in thought and conduct and dress which it forced into new moulds. A curtain descended to cut off the Victorian and Edwardian eras and invest them with a certain romance and mystery. They constituted a dream world nostalgically referred to as 'before the war'.

To a transformed Hawick corn exchange, where angry stocking-makers had once gathered and protested, short-skirted, short-haired, bosomless, hipless, thighless, cigarette smoking flappers in shapeless frocks and cloche hats went to 'the silent black and white flicks' to see *The Woman God Forgot* and *The Innocent Mrs Gordon* to the accompaniment of continuous piano playing; or to the town hall to see a live touring company performing *The Toodle-Oo-Girl*. There was a controversy over the design of a war memorial; there was unemployment—200 were out of jobs. A public subscription list was opened; the town council deliberated methods of relief. The Scottish Council of Textile Trade Unions considered amalgamating all the textile unions in Scotland to embrace 50,000 workers. The Rev James Wotherspoon was moved to give a discourse in Allars Church on the subject of Trade Depression which, he said, came in the wake of every war. He hit out at employee and employer alike. The former, he declared, were too often swayed by their savage instincts; but as for their masters 'it will not do for a man in these days to stroll into his office at ten, then out at twelve for a drink and a hundred up at billiards and so on, waltzing through a wasted day'. They should give a lead to their men. Privilege meant responsibility.

The anonymous 'Scotsman' making another of his periodic reviews in the *Hawick Express* said the trade in hosiery, underwear and knitted woollen goods—it is interesting to see him distinguishing the three

101

Opposite
Adrienne cashmere suit:
(1960s)

instead of lumping them all under 'hosiery'—had shared in the great depression that followed the war but had recovered more quickly than the tweed trade. 'This may be accounted for,' he remarked, 'by the fact that the underwear manufacturers are nearer the public.' They did direct trade with shopkeepers, while the tweed manufacturers acted through wholesalers. They had a great variety of goods to offer—fine underwear and 'special garments' (?), but a great deal of the machinery was employed on the production of sports coats, woollen jackets and vests, knitted costumes, scarves, etc. The home trade was very good and there was considerable business to the colonies, South America and Japan.

Pulling out of the depression was gradual. According to the report of the Hosiery Manufacturers Association for 1921, the dying year had been a disastrous one for the hosiery trade 'owing to the great slump in values and the famine in orders (for the first time in its history) and consequent lengthy period of unemployment and short time. For the past ten weeks orders have been more plentiful and, although as yet there are few signs of a return to normal conditions, the outlook is brighter and it is thought the year on which we are about to enter will generally prove to be better than the year just ended'.

In the year they were about to enter (1922) Robert Pringle embarked on his 60th year. It was a time to be thinking of releasing his grip and handing over the reins. He certainly had something very substantial to hand over if the record of the past decade was any indication. In the eight years 1910 to the end of the war (1918) the rise in sales receipts was steady. The obvious way to ensure the continuance of the Pringle enterprise was to turn the co-partnery into a private joint-stock company, and at the beginning of 1922 Robert Pringle seriously set about considering which of his acquaintances he would invite to join him, as directors. His choice fell on William Oddy and Robert L. Mactaggart.

William Oddy was a director of William Oddy & Sons, Bradford cloth manufacturers—he was known for having invented a lining for suit stiffening which he called 'Syddo' (Oddy's backwards). Robert Mactaggart was a director of the only firm in Hawick which processed wool for spinning into the yarn used in weaving tweed—partly Border fleece wool but also imported colonial skins. He had acquired the existing processing firm of Elliot, Mactaggart & Co, which, on being joined by his brother, he renamed Mactaggart Brothers Ltd.

Herbert Johnstone intimated that he was not prepared to take an active part in any new arrangement of Pringle, and asked that he should not be considered as a possible director. James Boyd Sime, however, was still game. Negotiations got under way in the middle of 1922, therefore, for the purchase of the co-partnery, its stock, cash, buildings, machinery and goodwill as a going concern by a private company yet to be incorporated, the subscribers to which would be Robert Pringle, James Boyd Sime, Robert Mactaggart and William Oddy.

The purchase of the co-partnery took place at the end of November 1922. It cost the new company £92,055. On December 1, a private company called Robert Pringle & Son Ltd was incorporated with a capital of £100,000 in £1 shares. Goodwill was finally assessed at £20,000. The first meeting of directors was held at 8 Forres Street Edinburgh. They appointed Robert Pringle chairman for one year;

102

Berwick backstage:
Pringle social event
(1960s)

Diamond sweater:
Pringle social event
(1960s)

Editorial:
Pringle fashion feature in
Bazaar magazine
(1960)

James Boyd Sime secretary and managing-director for five years; William Oddy and Robert Mactaggart non-executive directors. B. R. Chaston became the fifth member of the Board.

Boyd Sime set himself up at Walter's Wynd, now with only 120 employees; Robert Pringle continued his mainly outside sales activities. The war and the depression that followed it receded into the background. 'The year just ending,' stated the Hosiery Association in their 1923 annual report, 'has seen a very considerable improvement in the hosiery trade, and while business has not yet reached its pre-war steady flow, members have much to be thankful for.' Robert Pringle & Son Ltd was in a very healthy and entrenched position, well able to face competition from the French and Austrian garments now flooding into Britain at prices it was difficult to match at the exchange rates. The company focused on seven 'lines': dresses (combinations), underwear other than combinations, sweaters, skirts, knitting-machine coats, belts and scarves. In March 1923 they introduced a new line 'frame coasts' as distinct from 'knitting machine coats'.

Before they had been in the saddle for a year, the directors engaged two young men 'to learn the business of hosiery manufacturers' as special trainee-managers. These were Arthur Oddy, William Oddy's son, and William Mactaggart, nephew of Robert Mactaggart. This decision, made in October 1923, was followed by Robert Pringle announcing his intention 'of gradually retiring and not wishing to take such an active part in the management'. He was 62.

His wife and daughter Frances, who had married the Rev Chrystal Muir in 1912, attended the first annual general meeting at Walter's Wynd in January 1924 as shareholders. The profit for the year was declared to be £6,547 after tax, a 'not unsatisfactory' result in view of the fact that 'trading had been carried on under exceptionally difficult circumstances plus the usual troubles incident to a change of control'. But the directors were obviously more pleased with their first year's trading than the reserved 'not unsatisfactory' verdict might lead one to believe, for they at once authorised expenditure of £3,500 on factory extension. It was to be the first since the Nixon brothers moved out in 1867. Production was to be increased.

At the end of January 1925, Robert Pringle II told the Board that he intended giving up active work in connection with the company during the present year, 'probably in May but possibly not till November'. He went off to North America in March for a final business tour with a range of samples in his bag, while Robert Mactaggart acted as chairman. He was back in September to report on his trip, which had covered the United States and Canada where he had visited agents and appointed a new man for Eastern Canada. He suggested the company installed two cotton frames in America and manufactured garments there to save duty. He also suggested Pringle open a shop in New York. 'Neither of these proposals found much favour with the Board, but they decided to consider them at the next meeting,' ran the minute of those who never lived to see the elaborate way in which Robert Pringle II's second suggestion was eventually implemented.

The new line of battle was drawn up in the light of the chairman's intimated retirement. It was decided to advertise for an assistant to the managing-director. Already the second echelon was in position.

Trina two piece:
*In spindrift Pure New wool
a newly developed finish*
(1965)

Ruffle collared cardigan:
(1965)

103

Cashmere dress:
(1965)

The two new trainee managers took their appointments: Arthur Oddy in November 1924, and William (Willie) Mactaggart, who had left Sedburgh School the year before, in February 1925. A formal vote of thanks to Mr Pringle was passed on December 22, 1925 for all the work he had done for the company. The chairman recognised this as the formal moment for the CO to step down and join the ranks of his fellow officers, but saw no reason for his guns to stop firing—as the Board was soon to learn. Within months there was a head-on collision on the basic consideration of what could, and what could never, be a profitable line of business for Pringle.

Short skirts became the order of the day after the Armistice and never before—outside the music hall and the boudoir—had such an extent of female leg been actually *seen*. Overnight, stockings—and in flesh tints, none of that black nonsense—became outerwear. The working girl could not afford silk stockings—they were not for the likes of her in any case. The invention of 'artificial silk' (or 'rayon' as it was later called) and its application to stockings at half the price of real silk hose—'Aristoc' and the rest—rescued her from shaming dependence on coarse, unsophisticated cotton and unfeminine wool. But a 'lady' could never be seen in anything other than real silk stockings. They were still a social requirement for members—and aspiring members—of London 'Society' and the county set who patronised the high-class department stores of London and the provinces through which Pringle marketed most of their knitted overwear and underwear.

In August 1926, William Oddy, the non-executive director from Bradford who had been on a trip to China, told his fellow directors that he thought the manufacture of pure silk hose would be a paying proposition for Pringle and recommended the company installed the necessary machinery at once. The secretary (and managing-director), Boyd Sime, was asked to make enquiries. At the next Board meeting in October a Mr Bromley of Leicester addressed the directors on the subject of machinery for fine silk hose, and the Board decided to take the matter a step further by collecting all the information they could on prices and retail outlets. B. R. Chaston and Boyd Sime made a thorough investigation of the market so far as London was concerned, and interviewed buyers at leading stores such as Dickins & Jones, Harvey Nichols, Marshall & Snelgrove and Barkers. Their findings, communicated to the Board in December, gave them 'considerable encouragement'.

William Oddy was impressed and went so far as telling the Board that he would be prepared to take over the machinery and run it himself if the manufacture did not show a profit at the end of the first year. He then moved a formal resolution that they installed 42-gauge silk stocking machinery at once. Chaston seconded the motion.

Robert Pringle alone demurred. In his view it was not advisable to start what he considered 'an entirely strange trade in this district'. The money should be spent on purchasing three frames: a lace frame, a stupiry frame and a rib frame 'which were necessary for the trade at present being carried on'. No stocking frames should be bought, said Robert Pringle II. Quite so, one can hear a shocked Robert Pringle exclaim, but not *entirely* strange surely?

The oligarchy that now ran Pringle overruled the ex-autarch and pronounced in favour of buying stocking frames, but as a sop to the

104

Old Man agreed to buy the three he had recommended as well. Robert Pringle made no reference to the matter when he chaired the 1926 annual general meeting on February 9 at which a profit after tax of £4,505 was declared and a five per cent dividend. His main point was that the new fashion in ladies' underwear—the trend towards lighter and flimsier materials—was not helping the sales of Pringle vests and combs.

It was the year of the General Strike, but in spite of the dislocation of trade the results for 1927 were better than in the previous year. Robert Pringle withdrew to the South of France and was still there for the 1928 AGM when a profit of £9,107 was declared and a 7½ per cent dividend. There was no escaping the fact that the silk hose exercise was not proving the paying proposition forecast by William Oddy. To sharpen the edge of the marketing operation sales were concentrated on London through Herbert Johnstone, the one-time John Barker buyer and ex-partner, who was now living in Pinner in north London. This appointment of a single agent for silk hose was contrary to Boyd Sime's advice, who wanted it developed by *all* the travellers. The merchandise was given the brand name of 'Prinseta'.

Robert Pringle returned to England in October (1929) and attended a Board meeting. He is not reported as having actually said 'I told you so', merely as asking if the Board would consider disposing of the machinery. Red faces never find their way into minutes.

They were not entirely on the defensive, however. The position had improved of late. The machinery was now producing 'an excellent stocking' they said. Moreover they had to consider the press advertising series they had booked in *Vogue* and other magazines. The hosiery operation as a whole was being very rewarding—sales had risen from £85,000 in 1926 to £108,000 in 1929. The Board voted to give the pure silk stocking exercise another trial over the next season.

The man responsible for making the silk hose machinery turn out a saleable product was John Turnbull, who became a director in 1929 and the following year took over as managing-director from J. Boyd Sime who resigned in May (1929). In the summer of 1929 Turnbull persuaded the Board to buy even more machinery. But the silk stocking episode (as Robert Pringle had warned) was a diversion from the mainstream of the company's development which was now more firmly than ever in the field of outerwear.

'The period immediately following the War of 1914–18 was to women the age of the jumper, and in no sphere was it more appropriate than in the world of golf players,' wrote James Laver in his book *Taste and Fashion* (1937). 'It was worn in general with a coarse tweed skirt, reaching half way down the calf. It may be said that indeed the skirt and the jumper remained the accepted wear for golf until the end of the twenties.'

James Laver also remarked that the stylisation of sports clothes, their functional development and their tendency to become uniform had robbed them of any chance of influencing contemporary fashion, for a uniform was by its nature a dead end. 'It is regarded as something apart, and women are no more likely to be influenced in their ordinary dress by skating costume than by cycling shorts. The main stream of development lies elsewhere.'

The experience of the Hawick hosiery manufacturers was not to bear this out. It was from the so-called 'sportswear' that the greater

Pastel cashmere:
Coordination is a key fashion statement in this 1965 catalogue

Pastel cashmere:
(1965)

105

Lambswool advertising:
(1965)

part of their men's and women's fashion knitted trade developed.

'Jumper' is not as modern a word as it sounds. In Sam Johnson's dictionary of 1806 it appears as 'jump' (French 'jupe'), 'a waistcoat; a kind of loose or limber stays worn by sickly ladies'. A century later James Murray (of Denholm) defined it in his Oxford Dictionary of 1901 as 'a kind of loose outer jacket or skirt reaching to the hips made of canvas, serge, coarse linen, etc, and worn by sailors, truckmen, etc; also applied to any upper garment of similar shape, e.g. a hooded fur jacket worn by Eskimos'.

Looseness was the keynote. Garments came in profusion—the 'cardigan' with the buttoned front originally ordered by his Lordship for the fighting men of the Crimean War; the 'jersey' named after the wool from which it was first made which came from sheep bred on the Channel Island of that name, which got its name from Julius Caesar (Insula Caesarea); the 'pullover' named after the way it was pulled over the head; the 'sweater', the first of the names to appear in a Pringle price list, but now getting away from its exercising role. The generic term 'woollies' covered most of these knitted garments. From the United States came the college girl's favourite wardrobe item—the long, loose-knit sweater in Shetland-type wool later known as the Sloppy Joe, which perhaps had more influence than any other woolly of this time. Unlike the old 'V' cardigan, it was buttoned right up to the neck. Hawick began knitting heavy Sloppy Joe type of sweaters in a much finer and lighter weight, and teamed them with pullover jumpers having short sleeves and a simple round neck. The high button cardigan then became known as a golfer cardigan. Together they became the famous 'twin set' alike in colour, stitch and neckline. The age of 'classics' had begun.

But 'couture standards' did not apply. There was no conscious design as such; it was a question of producing the shape the frame foreman devised. In any event Pringle was not the leader here; this was the role of the brothers Innes. Throughout the 1920s outerwear was still the poor relation at Rodono Mill, as it came to be called, and took second place to underwear. A step in the right direction, however, was taken in December 1930—and a unique one for the time—by the appointment of Elizabeth Pringle, daughter of Douglas Pringle, as 'designer and styles adviser' for an experimental six months in London.

John Turnbull and William Oddy soldiered on with the silk stocking project—until it ran into what was known simply as The Crisis, the great economic depression which spread over virtually the whole world and made 2½ million unemployed in Britain. In 1930 silk hose production was reduced to one line only. The optimistic directors felt 'we would still get a firm footing in the market' but sales were very disappointing. George Mitchell, the new works manager, left at the end of 1930.

The type of customer which Pringle catered for—the highest class section of the trade—was the hardest hit by the depression. They found their taxes increased and their incomes decreased. It was the signal once again for Pringle to go into the market with an innovation, first with a new angle on the unhappy silk stockings and then with ladies' underwear.

The inherent weakness of all silk stockings and hose made of artificial silk, which was a preparation of wood pulp, was the ease

Amsterdam shopfront:
Opened in 1968

Amsterdam:
Opening party

Amsterdam:
Shop interior

with which they laddered and the fact that light flesh tint colour got spattered with mud in bad weather. There was not much to be done about laddering, but in the autumn of 1931 Pringle came out with a new version of their 'Prinseta' hose which they renamed 'Rodono Splashproof'. There was a considerable demand for these and more workers had to be engaged and trained. The Silk Hose Department went on double shift. Six girls were hired to tour retail stores and demonstrate the proof properties of the hose. A special drive was made at Christmas, packing the stockings in a tartan box bearing the portraits of five queens of Europe who, it was claimed, never wore any stockings other than 'Splashproof' hose from Pringle of Hawick. Advertisements were placed in the Glasgow *Bulletin*—an unprecedented step. There was a rise in wages. It looked as if Oddy's gamble was going to pay off.

In March, 1932—the month in which a loss of £138 had been declared for the year 1931—the firm obtained a patent for what they termed 'Slimfit' underwear. 'The special feature of this invention,' ran one of the company's advertisements, 'is the Rib Waist into which has been woven thin layers of India Rubber very closely covered with Silk, Wool or Cotton which, when combined with the ground work of the underwear makes a very elastic waist which can stretch to the figure and gives the desired effect of slimness, and at the same time an added support to the body ... This invention is unique in the trade and will give a new lease of life to this section of the Hosiery Trade which has been out of favour owing to the old style of underwear not coming up to the required standard of modern fashion.'

The project revolved round a material called 'Lastex'. 'When I heard this product was being made by the Dunlop Rubber Company,' wrote Robert Pringle, 'it occurred to me that it might be applied to the ladies underwear trade. I at once got in touch with the makers and had samples from them, which I had worked along with wool into samples of ladies combinations and vests. When applied to the waist this reduced the size very much, and our reduced waist garments were soon very well known. They were very well received by the trade, and a large demand was at once created. We secured the sole right from Dunlop to use this 'Lastex' yarn in Hawick for one year, but they would not extend the time as so many of the other Hawick firms wanted it. But we got a flying start and created a large trade during that time of grace.'

The young ladies of the 1930s wore backless evening dresses wrapped tightly round their posteriors—gowns designed mainly for their appearance from the back at a time when ballroom dancing was conducted by each partner holding the other closely in each other's arms. 'Rodono' Slimfit vests, knickers and combinations were available in low-cut backs to meet this essential fashion requirement, and the 'Lastex' ensured all-round smoothness in the lower regions.

What with 'Rodono' Splashproof and 'Rodono' Slimfit, Pringle were fighting back with a vengeance. There was a loss of £634 for 1932—but never again. Turnover which had been £108,000 in 1929 was down to £51,000. In the ten years' trading total gross profits, however, amounted to £48,000 and the average dividend was 2.7 percent.

Pringle Annual:
(1966)

Magazine advertising:
'The luxury of cashmere'
(1964)

107

When works manager George Mitchell left the company in December 1931, John Turnbull, the managing-director, arranged for young William Mactaggart to take his place for a trial period of six months. In March 1932, William Mactaggart and Arthur Oddy were appointed directors and the following year joint managing-directors. Each was 26. William Mactaggart at once proposed erecting a building next to the Milling House for shrinking and bleaching, processes which were being put out to the Hawick firm of Turnbull's. But it was one of the non-executive directors, Robert Mactaggart, Willie's uncle, who in July (1933) invited the Board to ask itself how it was that, at a time when all other Hawick firms were so busy with it, Pringle's trade in cashmere was so small. 'It was explained that we were being undercut in prices and also were not well-equipped with machines for that type of work, having 4-division machines whereas other firms had 6- or 8- divisions.'

Robert Mactaggart pointed to the direction in which the company should obviously now proceed; it was for his young nephew, now taking the reins into his hands, to make up for lost time and lay the foundations of the road along which the company was to find a new reputation.

'Cashmere' is the fleece of the Tibetan, or Mongolian, goat. Some say the word has only a phonetical connection with the Indian state of Kashmir and the shawls of its capital Srinagar, but it is hard to believe. Be that as it may, as one authority was writing in 1950, 'but little of the cashmere wool of today comes from Kashmir ... most of today's cashmere fleece comes from further north—the best grades from China, Inner and Outer Mongolia, Manchuria and Tibet'. Before World War I the finest fleece came from the remote southern frontiers of Imperial Russia, the mountains of the Caucasus and Turkestan; but in the 1970s the finest cashmere was Chinese, coming from a small district to the west of Beijing and another in Manchuria.

Like most animals living in cold climates, the 'Cashmere Goat' is provided by nature with long, coarse, outer hairs and a warm undercoat of fine fleece. The chief feature of this undercoat is its softness and warmth, partly real from its excellent non-conducting properties—ounce for ounce it has three times the insulation value of fine lambswool—partly imaginary from the satisfying sense of luxury and comfort which it induces. It gives warmth without weight. A quarter less weight is needed compared with other knitted garments. Apart from its warmth it is distinguished for its lustre—under wet brushing it develops a beautiful shining rippled surface. But as with other wools not grown on sheep, it is inelastic. Sheep's wool is resilient, returning to its shape after being stretched; not so the cashmere goat's wool. But it has perfect draping qualities.

Very small amounts are obtained from each goat—a male produces about four ounces, a female two ounces, a year. A year's yield from four to six animals is needed to make a sweater. It is never shorn (cut) with shears, as with sheep's wool, but carefully combed or plucked by hand from their underbellies by the Chinese or Tibetans in the mountains. The Chinese use it for making wind hats. Chinese cashmere wool in its natural state comes in three principal colours—grey, brown and, least common of all, white. The finest fleece is found on animals living in the heights of the mountain ranges. The higher the mountain, the sparser the vegetation, the finer the yield. From the Himalayas the

raw fibre is taken, as it travelled before Marco Polo explored the Great
Silk Road in the 13th century, in countless little loads on the backs
of men, yaks, camels and horses, across craggy wastes and steep paths.
On it goes, tied to rafts buoyed up with inflated skins down spuming
rapids, on boats floating down the rivers of majestic valleys, to the port
of Tien-tsin—a journey that takes the best part of a year. It is the way
it has followed for hundreds of years, for cashmere was known to the
ancient Romans whose aristocracy wore garments made from this costly
fibre at feasts and 'special occasions'. The French physician Francois
Bernier, who travelled to Tibet in the retinue of the Mogul Aurangzeb
in the 17th century, was the first European to see a cashmere goat.

Before the raw fibre is shipped, a first separation of coarse outer
hair from the outer fleece takes place by hand, but from the material
which reaches Britain a slow and expensive mechanical process
removes the considerable amount of coarse hair and much fine black
hair which still remains. By the time this stage is reached the fleece
plucked from the goats in the mountains has had its weight reduced by
a half to three-quarters. This preparation of the raw fibre is undertaken
in Britain by a processor who also dyes it, and then sells it to the
spinner, who sells it as spun yarn to the knitter. Unlike the South
American camels the Vicuna and the Llama, who in Australia breed
and behave as they did in the mountains of Peru, the Tibetan Goat has
never taken kindly to transplanting from its Himalayan fastness. The
animal manages to live and breed, but it ceases to grow a soft downy
coat on its tum.

There is no short cut to the long process of delivering cashmere
to the yarnstore at Walter's Wynd. As that connoisseur of The Rarer
Wools, E. S. Harrison, has said, 'the results are not, and never can be,
cheap but they have an individuality and charm, and are endowed with
an aristocratic air, quite beyond the reach of mass production'.

Garments knitted in cashmere had, of course, been appearing in
the Pringle 'Hosiery List' for some years. But it was all underwear.
In the 1899 list there were the Natural Cashmere and Fancy Shirts
and Trousers (vests and pants) for men; in the 1915 list, men's cashmere
socks. Most of the non-sheep's wool used at this time was Llama.
The Greensmith Downes *Book of Scotch-Made Underwear* of 1912
merely refers to cashmere in a footnote on the 'beautiful Australian
Merino golden fleece' which was the basis of nearly all their finest
productions in modern woollens. 'The fine Indian Cashmere wool,
which is also used in the manufacture of "Australlama" is only to be
procured from Tibet, and is indigenous to that country.' In another
section of the book the reader's attention is drawn to The Problem
of Shrinkage. 'The general impression is that all kinds of Wool are
equally liable to shrink; this is not the case. Lambswool is the most
liable; pure Cashmere is the least liable.' Examination of cashmere
fibre after soaking in water would show cuticles or scales very much
less pronounced. As far as shrinking was concerned it was linked with
silk, linen and cotton as 'unshrinkable'.

William Mactaggart at once set in motion the acquiring of the
machinery suitable for knitting cashmere outwear, and making enquiries
from the various spinning firms about the qualities and costs of cashmere
yarn available in Britain. One of the first spinners he approached was
naturally the Weensland Spinning Company whose John Hobkirk had

Princess Margaret:
*Photographed by Snowdon, for the
Savoy Gala fashion show programme
(1968)*

Savoy Gala fashion show:
Invitation and (below) cover

109

GALA FASHION
SHOW PRINGLE
OF SCOTLAND
AT THE SAVOY

directed Pringle down this new path.

The women's garments which Pringle began to make for the first time in the 1930s in cashmere were the range of 'sportswear', as they were still known, of jerseys, pullovers, slipovers, cardigans, jumpers, which the company had started making in sheeps wool on a small scale at the end of the 1920s. New was the combination of jumper and cardigan in the same stitch and colour and style which had been popularised in the United States—the 'twin set'.

In a typical catalogue of the time—'Pringle Sportswear'—the "Arklow Twin Set" is described as having that delightful combination of quality and style which had gone to make a perfect set for the out-of-doors girl. It was in the finest Pure Cashmere in a medium weight. It was in three colours, oatmeal, nigger and navy. There was no Race Relations Board in 1935.

What were advertised as the 'plain woollies you should never be without, so useful for any and all occasions' the cashmere jumpers and cardigans made in plain 'stocking stitch' with ribbed waist, cuffs and neck, became the Pringle all-the-year-round 'classic'. They were bought by the patrons of Harrods and Marshall & Snelgrove, and were worn at point-to-points and on the moors with pearls and 'sensible' shoes. They designed themselves and their appeal was limited. On the continent—in particular Austria and Italy—they were treated as *couture*, what would now be called 'designer-garments'. Jumpers and jerseys were being given the same treatment as blouses—unheard of in Britain.

The good sense of doing so dawned on the new management at Rodono Mill who, with a reputation second-to-none for Plain Woollies, decided to beat the imaginative hosiers of Southern Europe at their own game and apply to Hawick's products something of the magic implied by the word Design. They advertised for a designer.

When the unashamedly anti-semite National Socialist Party came to power in Germany in 1933, many German and Austrian Jews fled to Britain to escape the persecution which they saw must inevitably follow. One who came to England before the Nazis actually succeeded to power was Otto Weisz, the son of a Viennese surgeon, who had served an apprenticeship with the most famous of all Austrian manufacturers of knitted goods, Bernhard Altmann of Vienna. He settled in the first instance in Northern Ireland. His attention was drawn to the Pringle advertisement for a designer and applied. In June, 1934 at the age of 27, Otto Weisz was given the job of Pringle's—and Hawick's—first designer of knitted garments, with the brief to establish a Design Department and make women's knitted clothes fashionable.

Within a few years, with Otto Weisz's exceptional talents coming to bear on the whole range of women's 'sportswear', with considerable advances being made technically on the ability to knit very much lighter weight cashmere, and a sharp lowering of prices, Pringle twin sets, jumpers and cardigans, in a wide range of colours and well advertised, began to overhaul the well entrenched 'Braemar' lines. In fact, in 1934 Pringle pioneered the first collection of Scottish sweaters ever to be presented in fancy and novelty styles, with intricate detail work with collars, cuffs, 'peplums' and 'plackets', aimed at the American market.

The 'Nylan Jumper' of 1936 'in the sheerest of Pure Cashmere, almost featherweight in texture' was one of the first to depart from

110

Harrogate trade show:
Exhibition stand design
(1968)

Harrogate trade show:
Exhibition stand design
(1966)

Harrogate trade show:
Exhibition stand design
(1967)

the 'classic' high, round neckline with a floppy 'artist's' bow below an irregular shaped vee. It was the beginning of 'styling'.

'Pringle Sportswear,' proclaimed the spring 1937 catalogue, 'is designed for the woman of refined taste—for the woman who demands to be comfortably and faultlessly clad for an inexpensive outlay. The exclusive models shown in this booklet are made in purest Indian Cashmere and finest Botany Yarn; they are distinctively endowed with that subtle charm and inherent quality of good taste which has made them famous in the salons of London, Paris and New York. You may choose with confidence from this select assembly—for 'occasions' or for everyday, they are reassuringly RIGHT.'

The 'Sponor' jumper reappeared as the 'Primrose' jumper but in ten colours, at the same price of 29s 6d (£1.47). 'We created this garment to fulfil an oft-expressed wish of our customers. They asked us to design an "afternoon" garment which would be outstandingly smart, correct and becoming.' The 'Raymond' jumper—'a genuine inspiration'—also had the tie neckline but higher, and was described as a 'golfer coat' and jumper in one, in ten colours. For the less sporty types there were jumpers in the delicate lace stitch. A collar took the place of the traditional 'neck' cut round and high—the turn down 'Eton' collar of the 'Sylvia' jumper.

The type of customer to whom these clothes were appealing was spelt out in a typical brochure for the autumn of 1937—from Adderlys of Leicester.

'The "landed gentry" are never more distinguished than when they are in sports clothes—and why? Simply because their sweaters and tweeds are of the highest-class Scotch make, with the breath of the moors and outdoor life about them. Pringles have been making sweaters for the British aristocracy since 1815 and to have a "Pringle sweater" is to be correctly dressed for all but the most formal occasions. Each season the "Pringle" selection gives you something new which you can depend on as being only in the best taste.' The tone of the marketing approach was set by the illustration on the cover of Adderlys brochure, a black retriever with a pheasant in its mouth.

Signs of the times were the drop of underwear turnover in 1936, the rise in profit from £2,168 in 1935 with a dividend of 3½ per cent to one of £8,277 in 1937 with a dividend of 7½ per cent, and the plans to form a company in the United States in July 1937, where now the market potential was perhaps the greatest. In June 1937, Arthur Oddy said he felt the time had come to separate Underwear from Overwear, and have someone in charge of Underwear which was being neglected. The 'poor relation' was getting ideas above its station. Oddy proposed that George Mitchell who had begun as a framework knitter 30 years before, and was now a frame foreman, should concentrate on Underwear, but William Mactaggart was reluctant to take him off Overwear. The battle of Over versus Under was truly joined.

For this they recruited Jack Lyle of Lyle and Scott who was a specialist in the heavier wool combination side of the trade. It was even more important however to strengthen the Outerwear side of the company's output. When Maxwell Magnus of New York relinquished the agency for the 'Braemar' products of Innes Henderson, he agreed to represent Pringle. Known to all the leading outerwear specialists in the USA, Magnus brought Pringle new status in the American market place.

Harrogate stand design:
Harrogate an important fashion trade exhibition for Pringle is reported in the Bulletin (1963)

Harrogate trade show:
Bulletin report (1962)

111

Having hitched itself firmly, if belatedly, to Outerwear and Cashmere, Pringle's future in the late 1930s seemed bright and clear cut. Plans were made to step up production of outerwear—in August 1938, £7,500 was approved for a new four-storey extension—and to shift underwear, which still accounted for a substantial if decreasing part of the turnover, away from the centre of manufacture. The Old Mission Hall property was acquired and £1,500 allocated to re-fit it as an underwear 'frame flat'. Orders for the first five months of 1939 were double those of 1938. A new Ladies' Knitted Suit Department was started by Otto Weisz in conjunction with W. & O. Marcus of London.

Nothing, it seemed, could now stop the company from pushing right ahead—except a national catastrophe of the kind that stood in its way more than once before. The 'Munich crisis' of 1938 showed that unbelievably, after only 20 years, it *could* happen, and the next year it did—all over again, and with the same enemy.

But before World War II broke out on September 3, 1939, Pringle suffered a local calamity when, in April, fire destroyed the offices, and trimming flats over them, at the corner of Walter's Wynd and the road overlooking the Teviot—the lower section of the original brewery building which Walter Pringle had purchased from William Ainslie just over 100 years before. A safe containing all the records of the 107-year-old co-partnery fell from the top to the ground and burst open, committing the contents, which might have contributed so valuably to this history, to the flames. The loss in buildings, furniture, machinery and stock was estimated at £33,000. The knitting frames were stopped for 10 days while the debris was cleared.

Much of the knitting machinery came from Germany, and with the start of the war supplies from this source were naturally unobtainable. At the same time the supply of cashmere wool from China shrank to a trickle. The workers at Rodono Mill were given one week off in four. The shock of the declaration of war put an immediate damper on the demand for the kind of 'luxury' goods Pringle were now associated with, but after a lull during the 'phoney war', when to everyone's surprise no actual hostilities took place, there was a spate of buying abroad, particularly in America which at first kept out of the war. In fact, in the first ten months of 1939 the turnover of outerwear accounted for £48,000 out of £180,000 total sales. The number of employees which had been 200 in 1934 was now 585. Both William Oddy and Douglas Pringle died in 1939. Douglas's son John became editor of the *Sydney Morning Herald*.

It was a peak year in more sense than one; it was a time for reckoning, for re-shuffling the cards. Events had now caught up with the old guard, the men who had rallied the ranks of the co-partnery in the aftermath of the Kaiser's war. In the 17 years since 1922 society had acquired new values, new wants, new habits, new incomes.

The year 1940 found Robert Pringle II, the 77-year-old chairman, reluctantly facing his own withdrawal from the scene of action of which he had been the centre for 44 years since the death of his father in 1895, and, for the first time in its 125 years' history, leaving the enterprise without a Pringle at the helm.

Annual:
(1969)

Opposite
Egyptian theme:
London fashion shoot
(1960s)

12

KNITWEAR FOR THE AMERICAN COLLEGE GIRL

£1½ million turnover the year Robert Pringle II dies. (1940–1953)

R OBERT PRINGLE'S letter of resignation as chairman of Robert Pringle & Son was received and accepted by the Board on February 20, 1940. He went to live with his daughter, Mrs Frances Muir at Fetteresso Castle near Stonehaven in Kincardineshire, where the Pretender spent his first week in Scotland after landing for the 1715 rising, and was proclaimed James VIII of Scotland at the gate.

The new non-executive chairman was John Smith Wells of the Edinburgh firm of J. Aikman Smith & Wells which had been Pringle's accountants since 1895. All continental trade came to an abrupt end the day war was declared and export, which was to be the company's mainstay at a time of severe restriction on spending at home, meant principally North and South America.

The best market for Pringle goods in 1941 however was Argentina to which Otto Weisz paid a long visit in July. Uruguay came second. But the quantity of woollen clothing Pringle could make was determined by the amount of yarn they could get hold of, and with most of the raw wool coming from Australia on the other side of the world, output of knitted goods was restricted. So the company turned to making ladies' blouses, mainly in an artificial material called moss crepe, in conjunction with the Marcus brothers of Bradford, with whom the Knitted Suit Department had been started in June 1939. A branch factory for this was opened in another part of Hawick.

The blouses sold well, but demand for all wearing apparel was kept at a low level by the clothing coupon scheme. The government's policy was to reduce expenditure on clothing to the smallest amount

Opposite
Classic 'Crewe neck' pullover:
(1965)

'compatible with decency'. They needed all the space they could find for munition making, and factories on the Border as elsewhere were requisitioned for this purpose. The normal activities of these firms were 'telescoped' with those of similar companies in the same district. Under this scheme the Board of Trade allocated two small Dumfries firms to move in with Pringle at Rodono Mill, the Dumfries Knitting Company and S. A. Robertson & Sons.

Despite the rationing of yarn under the Limitation of Supplies Order, the introduction of Purchase Tax in November 1940, and the curtailing of all non-warlike industrial activities, shareholders at Pringle's annual general meeting of 1941 were heartened to hear that, for the first time, the quarter million mark had been passed in turnover—£258,855. It was an achievement not to be repeated till the war ended.

Growth was not an end in itself in the dark days of 1942. Contributing to the war effort was what most firms felt they wanted to be doing, and Pringle was in the happy position of being able to do this, when clothes were rationed by coupons, while keeping alive its traditional skills and expertise for when the conflict ended. For those whose duty lay on the home front the government prescribed a quality of clothing to which they gave the name 'utility'. A clothing manufacturer like Pringle was allowed to make a certain percentage of its output 'utility' and the rest 'non-utility', for which of course the purchaser had to give more coupons. Pringle's peacetime production could be said to have been entirely the latter. When they turned their hands to knitting, scouring and finishing garments to the government's wartime specifications, however, they found that the overall quality of their utility goods was so superior to those of most of their competitors that the demand for them was overwhelming. It brought full order books, full employment and financial stability. Moreover, a section of the community, who would never have read an Adderlys catalogue of the 1930s, got the feel of a Pringle jumper for the first time in their lives, and a taste of the indefinable way in which it differed from anything else they had ever worn—and they never forgot.

In addition to utility and non-utility garments for those in Civvy Street, Pringle were given big government contracts for underwear and jerseys for men and women in the armed forces. Otto Weisz and William Mactaggart soon had personal experience of such 'army issue' when they were called up in the summer of 1942. George Mitchell and Arthur Oddy were left as executive directors in Hawick with B. R. Chaston in London. The latter's son, A. G. Chaston, had joined the RAF in 1941. Some 115 men and 54 women had by now gone into the services from Rodono Mill.

War in the Far East cut short the supply of wool from Australia even further, and by the end of 1942 there was no shipping space for luxury articles like cashmere cardigans. Export orders flowed into Rodono Mill, but the use of yarn was restricted to 30 per cent. The making of cashmere goods stopped entirely after July 1, 1943; government contracts were halved.

The supply stage of the war was ending and it was now a question of getting on and winning it. It became permissible to imagine one could see a glimmer at the end of the tunnel, and to plan for emerging once more into the daylight. In mid-1943 the Board of Pringle

Pringle network:
Overseas agents for Pringle
(1962)

'Mayfair' twinset:
PR shoot in Savile Row
(1965)

'Mayfair' twinset:
Lace knit cashmere two piece
(1965)

deliberated 'putting the business on a different production basis in the immediate post-war period, having produced £6,000 more merchandise in the first eight months of 1943 with 310 workers compared with the same period in 1942 with 360 workers'. There was still the question of Under versus Over Wear to be settled. Arthur Oddy said he hoped the company would concentrate more on underwear after the war than it had done before it. Marcus proposed that after the war, with his help, Pringle should start a factory in London, where labour was more plentiful, for the mass production of girls' frocks and suits.

As an immediate positive step, the Board planned to put in a Pyjama and Night Dress department and engage a woman designer and manageress for it; but they had second thoughts and abandoned the idea. With Weisz in the army, however, they did appoint an assistant designer, Eugene Klappholz, another Austrian. They also had the foresight to place an order with William Cotton Ltd of Loughborough for the first eight Cotton Patent frames produced when the war ended.

Another of Arthur Oddy's ideas was to write to E. S. Harrison of Johnston of Elgin asking him whether his firm would consider co-operating with Pringle in the spinning and carding of hosiery yarn when the war was over. He also wrote to Joseph Dawson of Bradford asking him if he would supply Pringle with de-haired raw cashmere after the war if Pringle put down the most modern plant for carding and spinning and producing their own yarn.

At the annual general meeting of 1943—the private company's 21st birthday—Robert Pringle, who was attending as a shareholder, made it plain that his and Arthur Oddy's ideas on the future development of Robert Pringle & Son were not entirely in accord. This was the last meeting to be attended by Robert's wife, Edith. Mrs Robert Pringle died in 1944 at the age of 78.

On March 20, 1945, for the first time Pringle's directors allowed themselves to be minuted as discussing something called 'Knitwear'. The word emerged within six weeks of the end of the European War, a pointer to what the future was going to be all about. Arthur Oddy, made a last ditch stand in support of Underwear. He, for one, was not prepared to stand by and see Underwear left to struggle on by itself, he said, while all the real effort was concentrated on Knitwear.

The company was unable to install any new machinery during the war. There was still heavy restriction on non-utility goods, but there was an increase in output on government contracts and utility garments.

Victory in Europe came in May. William Mactaggart was demobilised and returned to Hawick in July to find that Arthur Oddy his pre-war partner and the man with whom he was going to build the new Pringle, had resigned and joined the board of a new competitor Caerlee Mills Knitting Company, a branch of Ballantyne Brothers of Innerleithen. So William took control as sole managing-director. He at once set off on a grand tour of the United States and Canada. Demobbed Otto Weisz re-established links with Paris, Brussels and Zurich. On his return home, Willie reported that the demand for British goods—of any description in North America was astounding. They were 'simply gasping' for them, he said. The Americans were very short of high-grade merchandise. With their rising wages, their manufacturers had to engage in mass production of clothing on a

Romans and Patersons:
Models at the Edinburgh boutique (1965)

Motor-racing star visits Pringle:
Jackie Stewart visits Rodono (1966)

Otto Weisz and models:
At the Edinburgh boutique opening (1966)

greater scale than ever before, thus lowering the quality and finish. The only complaint of Pringle goods was the narrowness of the shoulders. 'The fact that it was a Pringle garment was sufficient hallmark to dismiss any other question.' The plaint of the store managers everywhere he went was, 'Can't we have the Pringle line exclusive to ourselves in this town?' The Board discussed the point, and decided the policy would continue to be to sell Pringle goods to *all* high-class stores in each town.

At home, where clothes rationing continued in spite of the peace and the Board of Trade operated a quota scheme, Pringle received a licence to sell £12,000 worth of non-utility goods on the home market. On the strength of this, it was decided to appoint someone to handle the company's advertising, and in August 1946, Bill Rodger was made publicity agent (later director of publicity) based on London.

At the annual general meeting directors told shareholders the company would only be able to supply a fraction of the demand from overseas; they had a licence for £50,000 worth of non-utility exports (which was raised to £75,000 in 1947). Otto Weisz, who had gone to America in 1947, confirmed that Pringle was the most popular name in the States in the field of sweaters. The only serious competition came from Dalton and the Hadley Knitwear Company of Cleveland who made 100,000 sweaters a year, mainly for the college girl. These had a higher factory price than Pringle's sweaters, which became dearer in comparison after import duty had been paid. There was also competition from neighbours in Hawick. Pringle could not maintain its precious top position in the United States, reported Weisz, by selective styles, variation, originality and competitive prices. Above all, delivery dates must be kept.

The quality of American knitwear at this time was certainly not up to the Hawick product. In an attempt to cash in on the popularity of Scottish knitwear, American-made garments were marketed with names like 'Bonnie Briar'. For one thing few US manufacturers favoured dyeing in the wool. Spinning white yarn and then dyeing it was cheaper, but colours were not as fast as when the dye was mixed with the fleece, nor was it as easy to match colours. Spinning provided a second opportunity to vary a shade by adding white, if too intense, or colour if too pale.

The possibilities of the Scandinavian market were re-explored by Willie Mactaggart who, at the end of 1947, paid a first visit of a Pringle director to Norway, Sweden and Denmark since 1935. Weisz went to France, Switzerland and Italy. At home the London office and showrooms were moved from 136, Regent Street to 12a Savile Row, W1, a small, elegant Georgian mansion in this well-known West End street, famed for all that is best in men's tailoring. The house was built in 1733 and had been the home of author and politician George Grote, best known for his monumental *History of Greece*. He was a founder of London University and trustee of the British Museum who, on his death in 1871, was buried in Westminster Abbey. He was born in the same year as John Pringle was indentured to William Beck, 1794.

The same number of units were being produced at Rodono Mill in 1947 as there had ever been, but with 100 fewer workers—the result of simplified production techniques;—also the faster machinery which had been evolved with the manufacturers and improved works flow organisation on the factory floors. Fifteen of the latest frames

118

Mens fashion shoot:
(1965)

Illustrative campaign:
(1965)

were operating round the clock at the rented Weensland Mill. There
was a works picnic in the summer, a ball at Christmas and the 90
apprentices had an outing to Edinburgh all to themselves. With as big
exports as the government would allow to the hard currency USA and
Canada, turnover in 1947 was double that of 1939; and at home the
company had the satisfaction of knowing that its utility garments were
as much sought after as their high quality cashmere goods of pre-war
days. A better quality Chinese cashmere became available.

Robert Pringle & Son were riding high and their success was crowned
the following year when in March (1948) the company was granted the
Royal Warrant to Queen Elizabeth, wife of the reigning monarch King
George VI, and the right to display the queen's English coat of arms
with the words 'By Appointment, Manufacturers of Knitted Garments
to H. M. Queen Elizabeth'.

Advertising three shots:
From cashmere to Crimplene
(1966)

Pringle had made the underwear which the queen bought from
royal warrant holders Harvey Nichols & Co of Knightsbridge since
1938. The company had also made underwear and outerwear purchased
by other members of the royal family, including the queen's daughters,
Princess Elizabeth and Princess Margaret; Princess Mary (Princess
Royal), sister of King George V; the Duchess of Kent, widowed wife
of the king's brother, and her daughter Princess Alexandra. On the
occasion of their marriage both Princess Elizabeth and Lieutenant
Philip Mountbatten accepted wedding gifts of Pringle cashmere twin
sets and pullovers. Robert Pringle I of Whisky House Mill would have
been very proud.

Cashmere
(1966)

119

The number of women in Hawick able and willing to work in the
local knitwear mills had reached saturation point. If more hands were
needed to maintain the new levels of production, companies had to
open up branches outside the town. One of the first to do this was the
expanding Hawick Hosiery Company who acquired the old Catholic
School building in Walkergate, Berwick-on-Tweed, some 50 miles to
the west of Hawick. When they vacated it at the end of 1947 Pringle
took it over, and in February 1948 equipped it as a small branch factory
to which they could send garments from Hawick for collar binding.

Sales passed the half million pound mark in 1948, some 60 per
cent of which was export and most of that to the United States.
Owing to domestic financial rulings Scandinavia and Argentina had
been unable to take any goods at all. Italy was developing its own
knitwear industry. Italian tailored jackets with their detailed hand-sewn
decoration from houses like Dazza and Metelloni, and the long hair
Angora sweaters in brilliant colours from Perugia, were in a class by
themselves. But the company appointed an Italian agent, Gerolamo
Tidona, since, as Weisz reported, the label 'made in Britain' was a
laissez passer to the upper crust of Italian society. One day there
would be a market there, he said, even if they found difficulty in
pronouncing 'Pringle'. No one wanted to alter the name. On the
contrary, it was a stock-in-trade to be protected and proclaimed.
'Pringle of Scotland' was registered in 1947, and the following year
an advertising campaign was launched under the direction of the new
director of publicity, Bill Rodger, to make it a household name not
only in Britain but, as John Wells told shareholders at the 1949 AGM,

Man-made for men
'Crimplene'-wear from the world's top cashmere house

*From cashmere to Crimplene
a new 'man made' fibre
(1966)*

'throughout the civilised world—a fact which will stand us in good stead when those difficult times come along as I fear they must'. The by-now-familiar foreboding.

In 1949 clothing coupons were withdrawn, and the company's faith in its own future, Hawick labour shortages and economic storm warnings notwithstanding, was further demonstrated by the decision to buy another 75 ft of river frontage adjoining Rodono Mill and build a four-storey extension on it. At the back of the building was to be a new, one-story frame shed with a solid concrete, pillar-less floor to take the new-high speed machinery. William Mactaggart, aided by Ian Bell the youngest apprentice, cut the first sod on October 3, 1949 at an inauguration ceremony attended by the provost (mayor) of Hawick and a distinguished gathering which included that year's president of the Hawick Hosiery Manufacturers Association, Pringle's own George Mitchell. Notable absentee from the group of Pringle directors at the ceremony was Robert Mactaggart, prime mover of the joint stock company of 1922 and uncle of the managing-director, who had died earlier in the year.

'It would seem we are in the midst of a Knitwear Era, and in particular a cashmere one,' declared John Wells announcing a 53 per cent increase in export sales for 1950 over 1949. It was indeed a seller's market, but so far as cashmere was concerned the operation had to be exclusively overseas. For in 1950—five years after the war ended—the sale of cashmere goods to the British market was still prohibited. Immediately after the Japanese surrender, the UK-American wartime agreement known as 'lend-lease' was terminated, and Britain found herself in a grave financial crisis, with external liabilities increased by £3,000 million, only one-third of which was met by the sale of investments. Maynard Keynes negotiated a loan of $3,750 million from the United States to tide Britain over a transitional period during which her export industries would, it was hoped, develop sufficiently to enable her to pay her way. If Britain could raise its exports to 175 per cent of its pre-war level, it was reckoned it could make its finances balance once more, and this target, in which Pringle took its share, was in fact hit in 1950. The devaluation of the pound in 1949 also helped by cheapening exports, and increasing the demand for Pringle products in US and Canada.

While the demand for Pringle cashmere garments exceeded supply, the shortage of raw cashmere became acute. But in 1942 the company found itself with a stock of £30,000 worth and put £20,000 worth of it in cold storage 'for the duration'. This now stood them in good stead. But it was a warning against putting too many eggs in the cashmere basket. A marketing campaign was at once mounted to promote Fine Geelong Lambswool and Fine Botany from Australia on a bigger scale than ever before. To allow for exclusive concentration on knitwear and knitted suits, the Blouse Department which had brought Pringle considerable prestige and publicity, though not in its main line of business, was closed (1950).

The Knitwear Era had come into being as a result, to a large extent, of knitwear coming to be accepted as a fashion garment. Pringle realised that, if it was to survive in it and maintain its pre-eminence, it would have to superimpose on the reputation for quality and good

The persuit of luxury:
Pringle pioneered the technique of painting directly onto cashmere (£600 in 1967)

Irregular striped cashmere:
with colour co-ordinated 'A' line skirt (1960s)

120

taste for which it was already associated in the public eye, a highly developed sense of design and one that met the modern mood.

Design was destined to become an even more important ingredient in the marketing mix. In recognition of this the management engaged a young Scotsman on a two-year trial as trainee designer. This was R. Stuart Beaty who had just been awarded a six months Royal Scottish Academy travelling scholarship to Mexico. He was the first person to be appointed to Pringle with an art school training. Here was someone who could relate the idea of shape, style and decoration to the language of colour design in the abstract. His appointment provided the opportunity to build on the old classic garments, and develop the 'fancy' knitwear so successfully inaugurated by Otto Weisz, under whose aegis, of course, Stuart Beaty began his work in August 1950.

A prime object was to meet current American tastes. The reports of Otto Weisz and William Mactaggart indicated that the Americans wanted tighter ribbed waists, better packaging envelopes, mothproofing, a spare button tacked on each cardigan, and plenty of new colours. Attractive names for colours were very important. American college girls collected sweaters, particularly for colour. 'Carnival Ruby' and 'Arizona Gold' were in every collection.

American stores had separate domestic cashmere and imported sections, so there was no fear of one competing with the other. But in the first four months of 1949 Pringle's American soft apparel trade, as Weisz called it, was down ten per cent. Wide press advertising, he counselled, was to be avoided. American society women liked to think they were wearing clothes which were not seen in picture form every day by their neighbours, and by the wives of their husband's business acquaintances. He also warned against devaluing cashmere by mixing it with man-made fibres like 'Orlon' which would deprive it of its rarity appeal. The American public were more money conscious; they were buying cars and television sets and had little left over for knitwear. But when they decided to buy woollies, for every one enquiry they made to a sales girl for a competitive name, they made three for Pringle. Pringle were turning away business when other sweater manufacturers were asking for it.

Otto Weisz's old firm, Bernhard Altmann of Vienna, had started a factory in the United States and were turning out 'American' cashmere garments in 'Scots' styles. Knitting frames were now being made in the US. The Americans were demanding something different from the straight classic style, and it was up to the manufacturers of Hawick to meet their requirements or lose the market. Sweaters had ceased to be 'sportswear'. They were now smart afternoon and evening wear without the out-of-door severity of previous days or the shapelessness of the Sloppy Joes. They were what in America were called 'dressmaker' styles.

The ball was thrown at Stuart Beaty and he ran with it for all he was worth.

The increased dollar earning capacity which it would bring was emphasised when the Earl of Elgin opened the 21,000 square foot extension on March 22, 1952, giving additional floor space equal to a quarter of the existing area. Total exports for the year ending January 31, 1951, it was announced, were valued at £2,452,327, an increase of 37 per cent on the previous year. Seventy-three percent of production

Advertising:
Illustrative campaign for lambswool cardigan produced at the Glebe (1968)

121

went overseas in 1950, 58 per cent more than in 1949 and nearly ten times the 1945 figure. These achievements, it was explained, had been made with no great addition to the work force, but by improved production methods, some of which had been adopted from ideas submitted in the 'Suggestions Scheme', like mechanic Tom Gibson's proposal for stop and start mechanism for linking machines which gave foot, instead of hand, control and was introduced in April 1951.

The new machinery was soon making the luxurious dressmaker sweater jackets, golfer twinsets, short-sleeved pullovers and 'knitsuits' in cashmere, Angora and Botany wool in yellows, greys, ice blues, walnuts and blacks, being styled by the new Otto Weisz/Stuart Beaty design team. A couple of Pringle sweaters were given to Princess Margaret as a 21st birthday present, and one evening in January 1952, the Duchess of Buccleuch, with whom the princess was staying, telephoned to say her royal highness was wondering whether she could come over to Hawick, thank Pringle personally and meet the people who had made the sweaters. Princess Margaret duly appeared the next afternoon accompanied by her hostess, the Earl of Dalkeith, Lord Plunkett and Lady Rosemary Spencer-Churchill. She was welcomed by George Fraser, the provost of Hawick, and William Mactaggart. She made a tour of the mill and took a great interest in all she saw, chatting intensely with the Scots girls engaged on processes she could not understand or those which particularly interested her. Afterwards the party assembled in the canteen and everyone in the mill came to hear the managing-director tell the princess how greatly they had appreciated her gesture in coming to see them. Among them was Willie's son Bruce Mactaggart, who had joined the firm as a trainee in October 1951. 'Life in a factory can, at times, become very much routine and a little humdrum,' the managing-director said, 'but when we, know that the garments which have actually been made with our own hands are going to be accepted and worn by such people as yourself, then indeed this adds great zest to a working day and a very much greater pride to each worker's individual craftsmanship.'

He told her that turnover for 1951 had been well over a million pounds, and exports to the United States had been nearly half a million dollars. But in fact the year saw another cycle of prosperity starting on another downward dip.

In the United States the Korean War brought a buying spree for fear of shortages, but it had been followed by massive saving. There was a fashion for bejewelled cashmere sweaters. Retailers would take a couple of dozen sweaters from stock, alter them and cover them with artificial jewellery and beads. They sold at $35 to $65 each, whereas a Pringle plain cardigan cost $25 to $28 and gave a smaller profit margin. The kind of built-in colour designs knitted by a method known as 'Intarsia'* was all the rage—but it was impossible to buy Intarsia machines in Britain in the 1950s. In September 1952 a small workshop employing some 30 women was opened in Burnfoot, a new housing estate just outside Hawick. Here examining and hand-sewing was carried on right up to 1969.

*The skill of creating perspective designs and pictures by wood inlay (intersio or intarsia) was brought to Italy from the Middle East by the Certosini, and reached its high point as a pure art between 1460 and 1490.

122

The New York Times:
(1966)

A new factory branch:
Cumbernauld opens in 1969

Vogue editorial:
(1966)

On March 23, 1953 died Robert Pringle, the third generation of the founding family, who had been born in that far-off world of the 1860s which could claim virtually no resemblance to the era in which he died, save perhaps in the stubborn persistence of the practicality of the basic technique of William Lee's stocking frame.

His end came at Fetteresso Castle at the age of 91. He was the second Robert Pringle and the last Pringle to be associated with the firm. His sister Mary (Mamie), Mrs W. Johnson, died in 1950 aged 86. His daughter Frances, Mrs Chrystal Muir, who was 63 in 1953, moved with her 32-year-old daughter Geraldine, Mrs Maurice Simpson, and her grand-daughter Maureen, to Muchalls Castle, near Stonehaven.

In this same year also died Robert Pringle's old partner and the first managing-director of the private company, James Boyd Sime, at the age of 87. He had spent the last years of his life in retirement at the London home of his daughter Saida.

Robert Pringle & Son had come a long way in Robert's 91 years—from the co-partnery at Cross Wynd to the £85,000 company with the growing factory extending along the banks of the Teviot, its machinery and buildings valued at £645,000, an annual turnover of £1,600,000—and a royal warrant. Only the concept of quality was the same.

Mini skirts and twinsets:
Pringle social scene with Anne (centre) the Pringle house model (1965)

Men in pink:
Golfing go-togethers that will add colour to your game and even make you feel smooth in the rough (1966)

PRINGLE LEADS

Our collections are conceived with the most meticulous care, and it is our endeavour that they would be designed to suit discriminating women everywhere.

Our aim is to ensure that everyone who wears a Pringle sweater experiences a feeling of luxury and comfort, and we sincerely hope that an ever increasing number of well-dressed women all over the world will appreciate beyond all doubt that—"It's not only the name … that tells you it's a Pringle."

From the first **Pringle of Scotland** brochure, 1958

13

RAPID GROWTH IN SPACE & TURNOVER

Pringle change name, go public and discontinue underwear. (1954–1961)

I T WAS a seller's market no more. Sales girls from retail stores were brought to Hawick and shown how garments were made. 'Pringle Bars' were opened in leading London stores. A colour film *The Cashmere Story* was made to promote the Pringle story in every corner of the world. A new garment was brought out, the 'All-Wool Bouclé Sweater Suit'. Back opening was introduced on the continent.

There was trouble in the United States market from an unexpected quarter—political objection to the import of anything originating in the Republic of China. Joseph Dawson & Sons of Bradford, Britain's main importers of raw cashmere, discovered to their dismay that the US Customs were differentiating between cashmere from Outer Mongolia, which was part of Soviet Russia, and the cashmere from China. American manufacturers could only take Russian cashmere, and they took it all. So Joseph Dawson, who had bought from both countries, were now obliged to buy all its non-American supplies from China which in fact was superior to the Russian variety—better 'sorted'.

American manufacture of knitwear was now a real challenge to the Hawick trade. Though their finishing and fashioning was not up to Scottish standards—and the American girls were being persuaded to attach less importance to such things—they were successfully translating Paris fashions into economical and wearable knitwear. Pringle were certainly scared. In October 1954, they printed a leaflet headed 'Is Our Future Secure?—Hawick v. America Sweater Competition' and circulated it to all employees.

It drew attention to an article in the *American Knitted Outerwear Times* which showed the intense competition Pringle was up against.

Opposite
'Kalinka' cashmere and fur coat:
*Russian inspired winter collection
(1970s)*

It showed the drive in the US for perfection in quality, workmanship and design. One of the largest and most successful cashmere manufacturers in America, the Dalton Company, sold classic and dressmaker cashmere garments at two to four dollars (70p to £1.40) less than Pringle and other Hawick makes.

> We have seen and handled many Dalton sweaters and can tell you they are lovely cashmere sweaters and do present really serious competition to us. All the more astounding is the fact that they only entered the cashmere business seriously in October 1949—*only five years ago.*
>
> We must aim to be not only equal but to continue to excel in every department if we are to keep the position we have won with 140 years of experience behind us ... Don't make any mistake about it there are many manufacturers not only in America but in other countries too who present *serious competition.*

Worse, Japanese cashmere goods began to appear in America. Their top-grade knitwear sold at 24 dollars, where similar garments made in Hawick cost $28. Their low price came from using two-ply wool which covered up poor spinning and offering only dark colours. But by Japanese law, garments described as 'cashmere' had to contain ten per cent sheep's wool. So 90-per-cent-cashmere Japanese Cashmere Jumpers were not prized by the quality brigade whose custom it had always been Pringle policy to woo—and never more so than now. There could be no lowering of standards, or Pringle would cease to be Pringle. Technical support for such a resolve came in 1954/55 from the great engineering firm of Bentley Cotton.

In 1939 Cotton's knitting frames were seldom more than 8-division machines running at an average speed of 30 rows, or courses, a minute, capable of producing 17 dozen pieces a 45 hour week. (Needless to say, all machines were now powered by electricity, each with their own motor.) After the war, Bentley Cotton brought out their 8-division Fast Speed Frame which ran at 45 courses a minute and produced 25 dozen a week, and in 1952 they increased the speed to 65 courses a minute—30 dozen a week.

But the framework knitter still wasted time having to go from one end of the long machine to the other to set it or make alterations. In 1953 Cotton devised a 12-division Central Control Frame which cut out the need for these journeys and enabled the operator to make all adjustments from a single central point. On such a machine, to which had been attached their new automatic marking system, one frameworker with an apprentice helper could turn out 500 pieces a week—a far cry from the 200 of only 15 years before. The first of such machines to be installed in Scotland began operating at Rodono Mill in July 1954.

But there was more to come. Pringle had suggested to Bentley Cotton that perhaps the most important technical problem still to solve was a way of automatically transferring to the main fabric, comprising the body of a garment knitted in plain stocking stitch, the piece of fabric knitted separately on a machine for rib stitch—the collar, waist 'skirt' or cuff—instead of this being laboriously undertaken by hand, and

128

Printed cashmere maxi dress:
'Pisces' design with smocked waist and cuff (1970)

Fashion pages:
Competition featuring Pringle (1970)

Pisces re-created:
Pisces has been re-made for the 19 decades collection which celebrates the 190th anniversary of Robert Pringle founding the company in 1815

after having stopped the machine.

The Bentley Cotton Research Department took up the challenge. They patented a number of schemes, one of which met with Pringle's approval in the spring of 1955. Pringle sent down their most experienced framework knitter to help Bentley Cotton get the Automatic Rib Transfer Attachment to working production, and in the summer it was installed at Rodono Mill.

This, said William Mactaggart when the machine was formally set in operation by Mr James Stuart, MP, Secretary of State for Scotland, on July 18 (1955), was the biggest single advance since Cotton's Patent Power Frame of the 1880s. Compared with the new 12-division Central Control Machines installed the year before without the attachment, they were getting 30 per cent extra production with no extra labour—650 garments a week.

Printed cashmere:
Paisley designs
(1971)

> At the same time, while this is a great advance from the mechanical point of view, it is also a challenge to the Hawick trade in that to derive the full benefit from it there must be large and plentiful runs of garments. This is all the more difficult in these days when new colours and more colours are constantly demanded by the retail customers, and also the demand for dressmaker styles is greater than ever. However, we feel confident we can tackle the problem, as otherwise this latest step forward will prove more of an advantage to the Midland of England factories who are accustomed to knitting in greater quantities on more bulk production lines.

Paisley designs

129

By a device which appeared to be simple yet perfect, ribbed pieces were attached to the body on the main frame, and the finished garment removed, without stopping the machine. The rector of Calverton would have given his place in paradise to learn how they managed it.

Similar collaboration took place between Pringle's engineers and the manufacturers of the piece of apparatus known as the 'Paris Press', resulting in permanent modifications and improvements from which the whole industry benefited.

The Secretary of State also saw the second extension along Teviot Road which added another 14,000 square feet to the 21,000 built in 1951. Floor space at Rodono Mill was now double what it had been in 1946. It was going to be too much for Hawick's labour corps, and on August 8 (1955) the building of a new branch factory was started at Berwick-on-Tweed.

Paisley craze:
Paisley shirt with aviator shades

To meet the competition from America, all-out frontal attack was ordered. There was no mincing of words by Commanding Officer Mactaggart in his pep talk to the troops through the medium of the new *Pringle Bulletin* house magazine introduced in 1949. It was to be an open advance in the brightest array. The main strategy was diversification of styles, the operation shunned by Leicester and Nottingham as anathema to the profitable 'long run'. It was also likely to be avoided by the Americans for want of experience, skill and the right machinery, and a natural wish to play safe and ensure big returns quickly. The wages the American manufacturers had to pay for skilled labour were exceedingly high, so they could ill afford too much time spent on detailed hand work.

Many American firms were still reluctant moreover to involve themselves in the technically fussy business of knitting different coloured wool. By knitting and finishing nothing but white wool, all the settings on all machines could be standard and constant—the easy, quick, cheap way. Coloured wool varied—in thickness and stiffness for instance—from one colour to another. A machine adjusted to take dark brown wool, which was stiff and thick, had to be re-set to take pale blue which was flimsy and thin. Knitting an enormous choice of coloured wools, as Pringle did, as opposed to knitting one colour (white) took time, trouble, skills, money.

Each Pringle sweater became a 'dressmaker' garment of some complexity with its distinctive decorative features built into it by the designer, not imposed on a 'plain' jumper which was itself complete, by pouring over it a box of beads.

Pringle's policy was born of a belief that there were still people, albeit in a minority, with the taste and discrimination to know, and want, clothes of an informal kind which combined good design of a *couture* standard with the comfort and fit that came from being 'full-fashioned' in luxury materials which were 'dyed in the wool' in fast, delicate, unusual shades.

It was a policy which put a strain on every one of the 19 departments and processes then in operation at the enlarged Rodono Mill with its 1,100 employees. There had been different styles and colours before, but the new scale of diversification meant everyone involved doing his or her job in new gear—from the men in the yarnstore who had to cope with the literally hundreds of new shades and their fancy names, which changed every half year, to the clerical, invoicing and order office staff who had to be meticulous in making sure they had interpreted customers now varied orders into correct, working instructions. Habits accumulated over the years, when a comparatively few lines went through the department with some monotony in a state of near-automation, had to be discarded. Continuous belt thinking was out. Nothing was routine any more. Small lots took the place of big batches. Examining, pressing and folding of piles of identical garments with the application of a routine formula gave way to the attention being continually diverted from one design to another.

Above all, the men operating the knitting frames no longer set them to knit a particular shape and let them run for days. Runs became short as the number of 'working lines' became greater. Different types of garment came on and off the machine in quick succession. A man who today was making 'Brevis' shorts tomorrow was turning out 'Torso' sweaters. Be more nimble in your thinking, was Mactaggart's exhortation, and they responded with a demonstration of their adaptability which surprised even themselves.

Part of the new armoury were 30 Dubied '00' Intarsia machines installed at Rodono Mill, the first to be delivered to a British knitwear firm since the 1930s when Dubied discontinued making them. Within 12 months Pringle became the most skilled producers of Intarsia sweaters in Britain. Diversification of colours, multiplication of styles, elaboration of design, Intarsia knitting—it was putting a stick to their own back, but it was the broad, Scots back of an adventurer who had persevered

130

Printed cashmere:
Bold designs where a speciality in the 1970s

70's Geometric:
(1975)

Detail

before when the going was hard, and always been stimulated by challenges of the kind that now came from across the Atlantic. In 1956 there was no lacking the spirit which had buoyed up the house of Pringle through so many trials in the past. It was an impressive display of rising to the occasion which, as it gathered momentum, established the enterprise more firmly than ever before as the leader in its field.

Royal recognition of this came with the granting on January 1, 1956, of the warrant of appointment as manufacturers of knitted garments to Her Majesty Queen Elizabeth, who had succeeded her father King George VI on his death in 1952. The royal warrant from Queen Elizabeth The Queen Mother, as she had now become, granted during the lifetime of King George VI, had been renewed in February, 1952. Pringle was now the holder of two royal warrants.

The bold strategy succeeded. Turnover topped the two million mark—£2,091,146 in 1956. Profit before tax recovered after the setback of 1952, climbing, with a dip in 1954, to a peak of £248,807 in 1956 not to be reached again till 1962. Order books were full to over-flowing, the export trade had never been higher, particularly to the United States. Demand exceeded supply. But the price of raw cashmere was up again, approaching the excessive £6 a pound of 1951 which did not augur well for the determination to keep the selling price of Pringle cashmere garments in America to below $30.

The pace of development at Rodono Mill once more outstripped the number of women in Hawick available for the various processes. A bus collected 150 girls every morning from outlying villages. The eight-year-old Walkergate branch factory at Berwick-on-Tweed had been supplanted by the new building on the Tweedside Industrial Estate.

A special yarn was developed by Todd & Duncan, the big cashmere and wool spinners of Kinross, to the exclusive specification of Pringle and given the name of 'Spindrift'. To take its place beside the novelty 'dressmaker' styling came the 'Dyed-to-Match' look, with the sweater dyed to match the colour of woven skirt or trousers; bouclé knitted suits; 'Jacquard' knitted suits in mohair and wool yarn. Europe's taste differed from America's, and the knitwear which Stuart Beaty and his team designed for continental houses were more on classic lines in good quality and more sombre colours.

Style was now the primary concern of buyers in the States. Cashmere had to come down off its pedestal and compete with other fibres and qualities in the *way* it was used. It was no longer sought for its own value as a material. The Back-to-School trade had been seriously affected. Cashmere sweaters which had been traditional items of every college girl's wardrobe were now replaced by clothes of Shetland, lambswool and other less expensive materials. Everywhere there was a big price resistance. In the fall of 1956 a golfer jacket retailed at 29.95 dollars, the limit for most. When the price went up, customers ordered the less expensive three-quartered sleeve garment. There had been a rush by the stores to get rid of their stocks at any price. They had advertised in the papers 'Cashmere coats at give-away prices'. Cashmere had lost much of its prestige by being marked down in price in this way. It was no longer in a class apart. It had been *pushed* off its pedestal.

Care for you cashmere:
Expert advice from Pringle (1970)

131

For some years now the name 'Pringle of Scotland' had been used in press advertising and promotional literature, and on December 28, 1958 the name of the company was officially changed from 'Robert Pringle & Son Limited' to 'Pringle of Scotland Limited'. Even more important was the introduction of Pringle men's outerwear. One of the last brochures to bear the name 'Robert Pringle & Son Ltd. Sportswear and Underwear Manufacturers' showed a man in a yellow pullover under a jacket and Burberry, a soft hat pushed well over his eyes, filling his pipe and gazing out over a Lowlands landscape with a flock of sheep in the foreground. The caption at the top read: 'looking forward to the Pringle of the future!' Bill Rodger was right on beam.

In fact it had begun some years before. Demand for the kind of heavy men's underwear in which Pringle had specialised for a hundred years had fallen off and off, but as it did, the technique of the close, tight stitch on fine gauge machines used in the making of both men's and women's underwear was adapted to make a similar kind of garment but which, like the bathing suits, was both outerwear and underwear— a 'sports shirt'. Men's sports shirts—strictly the first male outerwear (nearer to what is today regarded as outerwear than the early 'sweaters') —were knitted in the Underwear Department alongside vests and pants. It began when in 1955 Pringle introduced in conjunction with the Ryder Cup Golf Team, the 'Ryder Cup' golf shirt.

The 1956–57 boom was, of course, all too good to last. First signs were the reduction in turnover in 1958 from the previous year's £2,285,936 to £1,821,547; and the profit before tax falling from £231,508 to £151,983. Chairman John Wells solemnly told shareholders at the 1959 annual general meeting that it had been 'the most difficult year of trading since the war'. In spite of this gloom yet another four storey extension was completed and occupied, along the Teviot river frontage, and another begun at the back to which to transfer the operations still being carried out at the rented Weensland Mill. In any case, it was only a minor tremor to an undertaking that had now assumed formidable proportions and rocklike stability. Nonetheless, its shareholders asked themselves whether a private limited company was the best form of commercial structure for either its present commitments or its greater future potential.

At the end of 1959 it was widely known in the hosiery trade and in the City of London that the Board of Pringle of Scotland were contemplating 'going public'. Such a state of affairs naturally enough attracted offers for the purchase of part or all of the company's share capital, and one came from Scottish and Universal Investments Ltd (SUITS). This was run by the Scottish financier Sir Hugh Fraser who had certain drapery interests—he took over 'Braemar' the following year—and another from Debenham & Freebody, the department store owners. Both were refused.

William Mactaggart assembled the whole staff of 1,300 on March 15, 1960, and told them what was in the air. Many of the bigger shareholders, he said, were reaching an age when large blocks of shares might have to be realised. Within the limitations allowed by the law governing a private company, this did not give the shareholders a fair chance. Turning the private company, in which shareholders could not sell their shares in the market but only to other shareholders, into a private company in which shares could be bought and sold

132

New fashion rules:
Break them!
(1972)

Printed cashmere:
'Aqua floral' designs
(1972)

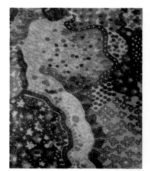

Printed cashmere:
'Aqua floral'

on the stock exchanges, would not only enable shareholders to receive a fair value for their shares, but would make for more efficient management. So many family firms, he said, had slipped back because of inefficient management. Going public would be an incentive and spur to keep Pringle in its present efficient and progressive state.

Three days later (March 18) 76-year-old John Wells took the chair at the last board meeting of the private company which had been formed from Robert Pringle's co-partnery in 1922. He was the only original shareholder left. In 1922, he said, sales had totalled £78,000 and salaries and wages £21,000. In 1959 sales had been 'within a kick of two million pounds' and the salaries and wages bill came to £600,000. Sales were to every country in the world except behind the Iron Curtain.

It was the last of the family gathering annual general meetings; next year there would be strangers within their gates.

With the backward reflections duly disposed of, the meeting proceeded to pass a resolution that Pringle of Scotland Limited became a public company. On March 21 the newspapers carried details of the Offer for Sale of 570,000 of the company's ordinary shares of 5s (25p) each at 14s (70p) a share.

The offer of sale told prospective shareholders that out of the existing issued share capital of £572,000 only £75,075 had been issued for cash, of which £20,000, written off in 1938, represented the Goodwill of the co-partnery which the private company had purchased in 1922. Authorised capital was £750,000.

Under the heading 'Profits, Prospects and Dividends' they learnt that the turnover for 1959 was nearly ten times that of 1945. 'The expansion was checked by the recession in the United States which resulted in severe decline in exports to that country in 1958. The profits for 1957 and 1958 were also affected by the substantial fall in the price of cashmere and of almost all other fibres used by the company.'

The accountants' reports took regard not only of the profits of Pringle of Scotland but of its two wholly owned subsidiaries, Pringle Johnston Imports incorporated in the US and Pringle Johnston (Canada). The profit before charging depreciation and taxation in 1959 for this 'group' was given as £247,093. It was the first of the Border knitwear firms to go public. The issue was open for one minute—from 10 am to 10.1 am. It was 50 times over-subscribed. There were 52,648 applications. Allotment was by ballot. The 11 applicants for 50,000 shares and over received 1,200 each. Employees were offered blocks of 100 shares at £70. They bought 104,650. At the start of dealing the 14s (70p) issue price rose to 16s 3d (81p) and then 17s 1d (85½p). By June the price of Pringle shares was up to 22s (£1.10).

At the first annual general meeting of the public company, shareholders heard that the Dyed-to-Match look, pioneered by Pringle, had caught on, and jumpers with skirts made by Pringle from Border tweeds and fine worsteds were having an enormous sale; and that, as it now represented only one and a half per cent of Pringle's total output, it had been decided to discontinue the manufacture of underwear and gradually to close down the Department which had once been the Factory. It was a sad, but necessary, decision. Demand had been decreasing for some years, and it was estimated that in 1961 turnover

Letter to Mr Barty-King:
Stuart Beaty writes to the author of this book in 1974 when the project initially began

Flower power:
Designed by students at Glasgow school of Art

133

Hand-screening:
Head of textiles at Glasgow School of Art, Robert Stuart was a major catalyst for the creation of the hand-screening department being created at Pringle in 1967

would only amount to £30,000.

Stockings had been the first to go. The manufacture of ladies' hose and tights with the new man-made fibres, the old artificial silk now made of plastic with nondescript brand names like 'Nylon' and 'Orlon', had become a separate industry undertaken by specialists with machinery that could make stockings and nothing else—like William Lee's frames in their early days. The knitting of men's socks in wool and mixtures of wool and man-made fibres, football stockings and everything that could come under the original term 'hose', now back to its proper meaning, fell to the stocking makers. Pringle, and others, were reluctant to disassociate themselves from the term. They still described themselves as 'hosiery manufacturers' in the prospectus of 1960, and the Hawick Hosiery Manufacturers Association only changed their title to Knitwear Manufacturers in 1966. In 1970 it was still the Hosiery and Allied Trades Research Association. Looping and not weaving—the stocking stitch—was still the common denomination.

Now Pringle, knitwear manufacturers in all but name, shed the making of that part of 'hosiery' which had developed from the making of *chaussés*, the vests and pants, chemises and knickers, which constituted 'Underwear', and had been the firm's entire output for 130 years. The Underwear versus Overwear contest was settled once and for all. Without any heart-searching decisions by management, it had settled itself.

Graphic look:
(1970s)

Washable luxury:
*First washable and shrink
resistant wool
(1970s)*

134

Opposite
Celebrating industry award
(1971)

14

'IS PRINGLE NEXT?'

With turnover at £4 million, Pringle is acquired by Joseph Dawson. (1961–1967)

B Y 1961 it was well and truly a buyer's market. In the United States
the demand for cashmere sweaters fell off. The criterion was now
the look, not the quality, of the material. There was keen competition
with flat knits from Italy, cotton knits, mohairs. The emphasis was away
from the Back to School Season to the Holiday or Christmas Season.

This, as much as anything else, prompted the formation, in
August 1961, of the Scottish Cashmere Association consisting of the
Hawick knitwear firms of Pringle, Braemar (Innes Henderson), Lyle
& Scott and Barrie, with Ballantyne of Peebles and Munrospun of
Edinburgh, supported by Joseph Dawson & Son of Bradford, the
leading importer to Britain of raw cashmere. Alan Smith, a director
of Dawsons, who was elected chairman of the association and was
its prime mover, said its formation was the fulfilment of the closer
co-operation which so many of them had advocated over the years.
'The grouping of resources by the six leading firms will enable all
the advantages of cashmere sweaters to be more widely recognised.'
In the co-operative publicity campaign that followed, Bill Rodger of
Pringle, chairman of the association's promotion committee, put the
emphasis on fashion and cashmere's all-round versatility.

Pringle now gave greater attention to overseas markets outside the
United States. The main outcome of the chairman's visit to Australia
was the taking over, on September 1, 1961, of the agency previously
held by H. Ide & Company, 'Pringle of Scotland (Australia) Pty Ltd',
a marketing company newly formed for the purpose, with a head office
in Pitt Street, Sydney, and Roy Ide as managing-director. There was
flattering indication of the popularity of the name as a sales leader in
the Far East when an enterprising Hong Kong establishment set up

137

Opposite
Men's co-ordinated fashion:
(1970s)

as 'Springle of Scott'. Sales to Europe increased by 15 per cent during 1961 and 1962—to Italy by 34 per cent. Pringle saw themselves well placed in the event of Britain joining the Common Market.

Tariffs against imports of knitwear by European countries were high in 1962. In theory it was 21 per cent against Britain, but most countries added other duties such as Luxury Tax or a Special Import Tax so that, as in the case of France, the 21 per cent became 54 percent. 'Despite the recent breakdown of negotiations for Britain's entry to the Common Market,' William Mactaggart told shareholders at the 1963 AGM, 'we see no reason to modify any of our plans for expansion.'

The principal of these was the acquisition of Glebe Mill in the Weensland area of Hawick—named after Parson Lee's vicarage at Calverton? In November 1962, Robert Noble, tweed manufacturers, amalgamated with Roberts of Selkirk, which meant closing their Glebe Mill at Hawick. Pringle offered to buy it for £27,000, and this was accepted. There were two 'flats' of 22,000 sq ft, each twice the size of the best flat at Rodono Mill. Altogether there were 70,000 sq ft and one and a half acres of ground for further expansion. Considerable structural alterations would be needed at cost of £55,000—the roof was removed and a second storey added. It was for the 'vertical' manufacture of men's knitwear that Glebe Mill had been purchased, a place where every aspect and process of production could be concentrated including design, instead of being regarded as a sideline in a factory devoted to women's wear. The final move to Glebe Mill was made on October 31, 1963 and it began with 200 employees. It was formally opened the following year by Edward Heath MP, Minister at the Board of Trade, who had been conducting the negotiations for Britain's entry into the Common Market. By December 1963, when Glebe Mill was in full operation, men's wear took up 25 per cent of all Pringle production. There were some three dozen styles in five different qualities in manly greys, naturals, blues, lovats, corn and cognac. The original 'Ryder Cup Shirt', which had been the spearhead of Pringle's men's outerwear, was still a big overseas seller. A more economic use of machinery both at Rodono and Glebe was introduced by double day shift working. The working week was reduced from 45 to 42½ hours in 1962, and to 40 hours in 1965.

The problem of finding enough labour to run these expanding mills was now very serious. Thirty-four families under a so-called Overspill Agreement were persuaded to leave Glasgow and come and live in the Meadows at Burnfoot. The men had been employed in engineering, shipbuilding, transport and the construction trades, and were given jobs at Rodono and Glebe on Intarsia work, folding, checking, etc. For further female labour the company was relying on the ladies of Berwick. A nursery was started at Glebe Mill. Here women workers both at Rodono and Glebe could leave their children in the care of matron Agnes Dodds and her staff who gave them a wholesome midday meal and kindly entertainment. The nursery helped to attract back to Pringle the girls in Hawick and local villages whom the company had trained when they left school and then, after a first year of marriage, had left the mill to start a family, but after three or four years wished to add to the family income by returning to employment.

138

The Queens Award for Industry: *(1971)*

Striped family: *Childrenswear makes a return to prodcution in the 1970's*

The royal and ancient game of golf, which originated in Scotland, had been the first link between Pringle knitwear and the male sex, and in 1964 it was decided to cement this relationship by the promotion of an annual Pringle of Scotland Professional Golf Tournament. The first one was held on the championship course at Carnoustie in August. A tented village was set up and there were daily fashion shows of Pringle knitwear. Harold Henning, the South African golfer, won the Pringle trophy designed by Stuart Beaty. The efforts of everyone concerned were greatly rewarded, and the tournaments became a regular feature of Pringle promotion. Later, an agreement was made with Palmer Apparel Inc for the exclusive right to use the name of American golfer Arnold Palmer, first for an alpaca cardigan, and afterwards for a jacket, sports shirt and pullover.

High quality goods of the kind made by Pringle had nothing to fear from the abolition of resale price maintenance in 1964; there was no price cutting. However, a more local event, the closure of the Edinburgh-Hawick-Carlisle railway line, under the government-inspired Beeching Plan, threatened the distribution operation of all the Border firms; Pringle certainly sent 80 per cent of its merchandise by rail at this time. But morale took an upward turn—not that it was down—when, in the 1964 Birthday Honours, the chairman Willie Mactaggart was made a Commander of the Order of the British Empire (CBE). He went to Buckingham Palace on November 17 with his wife and daughter, Mrs Claire Thompson, to receive the order from the sovereign lady for whom his company made jumpers and cardigans—which was more than the first Queen Elizabeth did for poor William Lee. It was regarded as a gracious compliment to the whole company.

It was the year for a general swap-round in the ownership of the Border knitwear firms. The well-known woollen clothing manufacturer, Wolsey, took over one of Pringle's principal competitors in Hawick, Lyle & Scott. They outbid offers from Sir Hugh Fraser and his Scottish and Universal Investments (SUITS), one-time bidders for Pringle, and from Stanley Field and his William Baird group. Fraser, however, was successful in acquiring both Ballentyne of Innerleithen and Braemar (ex-Innes Henderson) of Hawick, but then sold 51 per cent of his holding in these for £2 million to Stanley Field and the William Baird group, which had a 15 per cent interest in Dawsons of Bradford.

'Pringle next?' asked the City speculators.

The chairman denied all rumours. 'If a bid is made for Pringle,' William Mactaggart was reported as saying, 'the Board will give it the dusty answer.'

When a slight slowing off in the demand for ladies' knitwear occurred in 1965, the firm's 150th anniversary, it was reassuringly described as a 'temporary plateau'. A drop in orders from France, Italy and Switzerland was no great cause for alarm. There as much else to justify the view that the plateau was a platform from which the next leap would be made. Men were buying Pringle knitwear as never before, particularly in the United States. A 22½ per cent dividend was declared; five shilling shares changed hands at 25s; turnover went up another £600,000, and the value of stock in hand for the first time reached a million pounds, more than double that of 1955 (in 1935 it was only £27,800). For the first time in three years Pringle increased

Underwear inspired 70s style:
Summer jumper with placket detail taken from a traditional 'Henley' style underwear

Long line Jumper:
(1970s)

139

Knitted trousers suit:
Flared trouser fad did not escape knitwear designer Leslie Rankin (1970s)

prices but only between two and five per cent. Writing in the external news sheet *Pringle News* instituted in 1965, the chairman deplored the longer time it was taking customers to pay their accounts, implying that if the company had not to bear the burden of being owed more than a million pounds, as it was at that moment, they might not have had to raise the prices quite as much.

The cold wind of 1965, such as it was, put paid to Hawick's oldest knitwear firm, Walter Wilson & Sons, founded in 1789, 26 years before Robert Pringle I set up at Whisky House Mill with Waldie and Scott. It was a sad end to a distinguished innings of 176 years. Their going into liquidation left Pringle of Scotland the oldest Border knitwear firm by well over a century. Walter Wilson's mill also faced the Teviot, next door to Pringle's latest extension at the end of the Teviot Road cul-de-sac. It was inevitable that, in January 1966, Pringle should acquire these venerable premises—17,000 sq ft—and add them to their solid frontage along the river which spread from Walter's Wynd to the iron bridge.

For many years Pringle knitwear had been sold through agents and wholesalers to stores and boutiques literally all over the world. In 1965 the chairman and Mrs Mactaggart visited Pringle sales companies, agents and representatives on a whistle-stop tour of 13 cities in six countries—Athens, Beirut, Hong Kong, Sydney, Perth, Adelaide, Brisbane, Auckland, Wellington, Los Angeles, San Francisco, New York. There was never a week in which some senior executive or director was not on a visit to some quarter of the world. It was a matter not only of keeping alive old-established personal relationships in a way no correspondence or telephone calls could ever do—and keeping them on their toes—but often meeting for the first time representatives whose connection with the company covered quite a period. The first visit of a Pringle representative to South Africa and Rhodesia, for instance, was paid by Otto Weisz in 1965. Visits were made other than for sales promotion by engineering executives, and people like Stuart Beaty and members of the design team. Assistant designer Wallace Shaw spent four weeks studying American tastes in February 1965, and Lesley Brown, then the only lady member of the team, went to Italy in October.

A sales tool which had been doing a good job for the last 12 years, the film *The Cashmere Story*, seen by 25 million people all over the world, was replaced by a new film which included some beautiful scenes in full colour of cashmere goats grazing in the Himalayas.

But the best tools were of course the garments themselves. The 1965 Ladies' Stock Service contained details of 12 items, five in cashmere and seven in 'Spindrift' lambswool, available in 15 colours, actual samples of which were set into the pages of the catalogue. The sportswear connotation still survived, through the term 'twinset' and the brand name 'Princess' of underwear days. The cashmere 'Princess' Golfer Twinset and Cardigan (called 'Duchess' in lambswool), was all the rage among young ladies who would not know a bunker from a double bed.

Capping the two royal warrants and the chairman's CBE came the honour of being one of 115 first recipients of the new Queen's Award for Industry instituted in 1966. Pringle were one of 14 companies in Scotland and one of two knitwear firms—the other being Paine of Godalming, the town in the south of England where there was an early

140

Goucho style:
(1971)

Goucho twinset:
(1970s)

Knitted Midi skirt:
The new length
(1970s)

colony of framework knitters a couple of hundred years before stocking frames were heard of in Hawick.

Half a million pounds and more were the profits of this crucial year of 1966—at £511,244, 16 per cent more than in 1965—and the total sales for the first time reached four million pounds—at £4,346,121 10 per cent up on the previous year. There was another dividend of 22½ per cent. There had been a 47 per cent increase in men's wear sales, of which 69 per cent had been exported.

It was shortly after these impressive figures had been announced at the 1967 annual general meeting in March that the rumours began. 'Is Pringle next?' was a cry which, once raised, never entirely died, and in April 1967, it was heard again. The plateau the company now found itself not resting on but clinging to, was the top of a lofty pinnacle of independence built, secured and held by three generations of Pringle and their successors, which was now in danger of being knocked away from under them.

'There were some take-over rumours,' remarked the *Glasgow Evening Times* of April 25 when Pringle shares rose over the week-end by two shillings to 26s 3d (£1.31). Two days later (April 27) the *Daily Mail* reported, 'Pringle of Scotland touched 28s 3d (£1.41)—up 1s 1½d (5½p). This gives a gain of nearly 3s (15p) since Monday and rumours are that a 30s (£1.50) bid had come in. This is denied by Pringle who say that "no approach" has been made. "We can make no comment," say William Baird, tipped as likely suitors by speculators who feel that Baird would have liked to have taken Jaeger.' William Baird was Stanley Field's finance group which had an interest in Pringle's competitors on the Border—Braemar and Ballantyne.

The *Glasgow Herald* of April 27 remarked on the speculative buying in Pringle shares and named J & P Coats, Paton & Baldwins, William Baird and Sir Hugh Fraser's Scottish and Universal Investments (SUITS) as 'interested'. A Jaeger takeover offer from Coats and Paton & Baldwins was in the wind, said the writer. Robert Martin, the City editor, on another page quoted speculative sources as saying SUITS had already offered 30s (£1.50) for Pringle, but the Board were holding out at 35s (£1.75). It was hard to believe, he wrote, that Debenhams, who had shown some interest in the past and had a sizeable equity stake, would stand idly by. The *Scotsman* of April 27 got a Coats spokesman to say a Pringle bid rumour was 'nonsense'. Ernest Tait was reported telling the *Scotsman* that Pringle had had no approach whatsoever from anybody. But without a prospect of takeover, stated its correspondent, it was hard to justify the current high price of Pringle shares.

On May 2 Pringle shares went up another 4½d (1½p) to 27s 3d (£1.36). The *Sun* reported Pringle as denying a takeover bid. When the shares rose to 28s 1½d (£1.40½) on May 3, the next day's papers carried more denials. Ten days passed without any comment and then the *Glasgow Herald* made the topic its leading item in its chatty 'Investment Notes' feature on Monday, May 15, with the modest sized headline 'Will Joseph Dawson put in a bid for Pringle?'

'The shares of Pringle of Scotland,' wrote the diarist, 'finished the week at 27s (£1.35). They have been the centre of much takeover controversy in recent months. But few, if any, have mentioned the name of Joseph Dawson (Holdings), the leading processor of cashmere in this country. With Coats, Patons & Baldwins on the look-out for

London fashion shoot:
(1970s)

141

further acquisitions, Dawson must be worried about their own outlets. Expansion at Kinross and Selkirk will be completed by the end of the year, and the group would loathe to let one of their best customers disappear without a fight. Their own record stands comparison with Pringle's growth and the two companies are obviously complementary in many ways'.

No one thought this worth following up. It was an isolated tip which was never referred to by any other newspaper. Three days went by without any comment until the London *Evening News* of Thursday, May 18, made a one-line reference to Pringle shares rising another 3d (1p) to a 1967 peak of 29s (£1.45). Another week went by and the following Thursday the *Financial Times*, *Daily Mail*, *Sun* and *Evening News* ran stories. The *Financial Times* noted that after slipping 9d (4p) to 28s 3d (£1.41) earlier in the day, buyers moved in and forced the price up to a new 1967 high of 30s 3d (£1.66). They phoned the chairman in the evening who told them there had been 'no approach whatever as yet'.

But the *Daily Mail* and *Evening News* (both in the same stable) and the *Sun* all tipped Dawson as the likely wooer. George Welham of the *Sun* 'understood' the long-awaited bid for Pringle was very close and at 32s 6d (£1.61½) rather than the 30s 6d (£1.66) to which the shares climbed the night before. Dawson shares, he pointed out, rose 1s 9d (9p) to 17s 6d (87½p) when chairman Alan Smith announced the dividend would be five points higher at 17½ per cent. On the telephone on May 24 Alan Smith told Welham: 'No comment—as I said when I was asked about Pringle three years ago. But everybody is bidding for somebody these days.' Otto Weisz told Welham, 'There has been no bid and no approach from anyone as of this moment.' On May 25 Weisz was reported as telling the *Evening News* that no offer had been received and he was not expecting one.

But the following day (May 26) the story broke. Every morning paper reported that Dawson had made a cash and share offer for the £871,620 share capital of Pringle. They differed on its value. The *Daily Telegraph* put it at £6.2 million; *The Times* at £6 million; the *Financial Times* at £5.9 million; the *Yorkshire Post* and most English provincial papers at £5.7 million; the *Glasgow Herald* and most Scottish papers at £5.6 million. Dawson were reported as having made the offer 'well after market hours' on Thursday night, May 25.

The reported offer was of five new Dawson shares plus 15s (75p) in cash for every three Pringle shares. The bids put the value of the Pringle shares at 35s 5d (£1.77) in view of Dawson's closing price of 18s 3d (91p), reckoned the *Daily Telegraph*; but *The Times* valued the shares at 33s 10d (31.69), and so did the *Financial Times* which commented 'fancy prices are the rule for knitwear bids these days, and Joseph Dawson's offer for Pringle of Scotland is no exception'. George Welham of the *Sun* forecast a fight could develop. Closing prices of the Pringle 5s shares on May 25 was 31s (£1.55).

The formal offer went out from N. V. Rothschild & Sons, Dawson's financial advisers, on June 1. It was addressed to the shareholders of Pringle and offered five new Dawson 5s shares and 15s cash for every three Pringle 5s shares, as reported. On the basis of Dawson shares being worth 17s 3d (86p) on May 31, the offer valued each Pringle share at 33s 9d (£1.69). Alternatively, Rothschild offered to

Women's advertising:
(1971)

Stripe on stripe:
(1970s)

142

buy Pringle shares at 16s 6d (82½p). On this basis what they called the 'total consideration' which shareholders would receive would be 32s 6d (£1.62½) a share. George Welham of the *Sun* had got it just right. The offer was open until June 22 and was conditional on holders of not less than 51 per cent accepting it.

Who were Joseph Dawson (Holdings) Limited? In the letter to Pringle shareholders they described themselves as 'the largest processors and spinners of cashmere in the world', processing and spinning all forms of high quality wool and other natural animal fibres. The company was started in Bradford by Joseph Dawson in 1871, the grandfather of one of the present directors. In the early 1900s the company had evolved a secret process of de-hairing coarse outer hairs from the Tibetan goat, leaving only the soft, fine under down which could be used for spinning. The company sold processed raw wool to the spinners, one of whom in the 1930s was the Scottish firm of Todd & Duncan, who had a small mill at Kinross on the shores of Loch Leven, and sold their yarn to tweed firms mostly. Pringle first began buying Geelong Lambswool yarn from Todd & Duncan in 1938.

During World War 2 there was a Spitfire Training Aerodrome near Kinross and in 1942 a pilot called Alan Smith was posted there from Fighter Command to give instruction in serial gunnery. Miss Margaret Todd, whose father owned Todd & Duncan, operated a mobile canteen on the aerodrome as her war effort. This was the occasion of their first meeting, and before Alan was posted away from Kinross they had become engaged. He flew Spitfires in 1940 and was a member of Douglas Bader's famous squadron in 1941. He was awarded the Distinguished Flying Cross and won a bar to it in North Africa. He married Margaret Todd, and when the war was over, accepted an invitation from his father-in-law to join Todd & Duncan. He spent five months at the Galashiels Technical College to learn something about the business, and then took up his duties at the mill at Kinross, which in 1945 employed only some 42 workers. When Todd died, Alan Smith took charge.

Between 1946 and 1960 Todd & Duncan had expanded their business to the extent of taking some 60 per cent of the total output of cashmere of Joseph Dawson of Bradford. While the Dawson company was a public one, the majority of the shares were held by the Dawson family. With agreement on both sides, a reverse take-over bid was made by Todd & Duncan for the Dawson business. At the end of the day the Smith family and Miss Hilda Todd owned approximately 70% of the shares of Joseph Dawson Holdings Limited.

The main purpose of the move was to stabilise cashmere prices—an aim that was achieved. For between August 1960 and July 1968, when the pound was devalued, the price of raw cashmere never altered by one (old) penny in the pound. This was largely due to Alan Smith's twice yearly visits to Moscow and China to make his purchases personally.

In 1961 the Dawson, Todd & Duncan group bought Laidlaw & Fairgrieve, the Galashiels wool spinners, and Brown Allan the cashmere spinners of Selkirk. Both these had been owned by William Baird & Company who, on selling them, acquired 26 per cent of the Dawson Group capital. But Alan Smith still held 51 per cent of the voting power. By 1965 Pringle were buying 75 per cent of their spun cashmere,

Examples in 1971 men's advertising:

Pringle experiments with new fibres

143

lambswool and Shetland wool from either Todd & Duncan, Brown Allan or Laidlaw & Fairgrieve. In 1966 their purchases from the Dawson Group companies amounted to more than £1 million, which made them the Dawson Group's biggest customer. In the same year Dawson bought Barrie Knitwear of Hawick.

'The amalgamation of the two companies,' stated Dawson's letter to Pringle shareholders of June 1, 1967, 'will ensure the continuance and expansion of this trading relationship.' Pringle shareholders who accepted the offer would see an improvement in income of 54 per cent. Dawson's net profits after tax had risen from £435,000 in 1962 to £933,000 in 1966. Their net tangible assets were £6,288,000.

This printed letter was received direct by Pringle's shareholders in the post of the morning of June 2. As shareholders, the directors of Pringle studied the document in detail for the first time. Their first reaction was to draft a letter to shareholders saying they would do better in the long run to retain their Pringle shares, and advising rejection of the Dawson offer 'by those shareholders who are concerned to hold a long term investment'. This was never sent. Their second reaction was to write a letter, dated June 3, telling shareholders their directors had now seen the offer sent to them direct and the Board was in touch with their advisers regarding the terms and conditions of the offer. They were recommended to take no action until they had received further confirmation from their directors, which they would get in the very near future. The newspapers of June 5 printed this news with 'Sit Tight' headlines and no comment.

On June 7 a meeting took place in London at the office of N. V. Rothschild attended by William Mactaggart, Otto Weisz, and Ernest Tait representing Pringle, and Alan Smith and D. M. Clark representing Dawson. The same people met again in Hawick on June 12. At these meetings Pringle said it was essential that they should maintain versatility, and, for the good reputation and profitability of Pringle, that they should be allowed some freedom in the purchase of yarn. The basis for proceeding in this respect in the future, in the event of Pringle's directors advising acceptance of the Dawson offer, was that Pringle could buy from outside the Dawson Group up to the annual total of around 120,000 lb. But the part of it which was cashmere must be from raw material supplied by Dawson.

Alan Smith agreed to this, and so the answer to the 1967 takeover bid was not a dusty one. But the letter the directors sent to Pringle shareholders on June 14 was at pains to point out that they had not sought this offer, and that their own feelings had been in favour of retaining the independence which the company had enjoyed for more than a century and a half. Nevertheless, they were aware of the changes in the textile industry which caused one of their principal suppliers to make the offer. The chairman of Dawson had confirmed that it was his board's intention to let Pringle continue to operate as before under its own name as a separate unit with the existing management. The directors intended accepting the offer for their own holdings in Pringle—581,956 shares (17 per cent of the capital). Three Pringle directors already held shares in Dawson.

The shareholders took the hint, and on June 23, 1967 Joseph Dawson (Holdings) Ltd acquired the whole of the share capital of Pringle of Scotland for £5,800,000.

Catchy copylines were employed to seduce the shopper

(1970)

Cashmere for men

How it all happened was explained to the 2,000 Pringle employees by William Mactaggart in the *Pringle Annual*. 'Recently,' he wrote, 'Coats Patons, who spin cashmere and also lambswool, bought over Jaeger, and this made Mr Smith feel somewhat insecure, as many of the financial papers were putting out rumours that Coats Patons were still looking for firms to take over and that Pringle might well be the next on their list. Mr Smith therefore felt it imperative to protect the Dawson, Group's position by making an offer for Pringle which they did in May this year, because if we had been acquired by the Coats Patons Group they could have insisted on our buying all our yarns from them, thus causing very severe damage to the Dawson, Todd & Duncan Group.'

Catch-as-catch-can.

Men's advertising:
(1971)

'Bright Guy' campaign:
*Dramatic black background is used
to enhance the colour of the knitwear
(1971)*

15

WHICH SPRING WILL CATCH WOODCOCKS THIS YEAR?

Then, as now, satisfying the changing tastes and fashions of the world.

S O FAR as the Pringle manufacturing operation at the two Hawick mills and at Berwick was concerned, the event of June 23, 1967 brought no immediate change. The company image was, if anything, enhanced by bowing to the inevitable with swift dignity and a sound commercial sense respected by the City and all those with whom the company had dealings. The end-product, the superb knitwear, could not be affected, except for the better, through supplies of cashmere at stable prices being guaranteed as they had never been before.

William Mactaggart and Otto Weisz became directors of Joseph Dawson (Holdings) and as such attended the company's annual general meeting on November 30, 1967, at which a consolidated profit before tax was declared of £2,020,000 (£1,520,000 in 1966) and profit after tax of £1,258,000 (£933,000 in 1966). The latter included Pringle's £587,000 (£511,000 in 1966).

Alan Smith, chairman and managing-director, took the opportunity to admire 'the exemplary way in which the Chinese and Russians stood by all contracts negotiated at the old sterling parity prior to the devaluation announcement. This example of business probity caused me no surprise after several years of trading with them.'

He referred to the Pringle takeover by saying that no matter how excellent their spinning and thorough their service to the industry, if one of Dawson's customers was bought by a competitor, then that business was lost to them. 'Our knitting acquisitions have therefore been defensive, and we still look upon ourselves as suppliers of raw material and yarns to the industry generally.'

In December 1967, Dawson acquired the Dumfries knitwear firm of J & D McGeorge. The group now consisted of Joseph Dawson Ltd,

Opposite
Richard Gere in Pringle:
Men's Vogue
(1978)

Todd & Duncan Ltd, Laidlaw & Fairgrieve Ltd of Galashiels, Selkirk and Dalkeith; Arnfinn Strarme (Wools) Ltd of Bradford, wool merchants; Barrie Knitwear Ltd of Hawick; two companies in Switzerland and one in South Africa. Alan Smith and T.W.G. Ashdown came on to the Pringle board, attended the meeting of February 1968, and met the managerial group. The entente was entirely cordial, and the relationship of manufacturer and supplier was re-assumed with confidence and renewed optimism for what the partnership would bring in the future—to Dawson the assurance that their biggest customer would be continuing to place orders, to Pringle the backing of even larger financial resources and the sharing of much appreciated business expertise.

America was still being as big a market for Pringle as ever; Lewis Bannerman retired as president of Pringle of Scotland (USA) in 1969 and was succeeded by John Mendez. Retail shops were opened in Amsterdam, Tokyo, Hong Kong, Dusseldorf and Hamilton (Bermuda); marketing organisations established in South Africa and the Far East.

The big increase in sales outlets called for bigger production—and more floor space in places where there was the labour to fill it. Another two-and-a-half acres had been bought on the Tweedside Trading Estate, outside Berwick alongside the existing branch factory in October 1966. A 18,500 sq ft extension to Rodono Mill costing £70,000 was begun in May 1968, and a 24,600 sq ft extension to Glebe Mill in June, which was completed in the end of November. In February 1969, a small factory was leased from the Berwick County Council at Earlston to the north of Hawick, where the main employer had just closed his tweed mill. To start with, they put young women and girls there for trimming and finishing knitwear, but then took on older women as well, some 20 or so, to give a more even distribution of opportunity. Mrs Agness Greenhill was brought in to stat a training programme and then Miss Margaret Scott was appointed resident instuctor supervisor.

Similar work was undertaken in another 20,000 sq ft workshop opened on the Houston Industrial Estate at Livingstone, ten miles from Edinburgh, in May 1969 for 25 trainees soon raised to more than a hundred, with instructors from Hawick and Berwick-on-Tweed. Another 100,000 sq ft factory employing several hundred was planned in the same area. Bruce Mactaggart and Stuart Beaty presided over the opening of a new factory in the new town of Cumbernauld in September 1969 for skirt making. By this time, the company had 491,860 sq ft of floor space, of which 215,500 was at Rodono and 158,000 at Glebe.

Merging with Dawson coincided with Pringle's top management reaching retirement age—or 'retiral' as they say. In December 1968, Otto Weisz, the Austrian who had come from Vienna 35 years before and given Pringle knitwear its first sense of design and fashion, and been indefatigable in his sales missions to every country of the world, indicated that he wished to leave early in 1969, and in February he retired and went to live in the Channel Islands. Ernest Tait, financial director, retired in the same month after 31 years with Pringle, but retained his seat on the Board as a non-executive director, retiring finally in January 1970. While remaining on the Board, William Mactaggart gave up his position as joint managing-director in July 1968. Bruce Mactaggart, who had become a director together with Stuart Beaty and Alan Hopkirk in 1964, was appointed managing-director from March

Vogue editorial:
Gold medalist at the Montreal olympics star David Wilkie (1977)

80s fashion–four examples:
Layered geometrics (1980s)

Nostalgia for 'Old school' establishment

1, while his father continued as chairman and an executive member of the Board. Willie Mactaggart finally retired as chairman in July 1970 at the age of 63, and handed over to Alan Smith. Joining the company, as seen, in 1925 as a 19-year-old trainee, he had transformed the company. Few would dispute that if one man can be said to have made the Pringle of 1970, it was Willie Mactaggart. The men and women of every nationality who cherished the possession and wearing of a Pringle jumper or pullover as something out-of-this-world in comfort and luxury were in the debt of this resourceful, energetic and good-humoured man, the most dogged, untiring persevering adventurer of them all.

Producing high-quality knitwear however was a more down-to-earth operation than the word 'adventure' might imply. Nothing was left to chance. As will be seen later in this chapter, all was carried out according to a strict timetable.

But of course one man never makes an enterprise of this size and complexity. He inspires, guides and coaxes it; he sets the pace and the tone. But in the clothing business, he is led—by fashion.

In 1970 Stuart Beaty and his team of five designers of ladies' knitwear at Rodono Mill did not see themselves as fashion leaders—this was for the couturiers. They did not strain after novelty. It was a question rather of constantly maintaining the right balance in terms of the changing fashion silhouette—or at least not to go counter to the line of the moment. When skirts were long, to keep the right proportion, to maintain the balance prescribed by all that was meant by 'good taste', sweaters had to be shorter. When the whole female figure dripped downward towards the feet with trousers, then the sweater needed to be longer. Colour sense grew out of experience. It was easier to predict the direction in which colours were *not* going to move, than to know what they would be. Changes went in cycles. The very amount of fabric used and its general look—bulky, slim, stark, soft—inspired a certain kind of colour. Apart from this, in certain overseas markets many colours were out because the wearers were so sallow skinned.

Before Otto Weisz came to Pringle in the 1930s there were designs for hand-knit patterns, but so far as the mechanical knitting firms were concerned, the frame foreman was the designer. It was engineering design, not aesthetic design. There was no question then of balancing the proportion of a shoulder in relation to the depth of a ribbed skirt. If the finished product looked gross, no one cared particularly; couture standards were not applied. By 1934/5, when Otto Weisz produced Pringle's pioneer collection of 'dressmaker' sweaters, it was realised that perhaps design could sell and was not just a luxury. Knitwear needed designing just as much as blouses did.

The lesson was learnt—and had never been forgotten—that knitwear was a fashion commodity or nothing at all. Stuart Beaty's favourite description of the task of the fashion designer was the one given by Owen of Lachasse, 'working towards the fulfilment of an unknown desire'.

'By this of course,' said Beaty, 'he meant that the designer must commit his thoughts and his company's machinery to a course of action, the rightness or wrongness of which will only be known when, many months later, the customer sets, or fails to set, her seal of approval on his efforts. In other words, she either desires or does not

Layered geometrics and gilt details

Natural look

149

desire what is presented to her, and it is the designer's responsibility to ensure that in the majority of cases the customer simply cannot resist what she sees, even although she did not know what she was looking for when she entered the shop.'

Stuart did not place the knitwear designer on the same plane as the big names of *haute couture*.

It is given to them to create without restriction, but I regard myself as an industrial designer fated to work within the disciplines of our knitting machines and their full-fashioned process of increasing and decreasing width mechanically at pre-set points on the knitting. It is further conditioned by the fact that it takes anything up to six months from the spinning of the yarn to the delivery of the finished sweater, which means there must be a certain timelessness about our designs. It would be folly for us to strain after achieving complete up-to-dateness within the bounds of this inescapable timetable, and when fashion trends are liable to change every six days let alone six months. Furthermore, concentrating as we do at Pringle mainly on the conversion of cashmere and fine natural woollen fibres, the purchaser expects a garment which is more of an investment than a passing whim, to have a longer sojourn in her wardrobe than its less expensive neighbours.

Geometrics in hand intarsia:
Fashion in the 1980s was symbolised by a stylised glamour

It is largely a matter of applying the proportions constant in nature to such considerations as the depth of a neckline in relation to the overall length, the balance between the ribbed and plain parts of a sweater, the scale of the button, the curve or straightness of the silhouette. But it all has to be conceived within the narrow confines of a basically simple garment such as a pullover with its neck, arms and waist, and knowing that the trimming, the collar or any other part which the designer dreams up, is dictated by the limitations of the machine which will make them. It is the less successful designer who attempts to impose his will on the machine. The good knitwear designer will build his garments only with components which he knows each machine is capable of making. He seeks to create a piece of clothing which will be admired, not for any single feature, but for the logic of its construction as a complete and perfect piece of knitting.

Retro chic

For him every garment started with a basic shape, the body. Each variation was designed to fulfil a purpose or need, and was adjusted to the fashion silhouette of the time. Bouffant skirts called for short sweaters gripping at the waist. The Sweater Girl films from the United States had created a demand for tight fitters.

But designing as we do, not just for British tastes but for the world, we have to take note of the wide divergence, as might be expected, between what pleases a customer in Switzerland and one in California, one in Hong Kong or Australia. Our operation consists in putting together

150

collections tailor-made for each market to which we sell.
Its planning not only has to allow for the fact that nature's
seasons in the southern hemisphere is out of phase with
those in the north, but that the time of the fashion 'seasons',
two or three a year, differ from one country to another.
Added to this, of course, it is all projected very many months
in advance. The sense of timelessness comes fairly easily! To
help us sort out the needs of each market we all pay frequent
visits abroad, observing, talking with and listening to buyers,
customers, critics, other designers.

Considerations of colour, though less complicated than those of styling,
were, for Stuart Beaty, however, the start point of the design operation.
Colour for the knitwear designer meant yarn. In 1970, like other
Hawick firms, Pringle bought both cashmere and woollen yarn from
the spinners. Arthur Oddy's idea of setting up a spinning mill for
Pringle's exclusive use in 1943 was never followed up. (Oddy, who
had been managing-director of Ballantyne up to April 1968, died on
April 10, 1969.)

But though Pringle did not spin their own yarn they did specify
the colours and shades they wanted. The dyeing took place during the
processing in Britain of the raw wool which has been shorn from the
lamb in Australia or brushed from the goat in China. The designer had
to choose what colour he wanted 12 months in advance of the season
in which the garment would be offered for sale.

His task was eased by people called the French Colour Forecasters,
whose job was to correlate the colour choice of all the important fashion
houses, so that, when the time came, all manufacturers, independent
though they might be, would supply colours which complemented one
another. This made it easier for a woman to buy the correct matching
handbag or shoes. Such predictions, however, could only be a guide.
Since cashmere had its own unique qualities of softness and luminosity,
the rules did not always apply. It was mostly left to Pringle's own
experience to determine the families of colour best suited to it.
A material as soft as cashmere would rarely be right in a harsh colour.

Having taken all the advice and read all the omens, the moment
came when a particular colour in the spectrum had to be ordered, and
it was impossible to put a name or code number to it, since it was new!
The only way was to submit an object of a certain colour and say
'Match this!' Objects assembled by the Design Department for such a
purpose had been strange and various. One of Pringle's most beautiful
'ivory' shades was copied from a piece of string, a gorgeous brown
from the wrong side of a piece of leather, a best selling 'green' from a
tattered scrap of faded blotting paper. By 1970 Pringle's reputation for
good design was based not on individual style but on their capacity to
keep on producing day after day, year in year out, endless variations on
a classic and neo-classic theme so that their knitwear always belonged
to the particular age of the moment.

Stuart Beaty admitted:

Although Pringle tries to appeal to as many people as possible
we cannot please everyone. The styles with the highest design
content were invariably the ones which were at the same time

Boxy cut knits with shoulder
pad power

Batwing is back from the 1950s

151

Buffalo girl and modernist man

most liked by one group of people and equally disliked by another section. Some say that the future of full-fashioned knitting lies in tucks, in textures and in patterning generally.

To me the whole point of fashioning is not about surface, but about shape and the ability to retain that shape once it has been knitted. Surface effects are possible in almost all other fabrics apart from knitting, but there is something unique and special about the full-fashioned process whatever the superficial colour or texture. We aim to pinpoint the unique character of knitting that distinguishes it from all other fabrics, not to try and copy their textures and effects. Knitting stands on its own two respected feet. It has no need to lose its very splendid identity by masquerading as anything else.

As soon as one departs from the simple block shape of the familiar classic, the full-fashioned process begins to demonstrate its superiority. It is easy to cut fabric into a tube and call it a skinny sweater and allow the wearer to give it any shape it may assume. The subtler the shape the greater the need to have the garment retain it after cleaning, which is not one of the strong attributes of the cut garment. Apart from such technicalities, for some years now there has been a noticeable return to a craving for quality, probably a belated reaction to all the expensive rubbish thrown together in the early days of Carnaby Street and the King's Road boutique.

152

Men were not as fashion conscious as women—in 1970 at any rate—and did not feel it necessary to jump so quickly to keep up with changes in fashion as women did. There was nonetheless a men's fashion cycle; in 1970 the shaggy look was out and the tight look in. It was the job of the member of Stuart Beaty's design team in charge of men's wear to watch it and interpret it. Few men cared whether a garment was full-fashioned or cut, but went for colour and style. It was reckoned they wanted light, bright clothing for the evening and for week-ends which could be easily laundered in the home washing machine or sent to the cleaners. The men's design team at Glebe Mill created separate styles for the United States, South Africa, Hong Kong, as well as Britain and Europe.

Purveyors of apparel had to suit not only gender but race. And it was no simple task, considering the complexity of the manufacturing process.

Yarn for Pringle knitwear was ordered 16 weeks ahead. Delivery was normally promised within 14 weeks of the order being placed, and two weeks were needed for sorting and checking. In 1970 there was no standard method of accounting for yarn, either for its weight or circumference, or for how level or even it was. There was something called the Bradford Worsted Count which, for a reason which must be known to someone, was the standard weight of 560 yards of yarn. But there was also something called a Yorkshire Skein which was the weight of 256 yards of yarn, to say nothing of the Gala Cut and others. These were known generically as 'the count'. With the approach of metrification, an effort was made to bring the various methods together

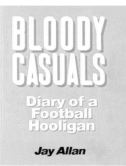

80s street fashion:
'The casual' Pringle was de riguer for the football hooligans in a bid to look respectable (1983)

under a single international count known as Tex, which was arrived at by the simple (?) process of dividing whatever figure the Worsted Count gave into 885.8. Jim Chalmers, yarnstore manager at Rodono Mill in 1970, wished such efforts the best of luck, for their success would greatly simplify his job of recording what yarn he took in and making sure he had received what he ordered.

There was a delivery of yarn to Rodono Mill every day, neatly wound on cones to fit the machinery on which they would be used. Every new batch was tested for 'count'—Pringle used the Bradford Worsted Count, in which the number increased as the wool became finer, and down as it became heavier. Spot tests were taken for moisture content. Six per cent of its weight should be natural oil and water—it is 'greasy' as they say. The whole of the first part of the manufacturing process took place with the wool in its greasy state, though well before the end it had lost it completely. On an average, 1,000 lb a month of one shade was delivered over a nine month 'season'. Cashmere yarn came from Kinross; Shetland and lambswool yarn from Selkirk.

As previously shown, 'Lambswool' was wool sheared from a lamb which was between 11 and 12 months old—the 'first year clip'. Since this was done in the warm climes of Australia, the animal did not feel the loss of his coat as it would have done if it was taken from him in Scotland where lambs are born in March when it can still be distinctly cold. As a lamb gets older, so its woolly coat gets less fine. Its second year clip, therefore, comes into a separate category and is known as 'Merino' or 'Botany'. This is spun in the worsted way, combing the raw wool before spinning so that all the fibres are smoothed down and faced in the same direction. These very fine wools, produced after an Australian lamb's first and second year, are suitable for knitting, but wool produced in subsequent years is only suitable for making blankets and carpets. What is designated 'Shetland' wool is the second year clip of lambs from the Shetland Islands and the North of Scotland, whose wool by the nature of their breeding is heavier than that of the Australian merino sheep. Pringle required a high price for their garments and one of the things the purchaser should expect in return was attention to detail. The high cost of Pringle garments in 1970 was due to a large extent to the expensive quality of the material from which they were made. Quality control made sure that what they called the 'handle', and the spinning of every batch of yarn bought in, were up to the standard Pringle was asking its customers to pay for, and their advertising led them to expect.

From every new batch of yarn, a test garment was knitted which had to pass muster with the knitting frame manager, while the yarnstore manager satisfied himself that there was no variation of shade between one batch and another, both labelled, for instance, 'Chameau Beige'. With 700 shades, differences within one red or grey were infinitesimal

In 1970 Bruce Mactaggart, the managing-director, announced that in future the range of Pringle men's wear would have to be even more diversified, as people were looking for more fashionable merchandise in a field which so far had been primarily 'classic' business. A successful innovation in 1970 was the introduction of a range of boys' knitwear which created great interest when shown for the first time at the Men's and Boy's Wear exhibition at Harrogate.

80s Sports fashion two examples:
Pastel power graphic

Geometric cashmere

153

Production of a greater variety of diverse styles was aided by the commissioning in August 1970 of an ICL 1901A computer. Following its initial use for the acceptance and confirmation of orders, it was later programmed to keep track of work as it flowed through the factories. This enabled points where delays occurred to be pinpointed immediately. All worklines came to be printed by computer.

A new order acceptance routine brought greater control during the critical bunched sales periods of the spring and autumn when the volume of orders overtaxed the manual capacity to handle them. All ladies' and men's orders were computerised for the autumn season of 1971. As soon as the first two systems were working, it was proposed to program the computer for such activities as the control of stocks of yarn and of finished garments. The new Information Technology was firmly harnessed.

The 200th anniversary of the founding of the Hawick knitwear industry by John Hardie which fell in 1971 found commercial competition between all but one of the leading Knitwear companies in the town virtually eliminated. In April 1970, Joseph Dawson (Holdings) had acquired from a group called Scottish Border Cashmere Limited three of their subsidiaries, Braemar Knitwear Ltd of Hawick and Arbroath, the former Innes Henderson founded in 1868 and incorporated in 1920; The Ballantyne Sportswear Company Ltd of Innerleithen and Galashiels of which Michael Oddy, Arthur's son, was managing-director; and The Ballantyne Spinning Company Ltd, also of Innerleithen (one of whose mills was sold at the end of 1970). The acquisition cost Dawson four million pounds. Scottish Border Cashmere was a subsidiary of William Baird & Company.

Thus the makers of Pringle, Braemar, Ballantyne, Barrie, McGeorge and Glenmac knitwear, with an annual turnover of more than £11 million, of which £6 million was export, had all become subsidiaries of the same Dawson group of which Alan Smith was chairman and managing-director. The group also still owned Todd & Duncan and other knitwear yarn spinners, and the Bradford wool processors, Joseph Dawson, which became a public company in 1950. Pringle of Scotland's articles of association were altered to make it once again a private limited company. As Alan Smith said in his letter to his company's shareholders about the Braemar-Ballantyne acquisition, the Dawson group had won for itself a position of outstanding strength in the markets of the world. All of it was going to be needed in the situation in which the group immediately found itself.

By the end of 1970 conditions in the textile industry were described by Alan Smith as the worst since the war. Profit before taxation of Joseph Dawson (Holdings) for the six months ended May 31, 1970 were £528,000 compared with £1,585,000 in the first half of 1969. None of the new knitwear acquisitions had of course begun to contribute. But 'the setback in demand for high-class knitwear in the major markets, the United Kingdom and North America,' wrote Alan Smith in his interim statement, 'has been of exceptional severity, reflecting the economic squeeze common to both areas and aggravated by an unusual degree of fashion uncertainty. In turn this has led to a major de-stocking movement seriously affecting sales of yarn and basic materials.'

154

Faldo signs his first contract:
(1981)

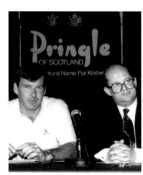

Faldo signs for a second time:
Nick Faldo and Graham Haywood sign a new contract in 1991

Signed contract:
Faldo's new ten year contract signed on Wednesday 22nd May 1991 at Wentworth Golf Club, Surrey

As far as Pringle was concerned, 1969 order books had been so full many deliveries had been late, and there had been cancellations which meant carrying over into 1970 a much larger quantity of merchandise than usual. Added to this was the 'fashion uncertainty' to which Alan Smith referred—whether skirts of mini, midi or maxi length would be in demand—which made store buyers reluctant to place large orders.

'We are living in fast changing times,' wrote Alan Smith in the Pringle Annual of 1970, 'and fashion particularly is tending to change much more frequently—indeed in as little as five or six months. In order to meet this, we can no longer accept time cycles of 16 or 17 weeks for knitting a sweater. We must be able to produce quickly and efficiently in order to meet these fashion changes and also to meet the very intense competition on price, not only from manufacturers in this country but from overseas.'

The theme was taken up by Bruce Mactaggart,

With fashion changing so rapidly it is vital that our customers have the right merchandise in their shops at the right time, and, if we can serve their needs more quickly now, then we are certainly going to benefit. This of course is not easy for us, but we will all have to learn to become much more flexible in accepting changes as there are going to be even more changes and faster changes in fashion than in previous years. The type of knitwear which we have been producing in the past is not necessarily correct today. For example, ribbed cut-up garments are in fashion, and at present we do not necessarily have the expertise to compete with others in these fields. Our plant consists of valuable full-fashioned frames which cannot be thrown out overnight and a plant for ribbed production introduced at once. The majority of our employees are experts in finishing full-fashioned knitwear by traditional methods, but we are going to have to learn to become experts too in assembling cut-up pieces of fabric by different methods. We will have to produce smaller, but possibly more, ranges with different merchandise so that what we offer is up-to-the minute in fashion.

Two years later Pringle of Scotland celebrated the fiftieth anniversary of the end of the old co-partnery and the birth of the private company Robert Pringle & Son Ltd. In 1972 it was the sole surviving Hawick hosiery firm of the Britain of King George III and the age of Waterloo.

'The principle that to shorten human labour by mechanical skill and power,' wrote William Felkin more than a hundred years ago, 'is to increase riches and capital, and furnish more and better paid employment and consequently comforts to the artisan, has not even yet become sufficiently understood in England. In Elizabeth's time the benign light had only just begun to dawn upon a few of the more advanced minds in the nation. It was reserved for a mere incidental circumstance to furnish the first striking example in modern ages of this beneficent operation. It will be anticipated that this example was the invention of the loom capable of perfectly imitating the hand-knitter's

Nick Faldo:
Defined the 80s and 90s
for Pringle Golf
(1993)

Geometric George:
Nick Faldo Golf branding
(1990s)

155

Detail

movements and producing the like results with manifold speed.'

The Aberdeen hand-knitting exercise was an undoubted success story, but it stands alone. It inspired nothing—no new technology, no new end-products. It merely led to the making and exporting of more and more hand-knitted stockings. It never harnessed itself to the revolutionaty development that came from the persistence of the country parson at Woodborough who freed knitting from dependence on the dexterity of human hands and fingers and enabled it to become an industry different in every respect from the domestic pastime it had been before.

To whatever extent the trade owed its development to mechanics, success depended on what it was that determined how women chose their clothing. Robert Burton had a shrewd idea. In his *Anatomy of Melancholy*, written about the same time as William Lee invented the stocking frame, he surmised:

> When they show their fair hand, fine foot and leg withal,
> they set us a-longing; and so when they pull up their
> petticoats and outward garments, as they usually do to
> show their fine stockings and those of purest silken dye,
> gold fringes, laces, embroiderings, 'tis but a springe to
> catch woodcocks.

It was the factor of which Bruce Mactaggart was only too aware. He knew, however, its influence could never be assessed, even by his ICL 1901A.

156

Scotland revisited:
*Two pages of the 1999 brochure
with model Honor Fraser*

Opposite
Nick Faldo in full swing:
*Golfing icon Faldo enjoyed a
long association with Pringle*

16

FOR SMART GENTS
AS WELL AS STYLISH LADIES

Not just sportswear but colourful, attractive, fashionable leisurewear for every social occasion.

I n Hawick's bi-centenary year of 1971, Stuart Beaty and his team
of Pringle of Scotland designers of ladies' knitwear at Rodono Mill
did not regard themselves as fashion leaders.

That was for the couturiers. They did not strain after novelty.
It was a matter of maintaining the right balance in terms of the
changing fashion silhouette—or at least not to go counter to the line
of the moment. When skirts were long, to keep the right proportion,
to maintain the balance prescribed by all that was meant by Good Taste.

Their market was now widespread, and their marketeers had
to cater for a highly varying range of conditions. As seen, in 1966
they had opened a shop in Vienna, in 1968 in Dusseldorf, in 1969
in Amsterdam; in that year also shops for customers in the Far East
with very different ideas of what was attractive in Tokyo and Hong
Kong, along with one in Hamilton, Bermuda, where customers would
wish to keep to the American fashion.

The next year 1972, they were celebrating the fiftieth anniversary
of the end of the old co-partnery and Robert Pringle & Sons incorporation
as a private company. Such changes to corporate structure and the rapid
expansion from 150 to 2,000 employees in 40 years in no way changed
the 'happy family' tradition of a community of workpeople engaged on
a craft with the ancient lineage of framework knitting, which since 1967
had been part of the all-embracing textiles group Dawson International.

It was up to the Pringle management to plough their own furrow
within the Dawson group and, with its help, achieve the enlargement
they were always aiming for, and the increase in their share of the
market. To this end they took full part in any activity by the government
designed to promote British knitwear in home and overseas markets

159

Opposite
Lily Donaldson:
*Up-and-coming super model washes
her cashmere with Pringle cashmere
pearls in the autumn and winter 2004
advertising campaign*

such as that of the Marketing Action Group of the hosiery and knitwear industry's National Economic Development Committee, at whose 1970 Harrogate conference Pringle had a high level delegation.

Associated Industrial Consultants predicted in July 1970 that total sales of the UK knitwear manufacturers should show an increase of seven per cent a year up to 1973, and four per cent up to 1978. This was due, they said, to the growing population plus the swing from woven to knitted fabrics. Knitwear 'is decidedly a growth industry' but, they warned, imports of knitwear were increasing. Forty-five percent of them were from Developing Countries. They suggested that with Britain's entry into the European Common Market, there should be overall scope for doubling or even trebling exports.

The 200th anniversary in 1971 found commercial competition between all but one of the leading knitwear companies in the town virtually eliminated and, as has been explained in the last chapter, conditions in the textile industry were alarming.

The Glebe:
Knitting machines
(2002)

JOSEPH DAWSON SLUMPS BADLY

A newspaper headline in 1971. Although poor figures were expected, they said, the actual results were a shock. Their £28 million 16-month sales had produced a pre-tax 12-month profit of only £392,000

The 'vigorous and enterprising' way the Pringle management tackled the challanges of the changing times was widely admired. As a Glasgow newspaper reminded its readers, remaining in the forefront of the fashion trade was a task which only the progressive and enterprising could achieve.

Wool cones at the Glebe:
The Glebe mill home to Pringle
from 1976 to the present day

One great opportunity which they recognised and grasped with both hands was in the world of Golf. For a long period Pringle's name was firmly associated with the royal and ancient Scottish game. The company's first male knitwear was a three-button shirt which was bought by the PGA and became the Ryder Cup Shirt which golfers purchased in large numbers from the professionals' shops at their club. As the game's popularity grew, so did the demand for golfing knitwear and in a short time the Pringle brand was selling all over the world—made of cashmere, lambswool, Shetland and merino in fresh colours, fresh styles.

Now it was said the days of any old sweater for golf were over. Not just the regulation pink, lime and orange, but co-ordinated outfits in every colour under the sun were the rage. Pringle of Scotland and Golf were now inseparable. In 1961 they decided to sponsor their own annual golf tournaments, at Carnoustie, at Edinburgh's Barnton course, at Royal Lytham—culminating with their taking over the sponsorship of the Seniors' Championship of Great Britain.

The most effective shop window for Pringle Golfwear at this time was the renowned British champion Nick Faldo who had turned professional at the age of 19. The firm signed him up in 1981 to represent its golf clothing for three years. He went on to win 39 tournaments and in 1989 they launched the Nick Faldo Sports Collection of leisurewear for both. The Faldo connection was so successful that he was given a 10-year contract.

The move to golfwear meant the downgrading of what was widely regarded as Pringle's exclusive concern with ladies dresswear. It was driven by young men whose interests were very different from that of

160

their parents—pop music, swift air travel, washing machines and cheap dry cleaning, different social habits and conventions, short working hours and higher earnings. It turned their attention to what they should wear at home, away, on special occasions and partying. As the Pringle designer Wallace Shaw wrote in a *Pringle Bulletin*, 'What could be more suitable than a fabric which gives both warmth and stretch, allowing its wearer both comfort and ease. Knitwear for men has to serve more requirements than that of merely something to pull on inconspicuously as the weather gets cold.'

The mainstream female market was kept alive and enhanced by the way the stars of showbusiness fell for what Pringle had to offer off-stage. Their high profile ensured plenty of top rank stars, such as the Scot Moira Shearer wearing her Pringle Minto twinset, were given full prominence in the press. Before embarking on their 1950s tour of America and Canada, members of the Sadlers Wells Ballet Company spent time in Pringle's London showroom at 12a Savile Row choosing knitwear to take with them. At the start of their tour, the firm's New York organisation Pringle Johnston Imports Ltd invited Ninette de Valois, the founder of Sadlers Wells, and Robert Helpmann, as guests of honour, along with ballerinas Margot Fonteyn, Beryl Grey and others, to a luncheon, after they viewed the new Pringle export range. It was all good publicity.

Then the Gala Fashion Presentation which they gave in London's Savoy Hotel in 1968 in the presence of HRH Princess Margaret (who had made several visits to the mills at Hawick), brought the public's attention to what Pringle had to offer young people in the UK, ski-ing, yachting and particularly golfing.

To help morale within the company a series of so-called Education Boards were posted in every mill and factory with a variety of headlines such as:

LIVING LIFE LA DOLCE VITA SCOTTISH STYLE

Eccentric personalities, who live life in a reckless manner but can't fully escape their good breeding, dress with one foot in traditional richness and the other in contemporary freedom. This strategy will firmly plant the Pringle brand back in Scottish soil among families with 15 generations of credibility. It will help keep the brand young, hip and authentic to its heritage.

ADDING VALUE TO YOUR PRODUCT

Staff were encouraged to invite visitors to their factory and to advise their product range and manufacture.

Once people realise the amount of work that goes into the making of a garment, and how many hands touch a single sweater, the perceived value of the product will greatly increase. If your luxury customer is willing to pay £500 for the ultimate two-ply black cashmere crewneck, they don't want to see the same brand of sweater purchased for £40 being worn in the High Street. They want to see their

David Beckham:
Bought his classic Pringle sweater in Selfridges
(2002)

Golfing girl:
Image from advertising campaign
(2002)

161

Kilt boy:
(Spring/Summer 2003)

friends wearing it at private parties. Luxury customers will
invest in heirloom quality garments if they can be worn
from season to season transcending the whims of fashion.
By using an established Scottish Borders family such as the
Pringles of Torwoodlee as inspiration, the correct flavour
of the collection will be reached—a collection based on
heritage, good breeding and the ultimate in good taste.

In 1962 Queen Elizabeth and the Duke of Edinburgh visited Hawick
and were given a private showing by members of the Hawick Hosiery
Manufacturers Association. The Queen was of course already well
acquainted with all that Pringle of Scotland stood for—her mother had
been a customer since 1937.

The firm had faithfully moved with the times through all these
years, but by the 1970s it seemed that it needed some other guiding
star to take it through the coming decades. Still beholden to Dawson,
the forward march was no longer as sure footed as it had been of
yore. The time had arrived for a major change of direction.

In 1976 Rodono Mill had become too expensive to run, and the
machinery was transferred to Glebe Mill, and the administration to
Victoria Mill. The volume of trade remained high, with 21 million
garments being turned out in Hawick and Berwick, 70 per cent of
which was exported, and in 1979 the company was given the Queen's
Award to Industry for Export Achievement, and again in 1983 and
1991. It all helped that Bruce MacTaggart took it upon himself to
acquire some practical experience in retailing by spending two months
behind the counter at B. Altman & Co's shop in New York over the
Christmas rush.

In 1984 annual turnover was up to £29 million, and the following
year they opened a new factory at Arbroath, with Pringle now producing
60,000 units a week. Steady customer Princess Anne took herself to
Glebe Mill in the summer of 1988, and five years later launched the
Pringle Autumn Collection at a gala presentation and banquet in the
National Gallery of Scotland; Princess Alexandra visited the Pringle
shop in Vienna and in 1993 Pringle sponsored the Edinburgh–Kiel
Yacht Race. On the surface and as the company moved its head office
from London to Scotland all looked set for as bright a future as its
remarkably successful past. However, forecasted in 1974, not long
after Dawson's acquisition of Pringle, the textile industry throughout the
world went into recession and continued to cause problems—faltering
economies, three day weeks, fuel shortages and everything that conspired
to make business more difficult.

Change became inevitable as the world celebrated the new
millennium. Pringle of Scotland's fortunes were at a low ebb, the
estimated turnover had fallen to below £ 10m and the company in
dire need of help. For anyone considering a take-over,
this was the moment. It was not now or never, but as Shakespeare
wrote, there is a tide in the affairs of men which taken at the flood
leads on to fortune, omitted and all the voyage of their life is bound
in shallows and miseries. Changing tack in an old established enterprise
such as Pringle of Scotland would never be plain sailing; it called for
determination and imagination of the highest order. Enter Kim Winser.

When Jorn Madslien, the BBC Online business reporter, talked

162

Handkerchief invitation:
*First London catwalk show
(2003)*

Sophie Dahl:
*Button print cashmere,
photographed by Jonathon Bookallil
(Spring / Summer 2003)*

Real men wear pink:
*photographed by Jonathon Bookallil
(Spring / Summer 2003)*

about the Pringle transformation from golf jumper manufacturer to hot fashion designer, he opened by saying, 'Meet Kim Winser, a woman whose visions of the future are both entertaining and impressive—and obviously totally unrealistic.'

Forty-five-year-old Ms Winser, who is Scottish, was born in Helensburgh on the Clyde in 1959. She joined Marks & Spencer from school in 1977 as a management trainee and was given the senior positions of Executive of Menswear and Divisional Director of their Women's Wear group. She created M&S's first marketing group, and held senior positions overseas with Brooks Brothers and the M&S Canadian business.

One day on a visit to Edinburgh in 2000 she had dinner with a gentleman she had known and respected for many years called Kenneth Fang who was chairman of the Hong Kong company S.C. Fang Brothers Knitwear Ltd. 'He said to me,' she told Madslien, "Would you run Pringle of Scotland if I bought it?"

'I was not sufficiently familiar with the current Pringle business to give him an immediate answer although I very much liked the idea of working with Kenneth, a gentleman of such integrity and skill,' she says, 'and told him I would like time to consider.'

I set about discovering all I could about a name, which I only knew about in a general sort of way, before making up my mind. Within no time I confirmed my first reaction that this was the chance of a lifetime. What a story! How could I turn down an offer to head an enterprise which had played so significant a part in the world of fashion, beginning as an underwear maker and going on to making very substantial changes in the ladies' wardrobe with innovations such as the knitted corset; and high-quality clothing for men, with the perfect 'Windsor' car coat at a time when fashionable women had started to drive around in motor cars. It had been one of the first brands to make cashmere outer clothing; it designed and developed the pattern which was an attempt to knit tartan for Edward Prince of Wales. This eventually developed into the intarsia pattern known to-day as the Argyle. Pringle had been at the forefront of the Sweater Girls glamour look in Hollywood in the 1950s. They were all wearing Pringle body-hugging twinsets and small sweaters, mostly in cashmere. Pringle had revolutionised men's clothing when dressing Noel Coward, playwright, actor, socialite, in pink cashmere. That turned some heads! In the 1950s when knitted outer clothing was just becoming the thing to wear, Pringle registered the name 'Knitwear'.

The idea became irresistible. How could she possibly fail to go along with such an intriguing a tide that had happened to flood in her direction? It was unlikely another opportunity as exciting or challenging as this would ever come her way. To give a new face to the old-fashioned discounted image then represented by the name of Pringle was not just a matter of change but metamorphosis. The treatment had to make Pringle 'cool' again, to be quality once more. It had to reflect its former

Backstage:
*London fashion week
Spring/Summer 2003 show*

Jodie Kidd:
*London fashion week Spring/Summer
2003 show*

163

Sophie Dahl:
*Recreates sweater girl glamour
photographed by Jonathon Bookallil
(Spring/Summer 2003)*

glory but in a style that was wholly relevant to the 21st century. The new brand image was vital—determining whether the revitalised enterprise would sink or swim.

The business had become a factory, no longer a brand. Indeed in 2000 the factory no longer manufactured Pringle sweaters, mostly discounted wool sweaters for the lower markets. The company that had brought cashmere to outer clothing, which became a favourite of the late 19th century aristocracy, no longer undertook cashmere production of any kind. In place of dressing the most famous of Hollywood's film stars, they were reduced to making nothing but the garb that golfers pulled over themselves in which to walk round the 18 holes of their local golf club.

The once innovative company no longer exported goods outside the UK except for a small amount of basic wools to the German markets. It was obvious to Kim that the brand needed repositioning; the structure and logistics dramatic readjusting. The company of the year 2000 had to be closed and a new company, reflective of its proud past, had to take its place.

Likewise Kenneth Fang was in no doubt whatsoever of Kim Winser's ability to effect the transformation without which he knew his purchase of Pringle would be money down the drain. And when she accepted his offer, he knew the risks he had taken in embarking on such a venture were reduced to a minimum. In 2000 Fang Brothers purchased the whole of Pringle of Scotland from Dawson International, and the loss-making group was withdrawn from the stock market.

Kim Winser resigned from M&S, and took over as chief executive, under Kenneth Fang as chairman, determined to lose no time in restoring the company's brand position by whatever means possible—and seemingly impossible. No holds barred. While doing so, she made sure the Pringle family were kept in the new picture, establishing a relationship with the younger members still living on the Borders of Scotland at Torwoodlee. James Pringle takes part in many of new Pringle's key social events, and now and again holds photo-shoots on his land. For Kim Winser and her colleagues, although the Pringle family are no longer involved in running the company, the link is a warm relationship.

Pringle had sadly become a UK only business with virtually no exports. Nothing less than a courageous, overall clean sweep would clear the company from the slough into which the previous management had let it drop. She cancelled most of the firm's long-standing licensing agreements with factories around the world, sales to mid-market retailers and 90% of all existing accounts. She headhunted top designers to re-invent what some had come to regard as Pringle's somewhat old-fashioned image, with new fashion ranges. In reviewing what equipment to purchase from the previous owners, Kim noticed that in the factory where they had once made Pringle cashmere they had covered over all their intarsia knitting machines which made the famous Argyle pattern in 1920 and was no longer fashionable. She asked them what they would charge for them. It seemed to her to be virtually nothing, so the company bought them all. They restored the factory to its former role of making cashmere sweaters which soon became in great demand from top stores all over the world.

She had no hesitation in taking steps which might be considered

164

Euan McGreggor:
In special edition Lion scarf for Scottish charity CHAS photographed by Julian Dufort (2004)

Pringle boutique Japan:
In the Aoyama district opened 2003

Raspini boutique:
Florence window with design inspired by Milan catwalk show (2003)

drastic, and by some as even ruthless, and holding firm if, as a result, things did not start to move at the right pace and in the right direction. All the while she remained wholly approachable, talking to all the different people engaged in the huge range of jobs which for so long had added up to the production and marketing of the remarkably diverse and remarkably high quality range of knitwear that had made the name Pringle of Scotland so highly regarded, but for some reason had gone astray. Kim had no time for layers; for big reporting structures; she was against having people feel that at every stage they had to report. None of her 300 employees, she said, should ever feel intimidated by the fact that she was chief executive. Once they got to know her, they would find she was 'just like anyone else really'. Out of working hours, that is what she was, a working mother who went home every evening and gave her six-year-old son a bath. The ailing company was in need of a new style of management, and this is what, under Kim, it got.

She was under no illusion that re-positioning a long established company like Pringle of Scotland back on a profit-making path would come quickly or easily. Difficulty arose in the Glebe factory over the new performance pay, and they had to face and solve a major delivery problem from a new supplier. In London many changes were happening too. The lease on the Savile Row offices, home to Pringle for over 52 years, had come to an end so new offices where secured just around the corner in Mayfair's Grafton Street. A small marketing team was created, Davina Payne who, straight from university, started on a six week placement and stayed five years and was crucial to Pringles' reinvention. Winser knew it was important with so much change that Pringle employees should be kept fully informed and Davina suggested re-introducing the Pringle Bulletin. So after a gap of 30 years the Bulletin returned, with news and views from every area of the business. Her Christmas Message for 2001 asserted that they had made a careful but well delivered start to their retail business. They opened the first ever flagship store in London's Bond Street, and a new local store in Hawick. Kim Winser set off on a Far East business trip on which she discussed with the chairman Kenneth Fang a five-year strategic plan, in which the priority was to restore Pringle's position as a luxury brand, cut the losses and then start making money. To this end they committed a substantial investment to see them through the tough time that lay ahead. The focus would be on excellent quality, design-led products, for which they brought in Stuart Stockdale who had worked for Romeo Gigli in Italy and as Head Designer for Jasper Conran in London. His task was to develop the small rail of men's knitwear into a full fashionable collection for men's and women's wear. He not only succeeded in achieving this but, with his team of designers, and Karen Thomson with her product developers, took the collection back into the fashionable luxury design sector throughout the world. He placed Pringle for the first time on the catwalks of both London and Milan, treading triumphantly in the steps of Otto Weisz 70 years before.

Delivery on time had to become a taken-for-granted feature of the Pringle brand wherever it was available. It was also made clear to everyone in the company that their objective, in whatever capacity they served, was to increase sales—and hopefully profits—particularly internationally. They saw the first area to develop as Japan, the world's

Bond Street flagship:
A chic new store opened in 2002 designed by architects Wells Mekereth photographed by Keith Parry

Bond Street:
Ground floor women's collection (2002)

165

Bond Street.:
Exterior with antler signage

biggest consumer of luxury goods. They appointed a distribution partner—the choice was the highly regarded distributer Sann Freres with their impressive trading house Mitsui. They would take Pringle into Japan and to some of the world's greatest fashion cities with a series of retail sites, and work with Pringle to develop a 'luxury brand for the Japanese market'. They also made a drive on developing sales in the United States of America. Having dropped their basic sweaters for male golfers, Stockdale relaunched their fashion collection and returned to cashmere and better yarns. As it turned out, it was through their official sponsorship of the European Women's Solheim Cup in Minneapolis USA that in 2001 Pringle golfwear re-entered the Golf international scene. The new ownership/management's tactics were having the effect that Winser and Fang, whose son Douglas and daughter Jean were now working with Pringle, had hoped. The family's commitment to the business has echoes of the Pringle family from so many years before with each having roles which suit their experience and passion. 'The founding years since 2000 would have been impossible without Douglas,' Winser stated. In May 2002 it was reported that Kenneth Fang would contemplate floating his acquisition on the stock exchange in a few years time although, as he said, there was no need to do so yet—'Kim has enough on her plate.'

There had to be no doubt in the mind of any of those involved in so vast an enterprise—workforce, customers, salespeople—just what they would be getting from the newly owned, newly managed Pringle, and that they were revitalising it from top to bottom. Kim at once entered on a new fashionable advertising campaign. She stole brand creative director Valerie Wickes, from New York. Wickes launched a very new look Pringle with a poster of a naked girl for the hoarding of their soon-to-open flagship store in Bond Street, described by Kim as a lady dressed only in her pearls waiting to buy her twinset when the Pringle doors opened. Wickes's creative, yet strategic hand has guided the look and feel of the new Pringle. Balancing old with new across new stores, showrooms, campaigns and packaging has turned Pringle from 'knitwear label' into a 'fashion brand'. Wickes put into work a programme that reinstated the hand drawn logo and rampant lion. The 'of' in 'of Scotland' was also restored. The new labels and packaging now reflected Winser's new Pringle and a sense of pride had been rediscovered. This work was vital in building Pringle's luxury position. The new image seemed to work, the national press regularly ran features on celebrities in Pringle, which they chose to buy themselves (not paid to do so): disc jockeys, rock stars, film directors and supermodels.

Kenneth and Kim's vision was to develop the company as an internationally renowned, luxury fashion business selling aspirational merchandise. 'We will use the heritage of nearly 200 years to illustrate our expertise in knitwear and the crafted product. Our attention to style, fit, pattern and colour will be second to none. The heart of the company is luxury knitwear and the vision is to focus on this but extend it into separates, accessories and lifestyle related areas.'

To keep the new-look Pringle on the rails required tight financial control, and a great deal of reorganisation. Tracy Chapman, Head of Finance, installed a high speed data communications network linking Hawick, London and the flagship stores, capable of managing deliveries

Pink Grease by Rankin:
Rankin, Scottish photographer and publisher of Dazed and Confused, shoots Autumn/Winter 2003 campaign

Heidi Klum :
Rankin shoots modern day pin up Heidi Klum for Autumn/Winter 2003 campaign

Milan men's catwalk show:
Autumn / Winter 2005 collection designed by Stuart Stockdale

and despatches to and from all European countries, Asia and America, in preparation for the all-important international growth. Their IBM computer was up-graded, based on the Movex system. In 2003 they acquired Pringle Distribution gmbh in Germany and established a U.S. Trading Company.

Links are also maintained with the recently knighted, one-time managing-director Sir Alan Smith. When he came to London in 2002 to take part in the Bader Celebrations for Spitfire pilots, he made a point of calling on Kim Winser and shaking her by the hand. If the Pringle family were alive today, he said, they would be so proud of the way she had re-positioned the firm and was now running things. 'It is a moment I shall never forget,' says Kim.

In an effective combination of donating to charity and publicising Pringle's shift from being mainly an Autumn business to a Spring business, they worked with Ewan McGregor and CHAS, the only Scottish children's hospice, to help fund the desperately needed second hospice. At their first t-shirt launch, Ewan modelled the Pringle t-shirt, and all profits were given to CHAS. A similar exercise was later mounted for accessories and a rampant lion scarf was designed.

In February 2001 the Princess Royal opened the new Pringle Learning and Development Centre. On September 15, 2002, as Hilary Alexander reported in the *Daily Telegraph*, 'a revitalised Pringle revealed its wake-up call to the fashion world' when it staged its first catwalk show at London Fashion Week. 'Like Burberry, it took a woman to turn a fashion label that nobody with any fashion sense wanted to wear into something that Madonna, David Beckham, Claudia Schiffer and Robbie Williams will want to fill their wardrobes with.'—for gents as well as ladies to wear when they wanted to look smart and not just when they were playing golf. They made Sophie Dahl their icon in place of Nick Faldo. Under the headline JODIE PUTS TINGLE BACK INTO PRINGLE, Caroline Redley told her readers that Pringle knitwear was once a staple item of their grandad's wardrobe, but it seemed that golfing jumpers had finally made it out of the style bunker. REVAMPED PRINGLE SAYS FAREWELL TO THE FAIRWAY ran another headline.

The products which were the objects of the designers' art, the marketing staff's energy and expertise of the merchandising team, still began life in the mills and factories on the Scottish borders, controlled with all the traditional Pringle exactitude and sophistication by Colin Anderson, Head of Manufacturing at Hawick. Tight cost control was the order of the day. 'We have turned this side of our business on its head,' he said, 'investment in technology, systems and people, a new research and development facility; focusing on Europe, Asia and the USA with Wovens, Separates and Accessories and other key products in addition to the mainstream knitwear.'

The latter, embracing knitted goods such as scarves, hats, socks and gloves, became the responsibility of Karen Thomson, Head of Product Development, who embarked on global procurement with a supply chain of more than 50 top-class suppliers. The Bently intarsia machines (so nearly lost in the sale of Pringle) and the knitters that ran them now found themselves runing 24 hours a day to meet the demands of Harvey Nichols, Selfridges, Isetan in Japan, and Fred Segal in Los Angeles, some of the best retailers in the world. Corso Como, one

Sloane Street flagship:
Opening in 2003, downstairs features a golf area for men and women

Golf Advertising 2003:
Featuring golfer and creator of new wave golf mag 'Putt' magazine Greg Stogdon, photographed by Masoud

167

Sloane street ground floor:
Real Silver birch trees punctuate the space

of Milan's most desirable stores, wanted to place the new collection of Scottish cashmere in their store, within a month and outside the planned manufacturing schedule. All hands came to the pump in Hawick and by stealing time at weekends and through the night the delivery was met. 'It takes 21 hands to make a Pringle Cashmere,' said Winser. 'I am very proud of the Pringle staff in Hawick; so many have given us so much skill, commitment and dedication in this turnaround.' With the collection becoming more complicated and trading moving more internationally, two further roles where added to the Pringle board: a Head of International Sales (Susie Murray) and an internationally experienced Head of Product Merchandise (Karen Schneider).

So far as Britain was concerned, from the end of September 2002 London shoppers could see the new designs in the £10 million 'castle' Pringle opened in New Bond Street, and another at 141 Sloane Street. Many Pringle 'corners' and bars in department stores like Selfridges and Harvey Nichols were set up by another member of the newly formed Pringle team, Bill Christie, who for many years had played a key part in the development of Burberry. Not long afterwards they established a shopping precinct at Heathrow Airport's Terminal 3. All this was the royal warrant-holding manufacturer's first venture into retailing—and there could be no doubt about its luxury goods, top drawer image. The castle was opened with due ceremony by the Princess Royal, a spectacular widely publicised event. The hoarding of the Pearl Girl in her birthday suit overlooking Bond Street, to which Westminster City Councillors finally gave their approval, presented the tabloids with just the kind of naughtiness which their readers found so titillating. It was in tune with the 'savage glamour', as Stuart described it, of his latest collection. To tickle the fancy of oriental customers, a more respectable Tea and Sympathy Salon show was staged in the British Ambassador's residence in Tokyo. A flagship shop was opened in Taiwan, and stores in Milan and New York were planned. When in 2003 a second flagship was installed in Sloane Street the opening ceremony was supported by the stylish, innovative Scottish actor Ewan McGregor. Here Pringle of Scotland's royal heritage effortlessly joined hands with the brand's modern, trendy position in the 21st century world of fashion.

Kim Winser, the Fang family and the team at Pringle put the brand right back up-market where, as this story has shown, it belongs, and from which it fell only temporarily. Kenneth Fang's intuition had paid off. Otto Weisz and Stuart Beaty would have rejoiced at this 21st century emanation of all they had striven to achieve, and that so successfully, in the context of their times. In 2005 Stuart Stockdale was succeeded as Pringle's Head Designer by Clare Waight Keller, who won an MA in Fashion Knitwear at the Royal College of Art, and spent the next four years working on womenswear at Calvin Klein—later moving to Ralph Lauren menswear, finally returning to London to work at Gucci. She became Pringle of Scotland's first ever Creative Director. The expectation of Clare's new role combined with the team already in place is substantial. Pringle has been put wholly back into the luxury sector. Clare is now developing creatively the brand for the future.

In Febuary 2005 the *Herald Magazine* printed a full-page head and shoulders photo of Kim Winser whom they described as 'Europe's

AW 2004 campaign:
Danny Beauchamp in boiled and felted cashmere jacket, photographed by Jonathon Bookallil

Royal Visit to Bond street:
Princess Anne opens the New Bond Street flagship with Kim Winser (2002)

Milan 190 anniversary event:
Set in 16th-century cloisters the gardens contained archive imagery and vintage pieces from the collection September 2005

third most successful businesswoman'. She has morphed one of the best fashion labels in the world from frumpy to fabulous in less than five years, said Cate Devine who interviewed Pringle's CEO, whom she called the Helensburgh Dynamo, at Sloane Street. Pringle's trump card was its Scottishness, an increasingly precious commodity in an era of increasing mobilisation.

In September 2005 Pringle of Scotland took one of Milan's oldest theatres in which to show the fashion world the reality of the great rejuvenation about which they had read so much. The theme of the 2005 show was Rural Scotland, described as a cutting edge blend of modernity and traditional craft, smooth chiffons and textured knits, frail and rugged. Many were embroidered with the famous lion rampant and Argyle diamond, but with a new twist. It followed a previous show in Milan when the *Herald Magazine* ran an article with the headline:

PEOPLE BUY ARMANI TO LIVE THE ITALIAN DREAM.
IT'S THE SAME WITH US. THEY WANT A PART OF SCOTLAND.

Pringle of Scotland continues its journey adapting to the ebb and flow of fashion, embracing new talent and innovation. 2005 is the 190th year since Robert Pringle founded his company and a reminder of the values and determination that began the tradition of quality Scottish knitwear, still a valuable commodity in the world today. Kim Winser's dynamism has enabled Pringle of Scotland to surge ahead. By rediscovering its heritage, Pringle has found its heart and its passion once more.

Claire Waight Keller:
Creative Director September 2005

Milan show AW05 collection:
Rose hand intarsia cashmere, made at the Glebe Hawick. A piece from the 19 collection

169

CHRONOLOGICAL TABLE

AD 256	Knitting of this date discovered at Dura-Europos, Iraq.
AD 500	Knitted socks of this date discovered in Egypt.
AD 711	Arabs introduce knitting to Europe—invasion of Spain.
1488	Act of Henry VII fixes price of woollen caps at 2s 8d in England.
1527	French stocking knitters form guild.
1530	Word 'to knit' in English royal grammar.
1532	Henry VIII's Privy Purse Expenses include 8s 6d for 'nyte hosen'.
1552	English Act of Parliament mentions 'knitte hose, knitte petticotes, knitt gloves, knitte slieves'.
1564	William Lee born at Woodborough, Nottinghamshire.
1571	'Cappers Act': 3s 4d forfeit for not wearing wool cap on Sundays in England.
1578	James VI, King of Scots, begins reign on own account.
1579	William Lee matriculates at Christ's College, Cambridge.
1583	William Lee graduates at St John's College, Cambridge.
1586	William Lee comes down from Cambridge University.
1589	WILLIAM LEE INVENTS MECHANICAL KNITTING FRAME.
1598	William Lee adapts his machine to make silk stockings.
1603	Death of Elizabeth I, Queen of England.
	James VI, King of Scots, also becomes King of England, but two kingdoms retain separate parliaments and laws. 11 stocking frames built by Lee and his assistants.
1609	Cloth manufacture begun at Bonnington, near Edinburgh.
1610	Death in France of William Lee, inventor of the stocking frame.
1612	James Lee and Aston make improved frames at Thoroton.
1625	Death of James I of England and VI of Scotland; Charles I succeeds.
1633	Spinning school established at Peebles.
1641	Scottish Act of Parliament encourages manufacture of fine cloth.
1642	Civil War breaks out between King Charles and Parliament.
	Cloth factories established at Ayr, Haddington (New Mills) and again at Bonnington.
1649	Execution of King Charles.
1652	Oliver Cromwell proposes 'Commonwealth' of England and Scotland.
1656	Ordinance of Union between England and Scotland.
	Lord Protector Cromwell grants charter to sewing needle makers.
1657	Cromwell grants charter to framework knitters of London.
1661	Restoration of monarchy: Charles II (separate parliament for Scotland again).
1663	Charles II gives framework knitters of London new charter.
1681	James Stanfield and Robert Blackwood establish New Mills Cloth Manufactory at Haddington, East Lothian.
	James, Duke of York, Royal Commissioner for Scotland, visits New Mills, and gives it royal patronage.
1682	JAMES STANFIELD INSTALLS STOCKING FRAMES AT NEW MILLS (silk hose).
1684	Woollen (worsted) stockings made at New Mills.
1685	French Government revoke Edict of Nantes and withdraw protection from French Protestants; Huguenot weavers flee to Scotland.
1687	Death of Sir James Stanfield.
1688	Public auctioning of New Mills stocking frames—no bids.
	Flight of King James II; William of Orange and his wife Mary invited to become joint sovereigns of Scotland and England.
1695	Darien Scheme fails.
1700	James Dunlop petitions Scots Parliament for permission to start operating stocking frames in Edinburgh.
1700–7	Andrew Cockburn, William Williamson, Mungo Smith and Alexander Clerk and others operating stocking frames in Edinburgh.
1702	Negotiations start for Treaty of Union between England and Scotland.
1707	UNION BETWEEN ENGLAND AND SCOTLAND. £2,000 Fund established for promoting coarse wool manufacture in Scotland.
1727	Board of Trustees created to encourage Scottish manufacturers.
	8,000 stocking frames in United Kingdom.
	Death penalty for destroying frames.
1728	Hawick bailies appoint Town Treasurer as liaison with Board of Trustees.
	Board of Trustees grant Hawick's request for wool sorter and send John Scot.
1733	Spinning School set up in Hawick.
1746	British Linen Company formed in Edinburgh.

1753 14,000 stocking frames in United Kingdom.
1756 'Incorporation of Stocking-makers in Glasgow' established.
1758 Jedediah Strutt invents ribbed frame.
1767 Hawick Flood which washed up Pringle family bible.
1771 JOHN HARDIE INSTALLS FOUR STOCKING FRAMES AT 37, HIGH STREET, HAWICK.
20,000 stocking frames in United Kingdom.
1772 George Haldane brings another four stocking frames to Hawick.
Walter Pringle I marries Betty Heiton.
1774 John Dixon introduces more frames to Hawick.
1775 William Beck engaged by John Hardie at 37, High Street, Hawick.
1777 William Beck sets up on own as master hosier.
1778 David Loch reports stocking frames being operated in Sanquhar, Laurencekirk, Stirling, Dumfries and Ayr, as well as Hawick.
John Pringle, son of Walter Pringle I, born.
1779 Sheep Fair started in Hawick.
1780 John Hardie retires; business taken over by John Nixon.
John Nixon abandons custom-work and makes stockings for market.
1783 British Linen Bank opens branch in Hawick.
1785 John Bramble makes first Hawick hose in lambswool.
1786 John Dixon introduces ribbed frames to Hawick.
1788 Whisky House Mill built.
1790 William Wilson sets up as master hosier in Hawick.
1793 Statistical Account reports Robinsons have 150 stocking frames at Banff and employ 560.
Walter Pringle I marries second wife, Anny Scott.
1794 JOHN PRINGLE APPRENTICED AS STOCKING MAKER TO WILLIAM BECK.
1795 ROBERT PRINGLE I, son of Walter Pringle I by his second wife, born.
1799 Combination Law passed.
1800 John Hardie dies.
1802 Alexander Laing sets up as master hosier.
1804 William Wilson and William Watson form co-partnery.
1808 Robert Pringle I apprenticed as stocking maker to Alexander Laing.
1809 'Waldie, Pringle, Elliot & Oliver' co-partnery in existence.
1812 28,155 stocking frames in United Kingdom (1,449 in 38 places in Scotland).
Death of John Nixon.
1813 First (oil) street lighting in Hawick.
1815 FORMATION OF 'WALDIE, PRINGLE & WILSON' CO-PARTNERY.
They acquire Whisky House Mill.
Dicksons, Beattie, Laings formed.
France defeated at Battle of Waterloo.
1817 Hawick framework knitters stand out against John Scot.
1818 Waldie, Pringle & Wilson receive £150 grant from Board of Trustees.
1819 Peter Wilson leaves Waldie, Pringle & Wilson.
Waldie, Pringle & Co move from Whisky House Mill to Cross Wynd.
1822 'The Lang Stand Oot' – Hawick framework knitters strike.
1823 Robert Pringle I marries Charlotte Paterson.
William Elliot & Son formed.
1824 Repeal of Combination Law.
1825 George Waldie dies.
1826 Introduction of Broad Frame – underwear as well as stockings.
Robert Pringle I's son, William Pringle II, born.
The Drouty Year.
Bank failures; collapse of William Beck's hosiery firm.
1831 Gravenor Henson publishes *History of the Framework Knitters.*
1832 Passing of the Reform Bill.
1837 Queen Victoria begins her reign.
1840 Hawick Framework Knitters Society formed.
1842 Walter Pringle II starts apprenticeship at Cross Wynd.
'ROBERT PRINGLE & SON' comes into being.
2,605 frames in Scotland (of which 1,200 in Hawick).
48,000 frames in whole of United Kingdom.
1859 DEATH OF ROBERT PRINGLE I, aged 64.
Walter Pringle II takes over firm.

1862	Peter Wilson dies.
	ROBERT PRINGLE II born.
1868	ROBERT PRINGLE & SON MOVE TO WALTER'S WYND.
1871	Centenary of Hawick Hosiery Industry.
	Frame rent dropped.
1872–3	Strike.
1873	DOUGLAS PRINGLE born.
1878	Robert Pringle II apprenticed.
1885	Robert Pringle II becomes a partner.
1887	Robert Pringle II marries Edith Price.
1892	Pringle make spun silk underwear—and in colour.
1895	WALTER PRINGLE II DIES, aged 69.
	Pringle introduce Seamless Gore for ladies' combinations.
1897	Douglas Pringle joins as partner.
1905	First experiments with outerwear.
1906	J. Boyd Sime joins as partner.
1909	Hawick Hosiery Manufacturers Association formed.
1910	Gerald Pringle, son of Robert Pringle II, starts apprenticeship.
	Knitted Coat Department started.
1914	Britain declares war against Germany (World War I).
1915	Robert Pringle & Son celebrate centenary.
1917	Gerald Pringle killed in action on the Somme, aged 24.
1918	Armistice signed with Germany (end of World War I).
	Douglas Pringle retires.
1919	Herbert Benyon Johnstone of Barkers becomes partner.
1922	Purchase of co-partnery of Robert Pringle & Son by incorporated private company formed for purpose, 'Robert Pringle & Son Ltd'.
1923	Pringle Board decide to appoint two trainee managers, Arthur Oddy and William Mactaggart.
1924	Arthur Oddy joins.
1925	William Mactaggart joins.
1927	Pure silk stocking manufacture started ('Prinseta').
1929	J. Boyd Sime resigns; John Turnbull becomes managing director.
1931	'Rodono Splashproof' silk stockings launched; 'Slimfit' underwear promoted.
1932	William Mactaggart and Arthur Oddy appointed directors.
1933	John Turnbull resigns.
	William Mactaggart and Arthur Oddy become joint managing directors.
1934	Otto Weisz joins as designer; A. G. Chaston made a director.
1935	Maxwell Magnus becomes New York agent; Lewis Bannerman goes out to USA.
1937	Otto Weisz and George Mitchell become directors.
1938	Adam Elliott, last of the handframe knitters, dies.
1939	Ernest Tait succeeds James Watherston as secretary.
	War declared against Germany (World War II).
	William Oddy dies; Douglas Pringle dies.
1940	Pringle Johnston Imports formed to represent company in New York.
	Ladies Blouse Department started in Hawick.
	ROBERT PRINGLE II RETIRES (FEBRUARY 20).
1943	21st birthday of Pringle as a private company.
1945	Word 'knitwear' used for first time in Pringle Board minutes.
	Arthur Oddy resigns; William Mactaggart becomes sole managing director.
1946	Five year lease taken on Weensland Mill; Kelso Branch Factory opened.
1947	Ernest Tait, Maurice Turnbull and George Sinclair made directors.
1948	Robert Pringle & Son granted royal warrant to Queen Elizabeth.
	Berwick Branch Factory opened.
	Sales pass £1½ million.
1949	Clothing coupons withdrawn.
	Death of Robert Mactaggart; death of B. R. Chaston.
1950	Blouse Department closed.
	R. Stuart Beaty appointed assistant designer.
1951	Turnover reaches £1 million.
	Bruce Mactaggart, son of William Mactaggart, joins as trainee.
1952	Extension to Rodono Mill opened; Burnfoot Branch Factory opened.
	Otto Weisz appointed assistant managing director.

1953	Death of Robert Pringle II, aged 91.
	Death of J. Boyd Sime.
1954	Bentley Cotton 12-division Central Control machines installed.
1955	Automatic Rib Transfer Attachment introduced.
	2nd extension to Rodono Mill opened.
	Start made on building new branch factory at Berwick.
	'Intarsia' machines installed at Rodono Mill.
	Men's 'Ryder Cup' golf shirt introduced – beginning of men's outerwear.
1956	Pringle granted royal warrant for Queen Elizabeth II.
	Turnover £2 million.
1957	Death of George Mitchell.
1958	Company's name changed to 'Pringle of Scotland Ltd'.
	'The most difficult year of trading since the war' (chairman).
	3rd extension to Rodono Mill built.
1960	PRINGLE BECOMES A PUBLIC COMPANY.
	William Mactaggart succeeds John Wells as chairman.
1961	Turnover £2,350,000.
	Underwear Department closed.
	Scottish Cashmere Association formed.
1962	Glebe Mill, Hawick, purchased.
1963	Men's Knitwear production started at Glebe Mill.
1964	Turnover £3 million.
	Annual Pringle professional golf tournament started.
	Bruce Mactaggart, Stuart Beaty and Allan Hobkirk made directors.
1965	Otto Weisz becomes joint managing director.
1966	Adjoining premises of Walter Wilson's acquired.
	Pringle receive Queen's Award for Industry for exports.
	First experiments in silk screening patterns on knitwear.
	Another 2 acres purchased at Berwick.
	Turnover £4 million.
1967	JOSEPH DAWSON ACQUIRE PRINGLE FOR £5,800,000.
1968	4th extension to Rodono Mill; and extension to Glebe Mill.
	William Mactaggart resigns as managing director; remains chairman.
1969	Branch factories opened at Earlston, Cumbernauld and Livingston.
	Otto Weisz retires; Bruce Mactaggart appointed managing director.
1970	Alan Smith of Joseph Dawson succeeds William Mactaggart as chairman.
	Queens Award for Industry is awarded to Alan Smith by Duke of Buccleugh
1971	200th anniversary of founding of Hawick Knitwear Industry by John Hardie.
1974	Stuart Beaty retires after 34 years at Pringle.
1976	Rodono Mill retires too due to cost, all machinery moves to the Glebe Mill Hawick.
1979	Queens Award for Industry Export is achieved
1981	Nick Faldo is signed to represent Golf clothing
	Rodono is demolished
1983	Queens Award for Industry Export is recieved
1984	£29 million annual turnover
1985	A new factory in Arbroth opened to increase capacity
1988	Her Royal Highness the Princess Royal visits Pringle at the Glebe
	Nick Faldo collection is launched
1991	Nick Faldo signs new 10 year contract
1993	Awarded British Gold award for outstanding export achievment
1994	Nick Faldo visits Japan, he is one of four of the world's top 20 golfers retained by Pringle
2000	SC FANG & SONS OF HONG KONG AND KIM WINSER ACQUIRE PRINGLE WITH KIM WINSER AS CEO
2001	Nick Faldo contract closed
	Virginia James appointed Head of Design
2002	A flagship store opens on Bond Street by Her Royal Highness the Princess Royal
	Stuart Stockdale joins, Pringle shows its first women's collection at London Fashion Week
2003	Sloane Street store opens
	Pringle menswear is shown in Milan Fashion Week
2004	Actor Ewan McGregor joins Pringle to promote Lion scarf for CHAS charity
2005	190th anniversary is celebrated in Milan
	Clare Weight Keller joins as Creative Director

173

BIBLIOGRAPHY

ANDERSON, Dr.
Observations on National Industry (1777)

BECKMANN, J.
A History of Inventions and Discoveries, translated by
William Johnston. 2nd ed (London: J. Walker & Co, 1814)

BREMNER, D.
The Industries of Scotland, Their Rise, Progress and Present Condition
(Edinburgh: A & C Black, 1869)

BREWSTER, Sir D., ed.
'Chainwork', The Edinburgh Encyclopaedia, Vol V (1830), p. 721

CHALMERS, G.
Caledonia, or an Account historical and topographic of North Britain
from the most ancient to the present times (London: T. Caddell, 1807–24)

COBBETT, W.
Rural Rides (1832)

DEFOE, D.
A Tour Through The Whole Island of Great Britain, 1724–6
(published in Penguin English Library, 1971)

FELKIN, W.
A History of the Machine-Wrought Hosiery and Lace Manufactures
(London: Longmans Green & Co, 1867; reprinted by David & Charles,
Newton Abbot, 1970)

GRAHAM, H. G.
Social Life of Scotland in the 18th Century (London: A & C Black, 1901)

HARRISON, E. S.
'Cheviot Wool' Scottish Woollens, no. 20 (Edinburgh: National
Association of Scottish Woollen Manufacturers, 1939)

HARRISON, E.S.
The Rarer Wools (Elgin: James Johnston & Co, 1940)

HENDERSON, T. F.
Old-World Scotland, Glimpses of Its Modes and Manners
(London: T. Fisher Unwin, 1893)

HENSON, G.
The Civil, Political and Mechanical History of the Framework-Knitters
in Europe and America (Nottingham: Richard Sutton, Bridlesmith Gate,
1831; reprinted with the help of the Pasold Research Fund Limited,
with an extract from the unpublished second volume, by David &
Charles, Newton Abbot, 1970)

LEVEY, S.M.
'Illustrations of the history of knitting selected from the collection
of the Victoria & Albert Museum', Textile Industry, Vol 1, no. 2
(Newton Abbot: David & Charles, December 1969—now published
by The Pasold Research Fund, Edington, Wilts)

LINDESAY, R.
History of Scotland 1436–1565 (Edinburgh: 1728)

LOCH, D.
A Tour through most of the trading towns and villages of Scotland,
containing notes and observations concerning the trade, manufactures,
improvements etc of these towns and villages (Edinburgh: The Author, 1778)

MACKIE, J. D.
A History of Scotland (London: Penguin Books, 1970)

MACKINTOSH, J.
A History of Civilisation in Scotland (1896)

MURPHY, W. S., ed.
The Textile Industries (London: Gresham Publishing Co., 1936)

PRYDE, G. S
Scotland, from 1603 to the Present Day (London: Nelson, 1962)

QUILTER, J. H.and CHAMBERLAIN, J.
Framework Knitting and Hosiery Manufacture, A Practical Work
on All Branches of the Knitting Industry (Leicester: 'Hosiery Trade
Journal', 1911–14)

RIDPATH, G.
The Boreer History of England and Scotland (1776)

ROGERS, Rev. C.
Social Life in Scotland, Vol 1 (Edinburgh: W. Paterson, 1884)

SCOTT, W. R.
New Mills Company of Haddington (Scottish History Society)

SINCLAIR, Sir J., ed.
The Statistical Account of Scotland drawn up from the
Communications of the Ministers of the Different Parishes
Vol. 8, 1793: Parish of Hawick, by Reverend Robert Gillan (also
serialised in bowdlerised form as 'Old Hawick' in the Hawick
Advertiser beginning January 1906)
Vol. 19, 1797: Parish of Roxburgh, By Reverend Andrew Bell
Vol. 19, 1797: City of Aberdeen, from the communications of
several Gentlemen of that City
Vol. 20, 1798: County of Aberdeen
Vol. 20, 1798: Banff, by Reverend Abercromby Gordon

SMITH, J.
Chronicum Rusticum-Commerciale or Memoirs of Wool & Co (1747)

SWINTON, J., ed.
An Abridgement of the Public Statutes in force and use relative to
Scotland from the Union in the 5th Year of Queen Anne to the 27th
Year of his present majesty King George III, 1788

WELLS, F. A.
The British Hosiery Trade, its History and Organisation
(London: G. Allen & Unwin, 1935)

WYATT, W.
A History of Aberdeen and Banff (Edinburgh: W. Blackwood, 1900)
A Collection of the Acts of Parliament establishing and relating to the
Funds under the management of the Commissioners for encouraging,
improving and promoting Fisheries and Manufactures in the Part of
Great Britain called Scotland, 1751

SEVENTEENTH AND EIGHTEENTH CENTURY PAMPHLETS

ANON.
A Representation of the Advantage from erecting and improving
manufactories (1683)

ANON.
The State of the Nation Enquir'd into ... (1688?)

ANON.
(Patrick Lindsay) The Interest of Scotland considered ... (Edinburgh: 1736)

ANON.
Observations on the method of growing wool in Scotland
(Edinburgh: 1756)

GENT, W. S.
The Golden Fleece (1656)

HAYNES, J.
Provision for the Poor (1715)

NAISMITH, J.
Thoughts on various objects of Industry pursued in Scotland with a
view to ensure by what means the labour of the people may be directed
to promote the public prosperity (Edinburgh: 1790)

SPRUEL, J.
An Accompt Current Between Scotland and England balanced (1705)

(Note: copies of all these pamphlets are to be found in the National Library
of Scotland, Edinburgh)

HAWICK

CRAIG, R. S.
Hawick and the Border (Hawick: 1927)

MURRAY, R.
History of Hawick (Hawick: 1901)

PIGOT.
Pigot & Co's National Commercial Directory of the Whole of Scotland
and of the Isle of Man, editions of 1825 and 1837, 'Hawick'

SCOTT, R. E.
Companion to Hawick (Hawick: Tweeddale Press, 1970)

VERNON J. J. and McNAIRN, J.
Pictures from the Past of Auld Hawick (Hawick: 'Hawick News', 1911)

WILSON, R.
('Lurgie'), A Sketch of the History of Hawick (Hawick: 1825)

CAMERON, A. D.
'Border Abbeys and Agriculture in the Middle Ages', Transactions, 1954
COWAN, A. (Mrs. John Smith),
'Recollections off Hawick', Transactions, 1935
MURRAY, A. D.
Untitled paper, Transactions, 1863
OLIVER, J. H.
'Framework Knitting in Scotland from 1682 to 1770', Transactions, 1970
PEACOCK, W. T.
'Early Stockingmakers', Transactions, 1960
WATSON, D. M.
'The Board of Trustees and the Early Manufacturers of Hawick', Transactions, 1898
WILSON, B. F. A.,
'The Industrial Development of Hawick', Transactions, 1953
Paper read by unnamed author March, 1868, p.221 (untitled)

HADDINGTON

GRAHAM, H. G.
Social Life of Scotland in the 18th Century (London: A & C Black, 1901)
GREEN, C. E.
East Lothian (1907)
GRAY, W. F.
A Short History of Haddington (1944)
MILLER, J.
The Lamp of Lothian, or the History of Haddington from earliest records to 1844
MARTINE, J.
Reminiscences of the Royal Burgh of Haddington (Edinburgh: John Menzies, 1883)

PRINGLE

PRINGLE, A.
The Records of the Pringles (The Author, 1933)
PRINGLE, R.
The Early History of Robert Pringle & Son, with some personal reminiscences (Hawick: Robert Pringle & Son, 1942)

FASHION

FAIRHOLT, F. W.
Costume in England (London: Chapman & Hall, 1846; George Bell, Bohn's Artist's Library, 3rd ed, 1865)
GREENSMITH DOWNES & SON.
The Book of Scotch-Made Underwear 6th ed, 1912 (Edinburgh: Greensmith Downes & Son, 1912)
HILL, G.
A History of English Dress from the Saxon Period to the Present Day, vol. 2 (London: R. Bentley & Son, 1893)
LAVER, J.
Taste and Fashion (London: Harrap, 1937)
MASON, S. G.
British Hosiery and Knitwear
MAXWELL, S. and HUTCHISON, R.
Scottish Costume (London: A & C Black, 1956)
WILLETT, C. and CUNNINGTON, P.
A History of Underclothes (London: Michael Joseph, 1951)

Back files of local newspapers in Hawick Public Library provided a considerable amount of information, in particular: the report of the Child Commissioners in the *Hawick Advertiser* of March 25, 1865; reports in the same newspaper of 1859 and of January 1899.

APPENDIX 1

Opposite
Festival revellers:
*Pringle lads standing outside
Rodono Mill celebrating the
Common Riding of 1973*

THE COMMON RIDING

The Common Riding at Hawick is an annual two-day June festival
which not only commemorates the town's reaction to a particular
English raid in the 16th century but also keeps alive the tradition
of 'riding the marches' or boundaries of the common lands gifted
to the town about 1511, when Hawick became a Burgh of Barony.
The annual vigilance of the boundaries was an old-time necessity
to prevent unlawful encroachment from envious neighbours.

For many months following the Battle of Flodden in 1513,
when the Scots army suffered a heavy defeat from the Earl of Surrey's
English forces, and the Scottish King James IV was killed, the whole
of the Borders was raided and plundered. In 1514, however, part of
another English army on a foraging expedition under Lord Dacre met
a setback when they had encamped for the night at Trows or Hornshole,
two miles down river from Hawick. A number of Hawick youths,
armed as best as they could, set out to resist the raiders and successfully
routed the intruders and captured their pennon to return to the town
in triumph. A replica of the flag, bearing the insignia of the adherents
of Hexham Priory in Northumberland, is carried at the festival by
a Cornet, or standard bearer, round the marches and at the various
ceremonials. Each year the Hawick Town Council elects a young
man from the town to act as Cornet and he becomes the central figure
for the Common Riding. For four weeks before the actual ceremony,
the Cornet with his mounted supporters ride out to villages in the area.

The two-day festival actually starts on the Thursday evening
at the Colour Bussing Ceremony where the Cornet's Lass ties her
blue-and-gold ribbons to the head of the staff of the flag as a favour
and sign of affection. On the Friday and Saturday the time-honoured
custom of Riding the Marches takes place with great ceremonial
followed by horse-racing on the Common Muir in a picnic atmosphere,
and on the last day by an athletic meeting, before the flag is returned
by the Cornet to the Town Hall, 'unstained and unsullied', where it
remains until the next festival.

Cashmere goat:
Wool from this animal is exquisitely soft, gentle and warm to wear. It is also beautifully light.

Lamaine Wool:
An ultra soft pure wool exclusive to Pringle of Scotland and handles much like cashmere

Lambswool:
Lambs are sheared when young to ensure the fleece remains soft and in perfect condition

APPENDIX 2

THE WOOLLY MINDED

Some object to the coat of any animal other than a sheep being called 'wool'. This may be current thinking in 'the trade' but is not supported by the Oxford English Dictionary which describes CASHMERE as a costly shawl (the first product in England) 'made of fine wool obtained from the Cashmere goat and the wild goat of Tibet'; and WOOL as the 'fleecy coat of the domesticated sheep (and similar animals)'. If cashmere is not considered wool in 1974, it is a recent distinction. In his booklet *The Rarer Wools* (edition of 1940), E. S. Harrison of Elgin wrote: 'Sheep are not the only contributors to the pure woollen cloths. There is a great host of animals scattered all over the world helping the sheep to supply our demands for clothes ... there are many cloths properly described as of pure wool that owe nothing to any kind of sheep. From this queer mixed herd of animals [camels like llama and vicuna, goats and rabbits] a great variety of raw materials is obtained—you may call them wools or furs as you like for there is really no line of demarcation between wool and fur, the distinction is purely arbitrary. The working of these materials forms a most interesting branch of woollen manufacture.'

There may be no technical demarcation between wool and fur and hair on the animal, but so far as clothing is concerned most people regard them as quite distinct. To a woolly minded consumer 'wool' denotes anything that is naturally 'woolly', as opposed to cotton, linen, silk and artificial man-made 'fibre' (a word associated with spikey materials like wood and asbestos). But 'fleece' has the same natural, warm, soft, woolly image as 'wool'.

Silk stockings:
Recreated for the 19 decades collection celebrating 190 years of Pringle. A piece from each decade was chosen to be re-created as a limited edition collection

OTHER BOOKS BY HUGH BARTY-KING

Maples, Fine Furnishers 1841–1991
GSMD, Guildhall School of Music and Drama 1880–1980
The Salters Company 1394–1994
HMSO 1786–1986
Girdle Round the Earth, Cable and Wireless
The Baltic Exchange 1823–1973
The AA 1905–1980
Water: The Book 1992 (for Water Services Association)
New Flame, social history of Town Gas, 1984
Making Provision, 1986 (Provision Trade Federation)
Round Table 1927–1977
Eyes Right, Dollond & Aitchison opticians 1750–1985
A Country Builder, Durtnell & Sons 1541–1991
Scratch a surveyor . . . Drivers Jonas 1725–1975
The Drum (for Royal Tournament 1988)
Cork on Cork, Sir Kenneth Cork Insolvency Accountant takes stock, 1988
Crash the Ash, Some Joy for the beleagured smoker, 1994
Friends At Court, Dunlop Slazenger, 100 years of tennis balls for Wimbledon
A Tradition of English Wine, 1977
Warfield, A thousand years of a Berkshire village, 2000
Rum Yesterday and Today (with Anton Massel), 1983
Sussex in 1839, 1974
Quilt Winders and Pod Shavers, English cricket ball and bat makers, 1979
The Worst Poverty, Debt and Debtors in Britain, 1991